THE ABSORBENT MIND

THE ABSORBENT MIND

Maria Montessori

AAKAR

The Absorbent Mind
Maria Montessori

First Aakar Edition 2012
Reprinted 2014, 2015, 2017, 2018, 2019, 2020, 2021
Reprinted 2022
Reprinted 2024

ISBN 978-93-5002-158-3 (Pb)

Published by
AAKAR BOOKS
28 E Pocket IV, Mayur Vihar Phase I
Delhi 110 091, India
www.aakarbooks.com

Printed at
Mudrak, Noida

Contents

Introduction

The present volume is based on lectures given by Dr. Maria Montessori at Ahmedabad, during the first training course to be held after her internment in India, which lasted till the end of World War II. In it she illustrates the unique mental powers of the young child which enable him to construct and firmly establish within a few years—without teachers, without any of the usual aids of education, almost abandoned and often obstructed—all the characteristics of the human personality.

This achievement by a being born with great potentialities, yet so weak in body, so lacking in all the usual faculties of the mind that it may almost be called a zero, and which after no more than six years already surpasses all other species, is indeed one of the greatest mysteries of life.

In the present volume Dr. Montessori not only sheds the light of her penetrating insight, based on close observation and just evaluation, on the phenomena of this earliest and yet most decisive period of human life, but also indicates the responsibility of adult humanity towards it. She, indeed, gives a practical meaning to the now universally accepted necessity of "education from birth."

This can be given only when education becomes a "help to life," and transcends the narrow limits of teaching and of the direct transmission of knowledge or ideals from one mind to another. One of the best known principles of the Montessori method is the "preparation of the environment." At this stage of life, long before the child goes to school, this principle provides the key to an "education from birth" and for the true "cultivation" of the human individual from the very beginning.

This is a plea made on scientific grounds, but also it is a plea validated by the experiences of one who has witnessed and helped the manifestations of child nature all over the world, manifestations of mental and spiritual grandeur which form a startling contrast to the picture of mankind today—a mankind which, abandoned during its formative period, grows up as the greatest menace to its own survival.

Karachi, 1949 **Mario Montessori**

1

The Child's Part in World Reconstruction

This book is one of the links in the unfolding chain of our thought, and of the movement to which we belong, for the defence of those great inner powers which children possess.

Today, while the world is in conflict, and many plans are afoot for its future reconstruction, education is widely regarded as one of the best means for bringing this about. For, no one disputes that mankind—from the mental point of view—is far below the level that civilization claims to have reached.

I, too, believe that humanity is still far from that stage of maturity needed for the realization of its aspirations, for the construction, that is, of a harmonious and peaceful society and the elimination of wars. Men are not yet ready to shape their own destinies; to control and direct world events, of which—instead—they become the victims.

But although education is recognized as one of the ways of raising mankind, it is nevertheless, still and only, thought of as an education of the mind. This it is proposed to train on the same lines as of old, without trying to draw upon any new vitalizing and constructive forces.

I do not doubt that philosophy and religion can bring to the task an immense contribution, but how numerous are the philosophers in this ultra-civilized world! How many have there not been in the past, and how many more will there not be in the future? Noble ideals and high standards we have always had. They form a great part of what we teach. Yet warfare and strife show no signs of abating. And if education is always to be conceived along the same antiquated lines of a mere transmission of knowledge, there is little to be hoped from it in the bettering of man's future. For what is the use of transmitting knowledge if the individual's total development lags behind? Instead, we must take into account a psychic entity, a social personality, a new world force, innumerable in the totality of its membership, which is at present hidden and ignored. If help and salvation are to come, they can only come from the children, for the children are the makers of men.

The child is endowed with unknown powers, which can guide us to a radiant future. If what we really want is a new world, then education must take as its aim the development of these hidden possibilities.

Our day has seen a great awakening of interest in the mental life of the newly born. Some psychologists have made special observations of the baby's growth from the first three hours after birth. Others, as a result of careful study, have come to the conclusion that the first two years are the most important in the whole span of human life.

The greatness of the human personality begins at the hour of birth. From this almost mystic affirmation there comes what may seem a strange conclusion: that education must start from birth. Strange, because, how, in a practical sense, can we educate a newborn babe, or even an infant during the first two years of his life? What lessons shall we give to this tiny being who understands nothing of what we say, and cannot even move his limbs? Or do we mean only hygiene, when we speak of this little one's education? Not at all. We mean far more than that.

During this early period, education must be understood as a help to the unfolding of the child's inborn psychic powers. This means that we cannot use the orthodox methods of teaching, which depend on talk.

It has been widely shown, by recent research, that tiny children are gifted with a psychic nature peculiar to them. And this points out a new path to the educator. It is something out of the ordinary, something not hitherto recognized, yet something which vitally concerns mankind. The child's true constructive energy, a dynamic power, has remained unnoticed for thousands of years. Just as men have trodden the earth, and later tilled its surface, without thought for the immense wealth hidden in its depths, so the men of our day make progress after progress in civilized life, without noticing the treasures that lie hidden in the psychic world of infancy.

From the earliest dawn of man's life on earth, these energies have been repressed and nullified. Not till today has any intuition of their existence begun to find expression. Only recently, for example, has Carrel written: "The period of infancy is undoubtedly the richest. It should be utilized by education in every possible and conceivable way. The waste of this period of life can never be compensated. Instead of ignoring the early years, it is our duty to cultivate them with the utmost care."[1]

Today we are beginning to see the value of these ungathered fruits, more precious than gold, for they are man's own spirit.

The first two years of life open new horizons before us, for here we may see the laws of psychic construction hitherto unknown. It is the child himself who presents us with these revelations. He brings to our knowledge a kind of psychic life totally different from that of adults. Here is the new path! No longer is it for the professor to apply psychology to childhood, but it is for the children themselves to reveal their psychology to those who study them.

This may seem obscure, but it becomes clear as soon as we go more deeply into details. The child has a mind able to absorb knowledge. He has the power to teach himself. A single observation is enough to prove this. The child grows up speaking his parent's tongue, yet to grown ups the learning of a language is a very great intellectual achievement. No one teaches the child, yet he comes to use nouns, verbs and adjectives to perfection.

To follow a child in his language development is a study of the greatest interest, and all those who have devoted themselves to it agree that the use of words, of names—the first elements of language—falls at a fixed period in the child's life, as if a precise timekeeper were superintending this part of his activity. The child seems to follow a severe programme imposed by nature, so faithfully and punctually as to improve upon that of any old-time school, however well organized. Still following this programme, the child proceeds to learn all the irregularities and grammatical constructions of his language with irreproachable diligence.

There is—so to speak—in every child a painstaking teacher, so skilful that he obtains identical results in all children in all parts of the world. The only language men ever speak perfectly is the one they learn in babyhood, when no one can teach them anything! Not only this, but if at a later age the child has to learn another language, no expert help will enable him to speak it with the same perfection as he does his first.

So there must be a special psychic force at work, helping the little child to develop. And this not only for language; for at two he can recognize all the persons and things around him. If we consider this, it becomes ever clearer that the child does an impressive work of inner formation. All that we ourselves are has been made by the child, by the child we were in the first two years of our lives. Not only has the child to recognize what he sees about him, and to understand and adapt himself to our way of life, but also—while still unteachable—he has to build up in himself all those complex formations that will become our intelligence, the foundation for our religious feelings, and of our particular national and social sentiments. It is as if nature had safeguarded each child from the influence of adult reasoning, so as to give priority to the inner teacher who animates him. He has the chance to build up a complete psychic structure, before the intelligence of grownups can reach his spirit and produce changes in it.

By the age of three, the child has already laid down the foundations of his personality as a human being, and only then does he need the help of special scholastic influences. So great are the conquests he has made that one may well say: the child who goes to school at three is already a little man. Psychologists have often affirmed that if our own adult ability be compared with the child's, we should need sixty years of hard work to do what he does in three; and this they have expressed in the words just used: "At three the child is already a man." Yet he is still far from having exhausted this strange power that he possesses of absorption from his surroundings.

In our first schools the children used to enter when three years old. No one could teach them because they were not receptive; yet they offered us amazing revelations of the greatness of the human soul. Ours was a house for children, rather than a real school. We had prepared a place for children where a diffused culture could be assimilated from the environment, without any need for direct instruction. The children who came were from the humblest social levels, and their parents were illiterate. Yet these children learned to read and write before they were five, and no one had given them any lessons. If visitors asked them, "Who taught you to write?" they often answered with astonishment: "Taught me? No one has taught me!"

At that time it seemed miraculous that children of four and a half should be able to write, and that they should have learned without the feeling of having been taught.

The press began to speak of "culture acquired spontaneously." Psychologists wondered if these children were somehow different from others, and we ourselves puzzled over it for a long time. Only after repeated experiments did we conclude with certainty that all children are endowed with this capacity to "absorb" culture. If this be true—we then argued—if culture can be acquired without effort, let us provide the children with other elements of culture. And then we saw them "absorb" far more than reading and writing: botany, zoology, mathematics, geography—and with the same ease, spontaneously and without getting tired.

And so we discovered that education is not something which the teacher does, but that it is a natural process which develops spontaneously in the human being. It is not acquired by listening to words, but in virtue of experiences in which the child acts on his environment. The teacher's task is not to talk, but to prepare and arrange a series of motives for cultural activity in a special environment made for the child.

My experiments, conducted in many different countries, have now been going on for forty years, and as the children grew up parents kept asking me to extend my methods to the later ages. We then found that individual activity is the one factor that stimulates and produces development, and that this is not more true for the little ones of preschool age than it is for the junior, middle, and upper school children.

A new figure had arisen to greet our eyes. Not just a school, or an educational method, but MAN himself: MAN whose true nature is shown in his capacity for free development, whose greatness became visible directly mental oppression ceased to bear upon him, to limit his inner work and weigh down his spirit.

Therefore I hold that any reform of education must be based on the personality of man. Man himself must become the centre of education and we must never forget that man does not develop only at the university, but begins his mental growth at birth, and pursues it with the greatest intensity during the first three years of his life. To this period, more than to any other, it is imperative to give active care. If we follow these rules, the child, instead of being a burden, shows himself to us as the greatest and most consoling of nature's wonders! We find ourselves confronted by a being no longer to be thought of as helpless, like a receptive void waiting to be filled with our wisdom; but one whose dignity increases in the measure to which we see in him the builder of our own minds; one guided by his inward teacher, who labours indefatigably in joy and happinesses—following a precise timetable—at the work of constructing that greatest marvel of the Universe, the human being. We teachers can only help the work going on, as servants wait upon a master. We then become witnesses to the development of the human soul; the emergence of the New Man, who will no longer be the victim of events but, thanks to his clarity of vision, will become able to direct and to mould the future of mankind.

REFERENCE

1. Dr. Alexis Carrel, *L'Homme cet Inconnu*, Paris 1947 (p. 222), 1st ed. 1935. English editions from 1935, and in Pelican Books, 1948 (A. 181).

2

Education for Life

In order to clarify at the outset what we mean by education for life starting from birth, it will be necessary to go more fully into details. One of the world's national leaders—it was Gandhi—announced not long ago that education must become coextensive with life, and not only this, but he said that the central point of education must be the defence of life. This is the first time that any social and spiritual leader has said such a thing. On the other hand, science has not only declared this to be necessary, but has been proving, ever since the beginning of our century, that the extension of education throughout life could be made a practical success. Nevertheless, no ministry of public instruction has yet adopted the idea.

The education of our day is rich in methods, aims and social ends, but one must still say that it takes no account of life itself. Among all the many methods officially used in different countries, no one proposes to help the individual from birth and to protect his development. Education, as today conceived, is something separated both from biological and social life. All who enter the educational world tend to be cut off from society. University students are required to obey the rules of the college to which they belong, and to follow in unison the programme of studies laid down by the authorities. But, till quite recently, it could be said that the university took not the slightest interest in the conditions of their physical or social life. If a student were underfed, or if defects in sight or hearing diminished his aptitude, he merely received lower marks. It is true that physical defects have now begun to receive attention, but only from the hygienic standpoint. No one yet asks whether the student's mind may not be threatened, or even damaged, by defective and unsuitable educational methods. The movement for New Education, so ardently championed by Claparéde, undertook an inquiry into the number of subjects in the curriculum, and tried to reduce these so as to diminish mental fatigue. But this does not touch the problem of how pupils can acquire the riches of culture without becoming tired. In most state-controlled systems, what matters is that the programme shall be fulfilled. If the spirit of an undergraduate reacts to social injustice, or to political questions concerning deeply felt truths, the order of authority goes out that young people must avoid politics and concentrate on their studies. What happens then is that young people leave the university with their minds so shackled and sacrificed that they have lost all power of individuation and can no longer judge the problems of the age in which they live.

Scholastic machinery is as estranged from social life as if this and all its problems were outside its compass. The world of education is like an island where people, cut off from the world, are prepared for life by exclusion from it. Supposing it happens that a university student becomes infected by tuberculosis and dies of it. Curious and saddening, is it not, that the university—the social *milieu* in which he lives—having ignored him while ill, should suddenly and unexpectedly make its appearance, in the form of a representative, at his funeral?[1] There are graduates so nervous that when they pass out into the world, they are useless to themselves, and a burden to their families and friends. Nonetheless, the academic body is not expected to take cognizance of this: an aloofness amply justified by the regulations which forbid it to take any interest in psychological cases, and only allow it to organize studies and hold examinations. Those who pass are awarded a diploma or degree. That, in our day, is the loftiest summit reached by institutional education. Meanwhile, research workers investigating social problems are discovering that university graduates and school licentiates are not prepared for life, and, not only this, but their capacity for engaging usefully in social work has been diminished. Statistics reveal a striking increase in the number of insane persons, of criminals, and of those whom their neighbours regard as "queer." Sociologists call upon the school to remedy these evils, but the school is a world apart, a world shut off from such problems. It is an institution of too ancient a lineage to alter its traditions from within. Only a pressure from outside can change, renovate, and find remedies for the faults that mar education at every level, just as they bear all too heavily on the lives of those subjected to it.

What about the period from birth to the sixth or seventh year? The school, properly so-called, takes no interest in this. Therefore, it is called prescholastic, meaning outside the range of official instruction: And what, indeed, could little newborn babies do in school? Wherever institutions have sprung up for the preschool child, they seldom depend on the central scholastic authority. They are controlled by unofficial associations, or have private managements which often pursue philanthropic ends. An interest in protecting the psychic life of babies, as a social problem, does not exist. Besides, society proclaims that young children belong to the home and not to the state.

The new importance now being given to the first years of life, has not yet extended to any suggestion for making practical provision for this. All that anyone thinks of, so far, is that home life could be improved, in the sense that a training for motherhood is now held to be necessary. But the home is not a part of the school; it belongs to society. So, in effect, the human personality, or the care of it, is broken up. On one side is the home which belongs to society, but which lives in isolation from society, and is neglected or ignored by it; on the other is the school, also shut off from society; and finally, the university. There is no unity of conception, no social solicitude for life as such; there are only fragments which ignore one another by turns and which appeal successfully, or alternatively, to the school, the home, or the university, the latter being looked upon as just another kind of school for the final part of the educational period. Even the new social sciences, which perceive the evils of this isolation, sciences like sociology and social psychology, are always outside the school. Hence, there exists no true system of help for the development of life. The concept of education as such a help is not new to science, as I say, but it still has no status or place in social organization. And this is the next step which civilization must urgently take. The path for it has already been charted. Criticism shows easily the errors of our present situation. Various workers have made clear what remedies are needed in all the phases of life. So all is ready; we have only to build. The various contributions for science are like stones from the quarry already squared for placing in the building. All we have to do is to find people ready to put them together and so erect the new structure which civilization so badly needs.

The concept of an education centred upon the care of the living being alters all previous ideas. Resting no longer on a curriculum, or a timetable, education must conform to the facts of human life. In the light of this conviction, the education of the newly born becomes suddenly of the first importance. It is quite true that the newborn infant cannot do anything, that we cannot teach him in the ordinary sense. He can only be an object of observation, of a study which we must undertake to find out his vital needs. This is just the kind of observation that we ourselves have been doing. It has a purpose. Its object is to find out what are the laws of life, for if we want to help life, the first condition of success is that we shall know the laws which govern it. Yet it is not enough merely to know them, for if we stopped there we should remain exclusively in the field of, psychology. We should never go further and become educators.

The knowledge of the little child's mental development has to become widely diffused, for only then will education be able to speak with a new voice, and say to the world with authority: "The laws of life are such and such. They cannot be ignored. You *must* act in conformity with them, for they proclaim *the rights of man* which are universal and common to all."

If society holds it necessary to make education compulsory, this means that education has to be given in a practical fashion, and if we are now agreed that education begins at birth, then it becomes vitally necessary for everyone to know the laws of development. Instead of education remaining aloof and ignored by society, it must acquire the authority to rule over society. Social machinery must be adapted to the inherent necessities of the new conception that life is to be protected. All are called upon to help. Fathers and mothers must shoulder their responsibilities; and if the home fails for lack of means, then it is required of society not only to give the needed instruction but also the support necessary for bringing up the children. If education signifies a protection of the individual, if society recognizes as necessary to the child's development things that the family cannot provide, then it is society's duty to provide those things. The state must never abandon the child.

Education will thus become obliged to act authoritatively upon the society from which it was formally excluded. If it is evident that society should exert a beneficent control over human individuals, and if it is also true that education is to be regarded as a help to life, then this control will never be restrictive and oppressive, but it must take the form of physical and psychic help. This means that society's first step must be to allocate a higher proportion of its wealth to education.

The needs of the child during his years of growth have been studied and the results of these studies have been published. Now, it is for society as a whole to take over conscientiously the responsibility of education, while education in its turn will liberally compensate society by the benefits resulting from its progress. Education, so conceived, no longer matters only to children and their parents, but also to the state and to international relationships. It becomes a stimulus to every part of the social body, a stimulus to the greatest of social improvements. Is there anything more immovable, stagnant, and indifferent than the education of today? When a country has to economize, education is sure to be the first victim. If we ask a statesman for his views on education, he will say it is no concern of his, that he has left his children's upbringing to his wife, who in her turn has entrusted it to a school. In the days to come it will be absolutely impossible for a statesman to give such an answer, or to show such indifference.

What are we to conclude from the reports of psychologists who have studied children from their earliest days? All are agreed that with proper care and help the child has it in him to grow to greater strength, to attain a better mental balance and a more energetic character. Instead of leaving everything to chance, the child's growth at this time should be a matter for scientific care and attention. This means that something more is needed than mere physical hygiene. Just as the latter wards off injuries to his body, so we need mental hygiene to protect his mind and soul from harm.

Science has made other discoveries about these first days. The infant in arms has far greater mental energies than are usually imagined. At birth he is nothing—psychologically speaking. And not only in his mind, for at birth he is incapable of coordinated movement. With his almost useless limbs there is nothing he can do. Nor can he talk, even if he sees what is going on about him. Yet, with the passing of time, the child walks and talks and goes from one achievement to another, till a man is formed in all the grandeur of his bodily and mental gifts. And this opens the door to an imperious truth:

the child is not an inert being who owes everything he can do to us, as if he were an empty vessel that we have to fill. No, it is the child who makes the man, and no man exists who was not made by the child who once he was.

The great constructive energies of the child, of which we have already said so much, and which scientists are now impelled to study, have hitherto been concealed beneath an accumulation of ideas concerning motherhood. We used to say it was the mother who formed the child; for it is she who teaches him to walk, talk and so on. But none of this is really done by the mother. It is an achievement of the child. What the mother brings forth is the baby, but it is the baby who produces the man. Should the mother die, the baby still grows up and completes his work of making the man. An Indian baby taken to America, and placed in the care of Americans, learns to speak English and not Hindi. So his language does not come from the mother, but it is the child who takes in the language, just as he takes in the habits and customs of the people among whom he happens to be living. There is nothing hereditary, therefore, in any of these acquisitions. It is the child who absorbs material from the world about him; he who moulds it into the man of the future.

To recognize this great work of the child does not mean to diminish the parents' authority. Once they can persuade themselves not to be themselves the builders, but merely to act as collaborators in the building process, they become much better able to carry out their real duties; and then, in the light of a wider vision, their help becomes truly valuable. The child can only build well if this help is given in a suitable way. Thus, the authority of parents does not come from a dignity standing on its own feet, but it comes from the help they are able to give their children. The truly great authority and dignity of parents rests solely upon this.

But let us think of the child's place in society from another point of view.

The picture of the labourer, extolled by Marxist theory, has now become a part of the modern conscience. He is seen as the producer of wealth and well-being, an essential partner in the great work of civilized living. Society has come to recognize his moral and economic value, and to accord to him the means and conditions needed for his work, as a matter of right.

Suppose we carry this idea over to the child. He, too, is a toiler, and the aim of his work is to make a man. The parents, it is true, provide the means essential to his life and creative activity, but the social problem in his regard is even more important, for the fruits of his labour are not just material things, but he is fashioning humanity itself—and not just a race, a caste, or a social group, but the whole of mankind. Seen in this way, the conclusion is irresistible that society must heed the child, recognize his rights and provide for his needs. Once we have focused our attention and our studies on life itself, we may find that we are touching the secret of mankind, and into our hands will fall the knowledge of how it should be governed and how helped. We, also, when we speak of education are proclaiming a revolution, one in which everything we know today will be transformed. I think of this as the final revolution; not a revolution of violence, still less of bloodshed, but one from which violence is wholly excluded—for the little child's psychic productivity is stricken to death by the barest shadow of violence.

What has to be defended is the construction of human normality. Have not all our efforts been aimed at removing obstacles from the child's path of development, and at keeping away the dangers and misunderstandings that everywhere threaten it?

This is education, understood as a help to life; an education from birth, which feeds a peaceful revolution and unites all in a common aim, attracting them as to a single centre. Mothers, fathers, politicians: all must combine in their respect and help for this delicate work of formation, which the little child carries on in the depth of a profound psychological mystery, under the tutelage of an inner guide. This is the bright new hope for mankind. Not reconstruction, but help for the constructive work that the human soul is called upon to do, and to bring to fruition; a work of formation which brings out the immense potentialities with which children, the sons of men, are endowed.

REFERENCE

1. Only in a few countries after the last war have attempts been made to improve this situation. In Holland, for example, there are now sanatoria for students. [Another exception is that of the tutorial system which has long been in use in British residential colleges of the older universities. But these are more like "boarding schools" with a corresponding loss of individual freedom.]

3

The Periods of Growth

Psychologists who have studied children's growth from birth to university age maintain that this can be divided into various and distinct periods. Following Havelock Ellis, and more recently W. Stern, others have taken up this idea, notably Charlotte Biihler and her followers; while, from another point of view, it figures largely in the work of the Freudian school. It differs very much from ideas previously in vogue. These held that the human being was of little account in the early years, but added to itself by growth. According to this, the tiny child was something small in process of development, something which increased gradually, but always preserved the same form. Giving up this older view, psychology now accepts that there are different types of mentality in the successive phases of growth.[1] These phases are quite distinct one from another, and it is interesting to find that they correspond with the phases of physical growth. The changes are so marked—speaking psychologically—that the following picturesque exaggeration is sometimes used: "Development is a series of rebirths." There comes a time when one psychic personality ends, and another begins. The first of these periods goes from birth to six years of age. During this time the kind of mentality remains the same, though it differs very much from those of later periods. There are two subphases, from birth to three and three to six. In the first of these, the child has a type of mind that the adult cannot approach, that is to say, we cannot exert upon it any direct influence. In fact, there are no schools for such children. In the second subphase (from three to six) the mental type is still the same, but in some ways the child begins to become susceptible to adult influence. During this period the personality undergoes great changes. We have only to compare the newborn babe with the six-year-old to see this. Leaving aside, for the moment, how these transformations have occurred, the facts are that the child of six has become—in popular parlance—sufficiently intelligent to go to school.

The next period goes from six to twelve. It is a period of growth unaccompanied by other change. The child is calm and happy. Mentally, he is in a state of health, strength and assured stability. "This stability, mental and physical," says Ross, writing about children of this age, "is the most conspicuous characteristic of later childhood. A being from another planet, who did not know the human race, could easily take these ten-year-olds to be adults of the species supposing they had not met the real adults."[2]

On the physical side, there are signs which seem to fix the boundaries between these two psychological periods. The changes are very visible. To cite only one of them; the child loses his first set of teeth and begins the second.

The third period goes from twelve to eighteen, and it is a period of so much change as to remind one of the first. It can again be divided into two subphases: one from twelve to fifteen, and the other from fifteen to eighteen. There are physical changes also during this period, the body reaching its full maturity. Man, after eighteen, is fully developed and no further marked changes occur in him. He grows only in age.

The curious thing is that official education has recognized these different psychological types. It seems to have had an obscure intuition of them. The first period, from birth to six, has clearly been recognized, because it is excluded from compulsory education. At six it is well known that a change occurs, making the child mature enough for school life. So it is accepted that by the age of six the child already knows many things. In fact, if children could not find their way about, could not walk, or understand what the teacher said, they would not be ready for collective life. So we may say that this transformation has been recognized in practice. Yet educational theorists have been slow to perceive that if a child can go to school, find his way about and understand the ideas put before him, this means that his mind has undergone a great development, for at birth he could do none of these things.

There is also an unconscious recognition of the second period, because in many countries children leave the preparatory, or primary, school at twelve and go on to the secondary school. Why is the period from six to twelve held to be suitable for giving children their first basic ideas of culture? This happens in all countries of the world, so it cannot be a haphazard matter of pure inspiration. Only a psychological basis common to all children can have made possible this type of school organization, which rests, beyond doubt, on conclusions reached by experience. In fact, experience tells us that in this period the child can submit himself to the *regime* of mental work demanded by the school: he can grasp what the teacher means, and is patient enough to listen and learn. Throughout this whole period, he is constant in his work and strong in health. That is why it is thought to be the best time for receiving culture.

After the twelfth year of age, a higher kind of schooling begins, which means that official education has realized that the individual is now entering still another kind of psychic life. This, again, has two subphases, indicated by the fact that the secondary school is in two parts, higher and lower; the lower one lasts three years, and the higher sometimes four. But it does not matter into how many years exactly the instruction is apportioned. What we are interested to see is the fact that in higher education, also, the six-year period becomes in practice divided into two. On the whole, this period is less calm and easy than the preceding one. Psychologists interested in adolescent education think of it as a period of so much psychic transformation that it bears comparison with the first period from birth to six. The character is seldom stable at this age; there are signs of indiscipline and rebellion. Physical health is less stable and assured than before. But the schools take no account of this. A timetable has been drawn up and the boys have to follow it, willy nilly. They also have to sit for long hours listening, they have to obey and spend much time in learning material by heart.

And, as a crown to these years in school, there follows the university, which also does not differ substantially from the kinds of school preceding it, except perhaps in the intensity of the work. There, also, professors talk and students listen. In my student days the young men did not shave, and it was comical to see them massed in the great halls, mostly with beards more or less formidable and all wearing moustaches of which the variety was legion. Yet these fully grown men were treated like children: they had to sit and listen; do as their professors told them; depend for their cigarettes and tram rides on the generosity of their fathers, who were only too ready to scold them if they failed in the examinations. And these were adults, men whose intelligence and experience would be needed one day to direct the world. The mind would be the instrument of their labours in the highest of the professions; they were the future doctors, lawyers, engineers.

And how far, we may add, does it take one to hold a degree in these days? Can one be sure of even earning a living? Who goes to a doctor only just qualified? Who trusts the design of a factory to a young engineer, or engages a lawyer only just allowed to practise? And how do we explain this lack of confidence? The reason is that these young men have spent years in listening to words, and listening does not make a man. Only practical work and experience lead the young to maturity. That is why we find young doctors who have to work for years in the hospitals; young lawyers who have to get experience in the offices of experts; engineers who must do likewise before they can practise on their own. And not only this, but to gain admittance to these practising grounds, graduates have to go in search of favours and recommendations, and to overcome no light obstacles. This happens, sadly enough, in all countries. A typical case occurred, once, in New York where a procession was organized consisting of hundreds of graduates unable to find work. They carried a banner, inscribed: "We are unemployed, and hungry. What are we supposed to do?" No one could answer that question. Education is out of control, and cannot change its inveterate habits. All it has done, so far, is to recognize in the growth of the individual different forms of development at the various stages of life.

In my young days, no one gave any thought to children between two and six years of age. Now, there are preschool institutions of various kinds, which take children from three to six; but today, as of old, the university is held in the highest esteem, since out of it come those who have cultivated most fully the essentially human faculty of intelligence. But, now that psychologists have begun to study life itself, there is growing up a tendency to do just the opposite. There are many who hold, as I do, that the most important period of life is not the age of university studies, but the first one, the period from birth to the age of six. For that is the time when man's intelligence itself, his greatest implement, is being formed. But not only his intelligence; the full totality of his psychic powers. This new idea has greatly impressed those with some insight into psychic life, and many have begun to study the newborn and the one year old child, who is the creator of the adult's personality.

Concentration on this, and its wonders, awakens in the student emotions not unlike those which people used to feel in earlier times when they meditated on death. What happens after death? No question had greater power to move men's hearts. But, now, it is man's entry into the world that captures the imagination. For we find in the newborn our own hidden nature.

Why should it be necessary for the human being to endure so long, and so laborious a babyhood? None of the animals has so hard an infancy. What happens while it is going on? Beyond question, there is a kind of creativeness. At first, nothing exists, and then, about a year later, the child knows everything. The child is not born with a little knowledge, a little memory, a little will power, which have only to grow as time goes on. The cat, after a fashion, can mew from birth; the newly hatched bird, and the calf, make the same kind of noises they will when adult. But the human baby is mute; he can only express himself by crying. In man's case, therefore, we are not dealing with something that develops, but with a fact of formation; something nonexistent has to be produced, starting from nothing. The wonderful step taken by the baby is to pass from nothing to something, and our minds find it very hard to grapple with this conundrum.

A mind different from ours is needed to take that step. The child has other powers than ours, and the creation he achieves is no small one; it is everything. Not only does he create his language, but he shapes the organs that enable him to frame the words. He has to make the physical basis of every moment, all the elements of our intellect, everything the human being is blessed with. This wonderful work is not the product of conscious intention. We adults know what we want. If we desire to learn something, we set ourselves to learn it consciously. But the sense of willing does not exist in the child; both knowledge and will have to be created.

If we call our adult mentality conscious, then we must call the child's unconscious, but the unconscious kind is not necessarily inferior. An unconscious mind can be most intelligent. We find it at work in every species, even among the insects. They have an intelligence which is not conscious though it often seems to be endowed with reason. The child has an intelligence of this unconscious type, and that is what brings about his marvellous progress.

It begins with a knowledge of his surroundings. How does the child assimilate his environment? He does it solely in virtue of one of those characteristics that we now know him to have. This is an intense and specialized sensitiveness in consequence of which the things about him awaken so much interest and so much enthusiasm that they become incorporated in his very existence. The child *absorbs* these impressions not with his mind but with his life itself.

Language provides the most obvious example. How does it happen that the child learns to speak? We say that he is blessed with hearing and listens to human voices. But, even admitting this, we must still ask how it is that, among the thousands of sounds and noises that surround him, he hears, and reproduces, only those of the human voice? If it be true that he hears, and if it be true that he only learns the language of human beings, then it must be that the sounds of human speech make on him a deeper impression than any other sounds. These impressions must be so strong, and cause such an intensity of emotion—so deep an enthusiasm as to set in motion invisible fibres of his body, fibres which start vibrating in the effort to reproduce those sounds

By way of analogy, let us think of what happens at a concert. A rapt expression dawns on the faces of the listeners; heads and hands begin to move in unison. What can be causing this but a psychic response to the music? Something similar must be happening in the unconscious mind of the child. Voices affect him so deeply that our response to music is nothing to it. We can almost see the vibrant movements of his tongue, the trembling of the tiny vocal cords and cheeks. Everything is in motion, trying in silent preparation to reproduce the sounds which have caused such turmoil in his unconscious mind. How does it happen that the child learns a language in all its detail, and so precisely and fixedly that it becomes a part of his psychic personality? This language he acquires in infancy is called his mother tongue, and it is clearly different from all the other languages which he may learn later, just as a natural set of teeth is different from a denture.

How does it happen that these sounds, at first meaningless, suddenly bring to his mind comprehension and ideas? The child has not only absorbed words and their meanings; he has actually absorbed sentences and their constructions. We cannot understand language without understanding the structure of sentences. Supposing we say, "The tumbler is on the table," the meaning we give those words derives partly from the order in which we say them. If we had said "On tumbler the is table the," our meaning would have been hard to grasp. We draw meaning from the arrangement of the words, and this is also something the child can absorb.

And how does all this happen? We say:"The child remembers things," but, in order to remember something, it is necessary to have a memory, and this the child has not. On the contrary, he has to construct it. Before one can appreciate how the ordering of words in a sentence affects its meaning, one must be able to reason. But this also is a power which the child has to make.

Our mind, as it is, would not be able to do what the child's mind does. To develop a language from nothing needs a different type of mentality. This the child has. His intelligence is not of the same kind as ours.

It may be said that we acquire knowledge by using our minds; but the child absorbs knowledge directly into his psychic life. Simply by continuing to live, the child learns to speak his native tongue. A kind of mental chemistry goes on within him. We, by contrast, are recipients. Impressions pour into us and we store them in our minds; but we ourselves remain apart from them, just as a vase keeps separate from the water it contains. Instead, the child undergoes a transformation. Impressions do not merely enter his mind; they form it. They incarnate themselves in him. The child creates his own "mental muscles," using for this what he finds in the world about him. We have named this type of mentality, *The Absorbent Mind.*

For us, it is very difficult to conceive of the infant's mental power, but there can be no doubt how privileged it is. How wonderful it would be if we could retain the prodigious capacity we had as children, of romping happily, jumping and playing while learning at the same time the whole of a new language in all its intricacy! How marvellous if all knowledge came into our minds simply as a result of living, without any need for more effort than is required to eat or breathe! At first, we should notice no particular change. Then, suddenly, the things we had learned would all appear in our minds like shining stars of knowledge. We should begin to realize they were there, become conscious of ideas that had unwittingly become ours.

Supposing I said there was a planet without schools or teachers, where study was unknown, and yet the inhabitants —doing nothing but live and walk about—came to know all things, to carry in their minds the whole of learning; would you not think I was romancing? Well, just this, which seems so fanciful as to be nothing but the invention of a fertile imagination, is a reality. It is the child's way of learning. This is the path he follows. He learns everything without knowing he is learning it, and in doing so he passes little by little from the unconscious to the conscious, treading always in the paths of joy and love.

Human learning seems to us a great thing; to be aware of our knowlege; to have the human form of mind. But we have to pay for this, for no sooner do we become conscious than every fresh piece of knowledge costs us effort and hard work.

Movement is another of the child's great acquisitions. When newly born, he lives for months in his cot. Yet, see him not long after, and he is walking, moving about in his world, doing things. He busies himself and is happy. He lives only for the day, and every day he learns to move a little bit more. Language in all its complexity becomes his, and with it the power to move as his needs dictate. But this is not all. Much else he learns with astonishing speed. Everything about him is taken in; habits, customs, religion, fix themselves firmly in his mind.

The movements the child acquires are not chosen haphazardly, but are fixed, in the sense that each proceeds out of a particular period of development. When the child begins to move, his mind, being able to absorb, has already taken in his surroundings. Before he starts moving at all, an unconscious psychological development has taken place in him, and when he initiates his first movements, this begins to become conscious. If you watch a child of three, you will see that he is always playing with something. This means that he is working out, and making conscious, something that his unconscious mind has earlier absorbed. Through this outward experience, in the guise of a game, he examines those things and impressions that he has taken in unconsciously. He becomes fully conscious and constructs the future man, by means of his activities. He is directed by a mysterious power, great and wonderful, that he incarnates little by little. In this way, he becomes a man. He does it with his hands, by experience, first in play and then through work. The hands are the instruments of man's intelligence. As a result of these experiments the child's personality assumes an individual, and therefore limited, form, since the world of knowledge is always more limited than the unconscious and subconscious worlds.

He enters upon life and begins his mysterious task; little by little to build up the wondrous powers of a person adapted to his country and its times. He constructs his mind step by step till it becomes possessed of memory, the power to understand, the ability to think. And here he is, at last, in his sixth year of life, Then, all of a sudden, it dawns on us educators that we have a being who understands, who has the patience to listen when we speak, while previously we had no way of reaching him. He lived on another plane, different from ours.

It is with this first period that our book is to deal. The

study of child psychology in the first years of life opens to our eyes such wonders that no one seeing them with understanding can fail to be deeply stirred. Our work as adults does not consist in teaching, but in helping the infant mind in its work of development. How splendid it would be, if we could, by standing ready, by treating the child intelligently, with understanding of his vital needs, prolong the period in which he has this capacity to absorb! What a service we should render mankind if we could help the human being to acquire knowledge without fatigue; if people could find themselves replete with information without knowing how they came by it—as it were by magic! Though it is true, is it not, that all the works of nature are, perhaps, magical and mysterious?

The discovery that the child has a mind able to absorb on its own account produces a revolution in education. We can now understand easily why the first period in human development, in which character is formed, is the most important. At no other age has the child greater need of an intelligent help, and any obstacle that impedes his creative work will lessen the chance he has of achieving perfection. We should help the child, therefore, no longer because we think of him as a creature, puny and weak, but because he is endowed with great creative energies, which are of their nature so fragile as to need a loving and intelligent defence. To these *energies* we want to bring help; not to the child, nor to his weakness. When we understand that the energies belong to an unconscious mind, which has to become conscious through work and through an experience of life gained in the world, we realize that the mind of the child in infancy is different from ours, that we cannot reach it by verbal instruction, nor intervene directly in the process of its passing from the unconscious to the conscious—the process of making human faculty—then the whole concept of education changes. It becomes a matter of giving help to the child's life, to the psychological development of man. No longer is it just an enforced task of retaining our words and ideas.

This is the new path on which education has been put; to help the mind in its process of development, to aid its energies and strengthen its many powers.

REFERENCES

1. For the latest information on this subject, and on the above mentioned points of view, see W. Stern, *Psychology of Early Childhood: Up to the 6th Year of Age*, 2nd ed., 1930 (1st German ed. 1914). Ch. Bühler, *Kindheit and Jugend*, 3rd ed. 1931. E. Jones, *Some Problems of Adolescence, British Journal of Psychology*, July 1922. For a deeper biological treatment, consult the works of Arnold Gesell.
2. J.S. Ross, *Ground Work of Educational Psychology*, London, 1944, p. 114 (1st ed. 1931).

4

The New Path

Modern biology is turning in a new direction. At one time all research was confined to adults. When scientists studied animals or plants, the specimens they took were always adult specimens. It was the same in studies made of mankind. Whether a question concerned man's morals or the form of his society, only adults came into it. One of the topics most often discussed was death, but this need not surprise us, since the adult, on his way through life, is going towards his death. The whole question of morality was one of law, or of social relationships in the grown-up world. But science is now beginning to take just the opposite direction. It seems almost to be going backward. For, whether it be in the study of man, or of other forms of life, the focus of interest is on the younger specimens, and even on their origins. Embryology and cytology—the study of cell life—have come to the fore, and from investigations made at this lowly level something like a new philosophy is springing up—a philosophy which is far from being wholly theoretical. Resting, as it does, on observation, one might well say it has a better claim to be called scientific than have many of the earlier conclusions drawn by abstract thinkers. For the unfolding of this philosophy is proceeding step by step with discoveries made in the laboratory.

Embryology, in fact, takes us back to the origins of the

adult being. At that early stage, there are things which do not exist at the adult stage, or if they do their manner of existence is quite different. Science lays bare a kind of life unknown to earlier thinkers, and this casts a flood of new light on child personality.

Let us start with one very simple reflection: the child, unlike the adult, is not on his way to death. He is on his way to life. His work is to fashion a man in the fullness of his strength. By the time the adult exists, the child has vanished. So the whole life of the child is an advance toward perfection, toward a greater completeness. From this we may infer that the child will enjoy doing the work needed to complete himself. The child's life is one in which work—the doing of one's duty—begets joy and happiness. For adults, the daily round is more often depressing.

The process of living is, for the child, an extension and amplification of himself; the older he gets, the stronger and more intelligent he becomes. His work and activity help him to acquire this strength and intelligence. But in adult life the passing of the years has an opposite effect. Again, there is no competition in childhood, because no one can do for the child the work he has to do to build the man he is making. No one, in short, can do his growing for him.

But if we go back still further in the child's life, to the period before he was born, we find him again in contact with the adult, because his embryonic life is passed in his mother's womb. Before that, there existed the first cell, which came from the union of two cells provided by adults. So, whether we go to the origins of human life, or follow the child in his work of growth, we always find the adult not far away.

The life of the child is a line joining two adult generations. The child's life, which creates, and is being created, starts from one adult and ends in another adult. It is the lane along which he passes, skirting closely the lives of adults, and the study of it brings us fresh rewards of interest and light.

Nature always sees to it that the child is protected. He is born of love, and love is his natural origin. Once born, he has the tender care of mother and father. This means that he is not born into discord, and that is his first defence from the world. Nature inspires both parents with love for their little ones, and this love is not something artificial. It is not just a love fed by reason, like the idea of brotherhood born of an intellectual wish to unite mankind. The love we find in infancy shows what kind of love should reign ideally in the grown up world: a love able, of its own nature, to inspire sacrifice, the dedication of one *ego* to another *ego*, of one's self to the service of others. In the depth of their love, all parents renounce their own lives to dedicate them to their children. And this devotion is natural to them. It gives them joy and does not feel sacrificial. No one ever says, "Look at that unfortunate man, he has two children!" On the contrary, they think of him as lucky. The efforts parents make for their children give them joy; they are a part of parenthood itself. The child awakens what adults think of as an ideal; the ideal of renunciation, of unselfishness—virtues almost unreachable outside family life. What businessman, in a position to acquire some property he needs, will ever say to one of his competitors: "You can have it, I am leaving it for you!" But if hungry parents are short of food, they will deny themselves the last crumb of bread rather than have the child go hungry.

So we see, there are two kinds of life, and the adult is privileged to share in both; in one, as parent, in the other as a member of society. The better of the two is that with children, for nearness to them brings out our best side.

These two different lives are just as plainly to be seen among animals. The fiercest and most savage of beasts turns tame and gentle with its young. How tender are lions and tigers with their cubs; how fierce the timid doe in protecting her dam! It seems as though with all animals, their usual instincts are reversed in the presence of their little ones. It is as if parenthood gave them special instincts, which override the normal. Timid animals, even more than men, have instincts for self-preservation, but these are changed to aggressive instincts, if they have young ones to protect.

Birds are no different. When danger threatens, their instinct is to fly away. But if there are offspring, they do not leave the nest; they remain motionless, covering it with their wings to hide the too visible whiteness of the eggs. Others pretend to be wounded, and barely escape the dog's jaws in luring him away from the nestlings, which thus remain unnoticed. In numberless fields of animal life we find the same thing, and it means there are two forms of instinct: one self-preservative, the other protective of the young. The great biologist, J.H. Fabre, gives most wonderful examples of this. He ends his great work by saying that the species owes its survival to mother love, and this is true, because if survival were due solely to the weapons evolved in the struggle for existence, how could the little ones defend themselves before they had grown these weapons? Are not tiger cubs toothless, and nestlings bare of feathers? Hence, if life is to be conserved, and the species to survive, the first thing necessary is a parental defence of the young, who are not yet armed.

If survival depended solely on the triumph of the strong, then the species would perish. So the real reason for survival, the principal factor in the "struggle for existence," is the *love of adults* for their young.

One of the most fascinating parts of natural history is the search for signs of intelligence which may be discerned even in the humblest of creatures. Each of these is endowed with various kinds of protective instinct; each is also provided with its own special kind of intelligence. But this intelligence is used mainly for the protection of the young. Also, the instincts of self-preservation are much less varied, and are accompanied by far less intelligence. They are far from that refinement of detail, which gave Fabre enough material to fill his whole sixteen volumes with the description of parental behaviour in insects.[1]

So if we study the different forms of life, we find the necessity for two kinds of instinct, of two ways of living; and if we make this assertion of human life, it becomes necessary—if for social reasons alone—to study children, because of the effects they have upon adults. It follows that to study human life effectively, we must begin with its beginning.

REFERENCE

1. *Souvenirs Entomologiques*. In English translation: *The Life of the Spider, The Life of the Fly, The Hunting Wasps*, etc.

5

The Miracle of Creation

Thinkers in every age have been struck by the astonishing fact that a being which at first does not exist, should end by becoming a man or a woman, able even to think and to have ideas of its own.

How does this happen? How do all these organs, of such wondrous complexity, come to be formed? What makes the eyes, and the tongue whereby we speak, and the brain—all the infinity of parts which make up the human being? Scientists at the beginning of the eighteenth century, or rather the philosophers of those days, believed in a pre-formation. They thought that in the egg cell there must be a miniature man (or woman) already made. True, it would be so tiny as to be invisible, but they thought it must surely exist and be destined to grow. This view was held for all the mammals, but there were two schools of thought, that of the "animalculists" and that of the "ovists." These were divided as to whether the minute individual was present in the germinal cell of man, or in that of woman, and much learned discussion raged around this point.

But a doctor of medicine, named G. F. Wolff, using the microscope which had only just been invented, decided to look for himself and see what really happened in the creative process. For this purpose, he studied fecundated germ cells in the eggs of chickens. By this means he arrived at the astonishing conclusion (see *Theoria Generationis*, by

G.F. Wolff) that nothing of this kind pre-exists. The being constructs itself, and he described the process as he had seen it. First, there is a single germ cell which divides into two parts; these two divide into four (see drawing), and it is by this multiplication of cells that the new being comes to be formed.

Naturally, the learned men arguing about pre-existence turned on him in fury. What ignorance! What presumption! This is heresy! It will undermine religion! And poor Wolff's position became so difficult that he had to fly the country. Indeed, the founder of modern embryology was obliged to live and die in exile.

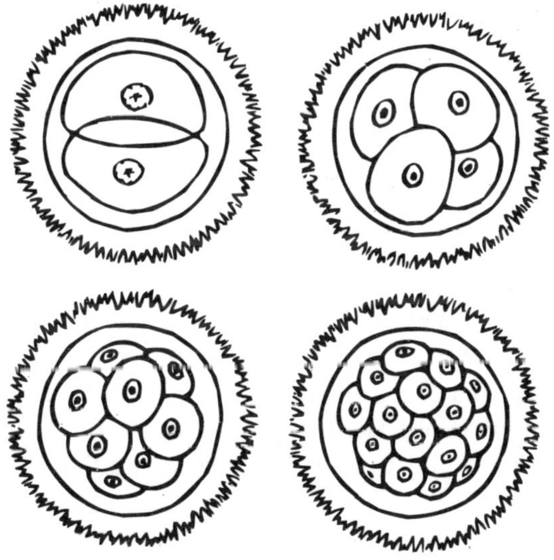

Fig. 1. *The multiplication of the germinal cell*

Although microscopes multiplied, no one else dared to investigate the secret for fifty years. Yet the assertions of this pioneer did make headway, and when another scientist, K. E. von Baer, repeated Wolff's experiments, finding them correct, everyone accepted the new truth, and a new branch of science was born—one of the most interesting—called embryology.

Embryology is undoubtedly one of the most fascinating sciences, inasmuch as it does not study the organs of a developed being, as anatomy does, nor the working of those organs, like physiology; nor does it study diseases, like pathology; but it has as its end and aim, to uncover the creative process, the way in which a body, which did not exist, comes to shape itself for entry into the world of the living.

Every animal, every mammal, even that most marvellous of creatures, man, comes from a single first cell to all appearances simple, like the most primitive of cells, undifferentiated and round. These germinative cells are amazing because of their smallness. That of man is no larger than a tenth of a millimetre. To get an idea of this, mark a point with a very sharp pencil and put ten such points close together side by side. However small you can make them, a millimetre will not enclose them all. So we see how microscopic is the cell giving rise to man. This cell develops apart from its progenitor, for it is protected and enclosed by a kind of capsule that keeps it separated from the body of the adult in which it is being carried.

This is true for every kind of animal. The cell is so isolated from the parent body, that the being to which it gives rise is truly the product of the germ cell itself. What an inexhaustible topic for meditation! The greatest of men, no matter in what field—whether it be an Alexander or a Napoleon, a Dante or a Shakespeare, or a Gandhi—no less than the humblest of their fellow beings, was each built up from one alone of these ultraminute cell bodies!

Viewing the germ cell through a powerful microscope, it is seen to contain a certain number of corpuscles. These, because they can readily be coloured by chemical means, have been named "chromosomes." Their number varies in the different species. In man there are 46 chromosomes. Other species have 15, others 13, so that the number of chromosomes is one of the fixed characters of the species. The chromosomes have always been regarded as depositories through which hereditary features are transmitted. Recently, new microscopes of greater power, called ultramicroscopes, have enabled it to be seen that each chromosome is a kind of box containing a chain, or necklace, composed of about 100 very small granules. The chromosomes open, the granules are freed, and the cell becomes a storehouse for some 4,000 corpuscles called *genes* (see drawing). The word, *gene,* implies the idea of generation, and by common consent the intuition is accepted that each gene may be the bearer of some particular hereditary feature; for example the form of the nose, or the colour of the hair.

It is plain that this scientific vision of the truth has not been reached solely by the help of the microscope, but because man's mind is creative. It does not just retain impressions like so many photographs, but they act as stimuli to its imaginative powers. It is by imagination, or, thanks to an intelligence which can "see behind the things of sense," that man can make conjectures as to what is happening, and it is from these powers of the human mind that all science and all discovery derive the impulse that sends it on. If we reflect on these disclosures of the genesis of all things living, we cannot fail to see how much mysticism there is in the bald statements of science. For this germ cell, so small as to be invisible, contains in itself the accumulated heredity of all past ages. Within this tiny speck, there lies embodied the whole of human experience, all the history which made the race.

Before any change becomes visible in the primitive cell, and before this begins its work of segmentation, the genes have already come to an agreement among themselves. There is a kind of competitive struggle between them, from which a choice results. For not all those present in a given cell can play a part in the production of the new being. This comes only from the genes which have prevailed in the contest. They carry the "dominant characteristics."

Others, instead, remain concealed. They carry the "recessive characters." This curious phenomenon, which

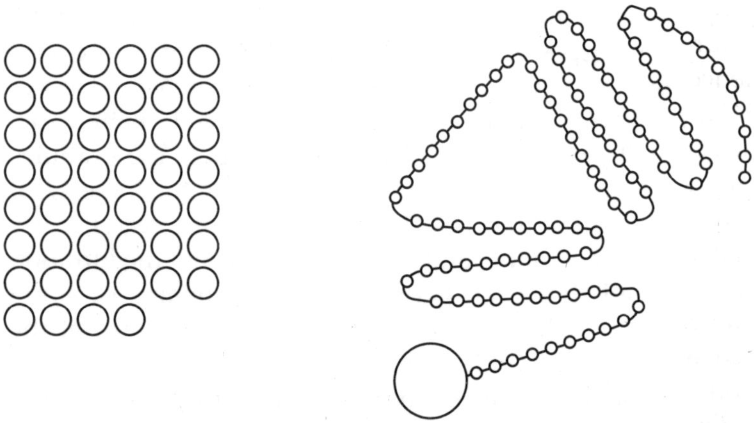

Fig. 2. *A chain of 100 genes pictured as a line; these are all held within each of the 46 chromosomes arranged geometrically on the left.*

occurs in preparation for the creative work of the germinative cell, was first noted by Mendel, who expressed it in the shape of a scientific hypothesis based on his famous and revolutionary experiments in the crossing of plants of the same family, one of which had red flowers and the other white. On sowing the resulting seeds, he obtained three plants with red flowers to one plant with white flowers. The dominant red genes had supplanted the recessive white in three cases out of four. It is easy to show that the proportion which results from a struggle between rival characteristics must follow inevitably the laws of mathematical combination.

Studies which have since been based on mathematical assumptions concerning the combinations possible among genes, are much more complex, but the conclusion remains that any germ, under given conditions, may turn into an individual more or less beautiful, more or less strong, according to the priorities reigning among its genes.

It is due to these differing combinations that every human being is different from every other. So we see in the same family, between children of the same parents, innumerable varieties of beauty, physical strength and intellectual attainment.

Special interest attaches to studies of the conditions which favour the emergence of the best types, and from this a new science has been born, that of *Eugenics*.

Nevertheless, this has been a chapter in scientific history (the science of genes and their combination) which rests on many suppositions. It plays no part in the direct study of what happens after the combining has occurred.

It is here that the true biological process of building up a body begins. This is a matter of cellular segmentation, so clear and easy to follow, that even Wolff, observing it microscopically for the first time, could describe the phases through which the developing embryo passes in succession.

The cell begins by dividing into two equal cells which remain united. Then these two become four, the four eight, the eight sixteen, and so on. This process continues till hundreds of cells have been produced. It is as if a building were being started intelligently by the accumulation of enough bricks to build the house. In due course, the cells are arranged in three distinct layers, as if the bricks were being built into walls (this comparison is due to Huxley). What follows is common to all animals. First, the cells form a kind of empty sphere, like the sides of an indiarubber ball (the *morula*). Then the shell is bent inwards forming two walls opposed to each other. Finally, a third layer is infiltrated between the other two. So here are the three walls, from which the whole of the final structure is about to unfold (see drawing).

These layers, the "germinative leaves," are therefore as follows: one is external, the ectoderm; one is medial, the *mesoderm*, and one is internal, the *endoderm*. Together, they form a tiny elongated body in which all the cells are of equal size, though somewhat smaller than the first cell from which all have come.

Each of these three walls produces a complicated system of organs. The outer gives rise to the skin and to the sensorial and nervous system. Indeed, this is to be expected, since it is the layer in contact with the outer world, from which the

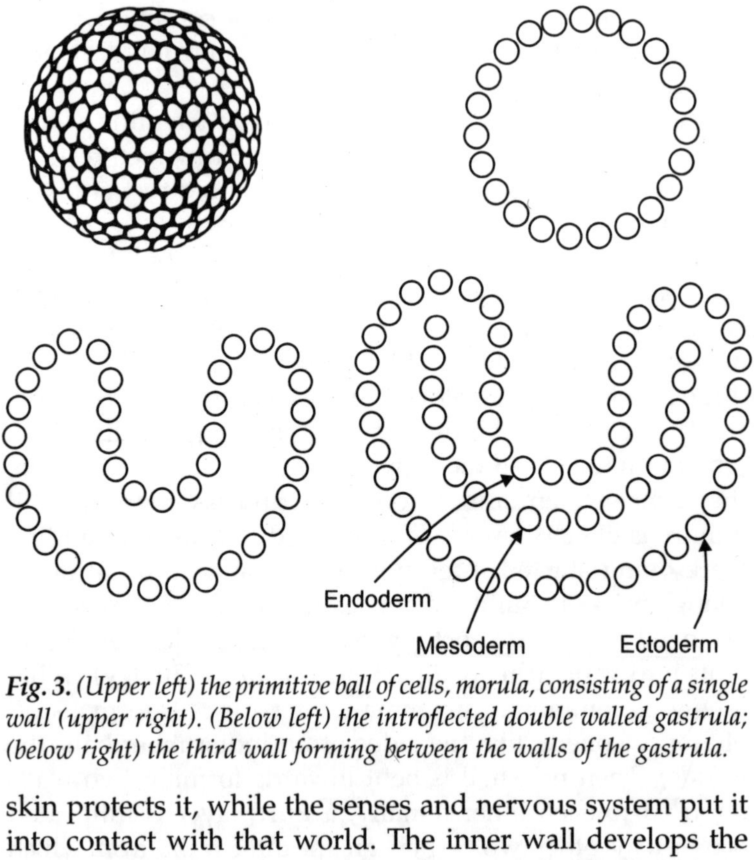

Fig. 3. *(Upper left) the primitive ball of cells, morula, consisting of a single wall (upper right). (Below left) the introflected double walled gastrula; (below right) the third wall forming between the walls of the gastrula.*

skin protects it, while the senses and nervous system put it into contact with that world. The inner wall develops the organs which provide nutrition; for example, the intestines, stomach, digestive glands, liver, pancreas and lungs. The third, or medial, wall produces the skeleton which supports the whole of the body and the muscles. The organs of the nervous system are called "organs of relationship," because they govern our relationships with the outer world. The organs of the digestive and respiratory system are called "vegetative organs," because they minister solely to the vegetable, or nonactive, part of living things.

Only recently have further studies shown how the organs themselves develop. What happens is that points, or centres, appear in the uniform layers, and these points suddenly manifest great biological activity. Cells emerge from the mural matrices, and commence to construct an organ, or the design for an organ. Whatever the organ is to be, the same procedure marks its emergence, and the different organs all come from such centres of increased activity, even though the latter may be out of touch and quite separate from one another. It was Professor Child of the University of Chicago who discovered this. He called the centres "gradients."[1]

Almost at the same time another embryologist, Douglas, working in England independently of Child, made a similar discovery, though his observations were restricted to the

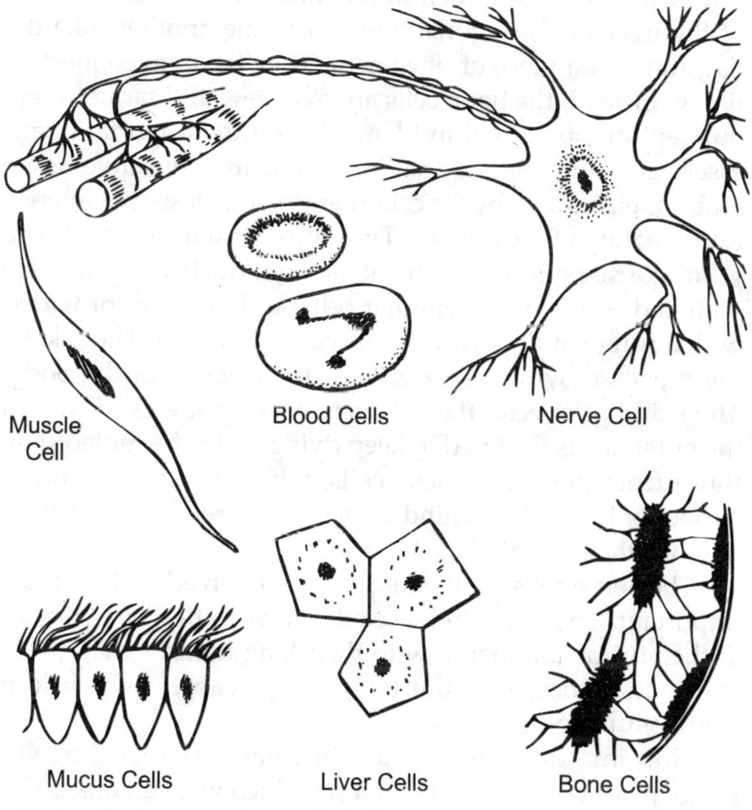

Fig. 4. Types of cells.

nervous system. He called the active points "sanglia,"[2] attributing to them a special degree of sensitiveness.

At the moment when the organs are beginning to appear, the cells themselves, which at first were all alike, begin to change their type and to undergo profound differentiations. This corresponds to the functions which the organs are going to perform. Thus, there occurs a "specialization" by which the cells become suited to do the work of the organs they are building up. Yet, this delicate specialization, although it occurs for the sake of a particular function, does so *before the function begins to operate*.

In the accompanying drawing are shown some of these cells to give an idea of their tremendous differences. The cells of the liver are hexagonal and touch one another, like the flagstones of a piece of pavement. They have no connective tissue. Instead, the bone cells are oval, few and far between, but kept in touch by thin filaments; but the important part, essential to the bone, is that kind of solid connective tissue which is elaborated by the cells themselves. Of special interest is the coating of the trachea. Tiny cups constantly excreting a gum-like substance which catches the dust of the air, are scattered among the triangular cells, and these are provided with a fringe of fibres always in vibrant motion. These keep the mucus moving along toward the exterior of the body. The skin has special flat cells arranged in layers, of which the outer one is destined to keep dying and to be replaced by those from beneath. These cells, which protect the outer surface of the body, remind us of soldiers ready to give their lives for their country.

The nerve cells are the most highly evolved and the most important. They are irreplaceable. Always they are present at the post of command, with their long tendrils that go for great distances, like the telegraphic cables which join continent to continent.

How interesting is this vast difference between the cells, for each has come from the first set which were all alike. Yet, in preparing themselves for their future missions they have changed, so that each can do something it never did before! But, once they are altered, they can never change again. A liver cell can never become a nerve cell. It follows that, to do their work, they have not had—as we used to say—to prepare themselves, but to transform themselves.

But does not much the same thing happen in human communities? Here we find specialized kinds of folk, who may be compared to organs in the body. In primitive times, everyone did many kinds of work. The same person might be a builder, a carpenter, a doctor; in short everything. But, as the community develops, work becomes more specialized. Each person chooses one kind of work, and becomes psychologically unfitted for other kinds. Practising of a profession does not just mean learning a technique. Dedication to it produces inward changes necessary to success. More important than technique is the acquisition of a special personality suited to the work. This makes it a man's own ideal. It becomes the goal of his life.

Returning to the embryo, each organ is made of specialized cells and has its own functions to perform, different from those of the other organs. Yet each of these functions is necessary for the health and well-being of the organism. Each organ, therefore, exists and works for the sake of the whole.

Not only does the developing embryo produce the organs, but it provides for intercommunication to occur between them. This is done by two great systems; the circulatory system and the nervous system. These are far the most complex of all the organs. Also, they are the only ones engaged solely in uniting the others.

The first is like a river which carries substances to all parts of the body. But it acts also as a collector. In fact, the circulatory system is the general vehicle of transport which carries nourishment to every cell in the body, while, at the same time, it takes in oxygen from the lungs. Blood also carries certain substances, secreted by the endocrine glands. These are known as hormones, which exert an influence on the organs, stimulating their activity and, above all, controlling their operation so as to produce a certain harmony of action necessary to all.

Hormones are substances necessary to organs lying at a distance from those in which the hormones are produced. What perfection is achieved, therefore, by this circulatory system in the doing of its work! Every organ lives, as it were, on the banks of a river, from which it draws all that it needs for its life, and then pours back its own products, some of which are needed by organs elsewhere.

The other great organism which harmonizes the body's total activity is the nervous system. This is what directs, concentrating in the brain a kind of directorate, or "controlroom," whence commands are transmitted to every part of the body.

Even in the life of humanity, a circulatory system has developed. Things produced by different peoples and countries go into circulation, and every one takes from it what is needful for his life. The great river of trade makes them available to other persons and countries. Merchants and travelling salesmen, what are they but the counterparts of the red corpuscles in the blood? And in the great human society, are not the goods produced in one place constantly being consumed in another?

In recent years, we can even see the growth of arrangements doing the work of hormones.

These are the efforts of large states to plan the environment, to control commerce, stimulate, encourage, and direct the undertakings of all nations, simply with a view to achieving the greater harmony and well-being of all. One may say that the defects that have shown themselves clearly enough in these attempts merely prove that the embryonic development of the social circulatory system, though it has made a beginning, is still far from perfect.

As for the specialized cells of the nervous system, anything corresponding to these is still woefully lacking in human society. From the chaotic state of today's world, we might well infer that what is needed to carry out their function has not yet been evolved. For lack of it, we have nothing that acts simultaneously on the whole social body, and guides it to harmony. Democracy, which is our civilization's highest form of government, permits everyone to vote, and so to choose the Head of Affairs. For this to happen in embryology would be absurd beyond belief, for if each cell has to be specialized, then the cell able to direct all the others must be even more specialized. To rule is the most difficult task of all and requires a higher specialization than any. So there is here no question of election, but of being trained and suited to the work. Whoever directs others must have transformed himself. No one can ever be a leader, or a guide, who has not been prepared for that work. This principle, which links specialization with function, may well engage our active attention—all the more so as it seems to be nature's way, the plan she follows in all her works. One can see the wonders it brings about in living organisms.

So embryology can point a direction for ourselves. It becomes a source of inspiration. Julian Huxley well sums up the miracles of the embryo. "The passage from nothing to the complex body of the fully grown individual is one of the constant miracles of life. If we are not struck by the greatness of this miracle, it can only be for one reason, that it occurs so often under our eyes in the experience of everyday life."[3]

Whatever the animal we study, bird or rabbit, or any of the other vertebrates, we find it to be composed of organs each of the utmost complexity. And, more marvellous still is the fact that these organs, in themselves so intricate, are strictly interconnected. If we contemplate the circulatory system, we find a form of drainage so delicate, complex and complete, that no system, invented by the most advanced type of civilization, can be compared with it. Also the mind, the instrument of thought, which collects through the senses impressions from the outside world, is so marvellous that no modern mechanism bears it the slightest resemblance. Can any of our mechanical devices match the hidden marvels of the eye, or the ear? And if we study the chemical reactions that occur in the body, we are obliged to face the existence of whole laboratories, so well-equipped that substances can be manufactured and their components held together, which defy the most elaborate of our own techniques.

Beside the network of communications in the nervous system, even our most brilliant triumphs, the telephone, radio, television, wireless telegraphy, and so many others, seem clumsy and inept.

And if we inspect the best trained troops in the world, we shall not find an obedience like that of the muscles, which respond immediately to the commands of a single controller and strategist. Docile servants, they practise a special craft of being always ready to carry out exactly the orders they receive. If we let our minds dwell on these facts, and realize how these complex organs, these organs of communication, these muscles, and the nerves which make contact with every tiniest cell in the body, and if we remember that all this comes from a single cell, the primitive round germinal cell, then we feel upon us the spell of the wonder and majesty of nature.

REFERENCES

1. C.M. Child, *Physiological Foundations of Behaviour*, New York, 1924.
2. A.C. Douglas, *The Physical Mechanism of the Human Mind*, Edinburgh, 1925.
3. J.S. Huxley, *The Stream of Life* (1926).

6

Embryology and Behaviour

Each of the phases we have traced in the embryo's development is common to all the higher animals including man. Lower animals differ only in the sense that their development is incomplete. It is arrested in one of the earlier phases.

For example, *Volvox* is a creature which has not developed beyond the globular stage. It remains a tiny empty ball which rotates in the waters of the ocean. On the outer side of its single layer of cells there is a coating of tiny vibrant hairs by waving which it turns about and moves.

Coelenterates are those animals which correspond to the next or double walled stage, when the coating of the hollow sphere has bent inwards forming two layers of cells, the ectoderm and endoderm. And once all three layers have developed, the stages which follow are so similar in many species that it is easy to confuse the embryo of one with the embryo of another. Fig. 5 makes this very clear.

This last fact has been regarded as one of the clearest proofs of the theory of descent through the various degrees of "animality." Thus, man was said to have come from the apes; mammals and birds from the reptiles; these again from amphibia; the latter from fish, and so on, right down to the simplest forms in which the creature consists of one cell only. By the process of inheritance, each embryo had therefore to pass through all the stages of its predecessors, so that in the embryo was summed up, or synthesized, the whole evolution of the species. This was called the recapitulation theory, by which Ontogenesis repeated Phylogenesis.

For this reason, embryology became incorporated in the theories of Darwin, of which it was held to be one of the most convincing proofs. But later on, after the discoveries of De Vries, embryology found itself obliged to embrace a wider view, if living things were to be explained.

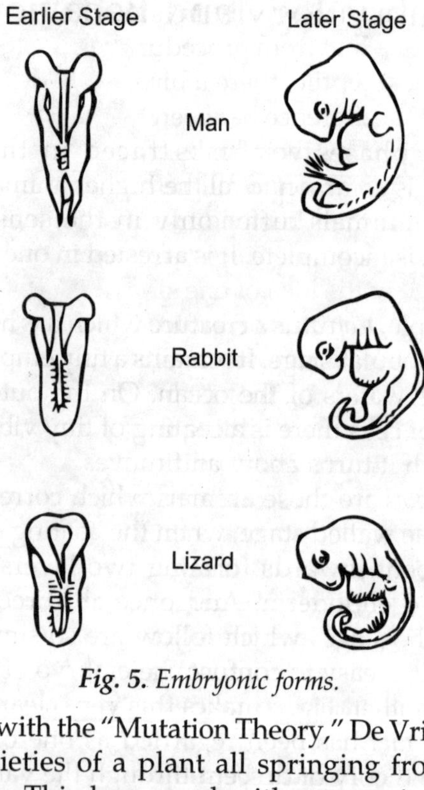

Fig. 5. Embryonic forms.

To begin with the "Mutation Theory," De Vries[1] observed different varieties of a plant all springing from the same parent forms. This happened without any influence that could be attributed to the outer world, and it made people speak of spontaneous variations. If the causes of these changes could not be found in the environment, they could only lie in the interior activities of the embryo, for here alone could rapid evolution take place.

Thus, it became possible to envisage other possibilities than that of the slow adaptive transformations of the Darwinian hypothesis, which required immense periods of time, and this permitted thinkers to move more freely toward other intuitions, to accept the possibility of more problems.

In fact, the building up of the embryo, which the microscope reveals, is merely the mechanical part, for living beings are not just an assemblage of organs working together for a common end. The really mysterious thing about the higher creatures is that from procedures so alike there should come forth here a reptile, there a bird, a mammal or a man.

For the main difference between these animals lies in the final form reached by their limbs, their bodies, their teeth, and this final form is not at all related to their embryonic past but rather to their behaviour in the surroundings they inhabit.

This had led to the idea of one single constructive plan in nature: a single manner of building, much as in man's handiwork, where the most varied structures—simple or monumental—are all begun, first by collecting the materials (stones and bricks), then building these into walls. But what really causes our buildings to differ, both in shape and in ornamentation? It is not the materials from which they are made but the different purposes they are designed to serve.

But, all this apart, the truly important thing is that embryology has been able to emerge from the stage of abstract theorizing. It does not lead merely to fresh ideas, but a path has been opened for experimental research, and along this enough progress has been made to found a science with practical applications.

The embryo, in fact, can be subjected to influences which are capable of working changes in it. This means that man, by acting on the embryo, can experimentally alter the course of life. Already this is being done.

By means of the genes and their combinations we can intervene in vegetable heredity—then in that of the animals—with results of the first importance. A new field of vast and varied interest, not just academic, but useful in practice, has been opened up. The importance of the embryo lies in the fact that it has not yet fully constructed its organs, and so can be made to change them with relative ease. This is the secret of which man has now become possessed.

A few years ago, the first patent was granted in America in the field of embryology. A variety of bees had been produced without any stings, and able to collect much more honey than ordinary bees. In the same way, various plants have begun to yield more fruit, or to develop stems without thorns. Others produce roots far richer in food value, or some already rich have ceased to be poisonous.

The best known results are in the improvement of blossoms. But, although this is not so well known, man's intervention now extends beyond the dry land, to the animal and vegetable kingdoms which exist under water. Hence we can say that man, by using his intelligence, has been able to beautify and enrich the earth. And if, as biologists do, we study all life as such, and consider the influence on one another of the forms it assumes—and the effects of these—we begin to see one of the purposes of man's life on earth, and to understand that man himself is one of the great cosmic forces of the universe.

With the harvest of his intelligence man is seen, in fact, as the continuer of creation, as if he had been sent (as Huxley says) to use this power to help creation and accelerate its rhythm. By exercising control over life itself, he helps to perfect it.

So the study of embryology is no longer abstract or sterile.

If, by an effort of imagination, we visualize mental development as following similar paths, it would be natural to suppose that man, who today can act on life to create new types of a higher order, must be able, also, to help and control man's mental formation.

For mental development, as well as bodily development, seems to follow nature's same creative plan. Just as the body begins with one primitive cell, differing in no apparent way from others, so the human mind also proceeds from nothing, or from what appears to be nothing.

Just as there is no complete man already formed in the original germinative cell, so there seems to be no kind of mental personality already formed in the newborn child. The first thing one sees on the mental plane is an accumulation of material, which may be compared to the multiplication of cells that we saw to occur on the physical plane. It is done by what I have called *the absorbent mind*, and on this plane, also, we see the formation of psychic organs around about *points of sensitivity*, which appear in turn. These are of such intense activity that the adult can never recapture them, or recollect what they were like. We have already hinted at this in the child's conquest of language. For it is not the mind itself that these sensitivities create, but its *organs*. And here, too, each organ develops independently of the others. For example, while language is developing on the one hand, the judgment of distances and of finding one's way about, is developing quite separately; so is the power to balance on two feet, and other forms of coordination.

Each of these powers has its own special interest and this form of sensitivity is so lively that it leads its possessor to perform a certain series of actions. None of these sensitivities occupies the whole period of development. Each of them lasts long enough for the construction of a psychic organ. Once that organ is formed, the sensitivity disappears, but, while it lasts, there is an outpouring of energy incredible to us, who have outgrown it so completely that we can no longer remember ever having had it. When all the organs are ready, they unite to form what we regard as the psychic unity of the individual.

The occurrence of passing sensitivities, not unlike these, has been discovered in the life cycles of insects. The same De Vries who enunciated the mutation theory, showed how these temporary states begin to guide the insect immediately after its birth through a changing series of activities, each of which in turn is necessary to its survival and development. This second discovery of De Vries led to many biological and psychological studies of other animals. And these gave rise to a quantity of theories, heatedly championed by different groups, until Watson, an American psychologist, tried to cut a new path through the somewhat chaotic tangle of hypotheses.

"Let us drop everything we cannot verify," he said, "and cling only to what we can prove. Now there is one thing of which we can be quite sure, because it is an observable fact, and that is the animal's behaviour. So let us make this the basis for a new line of research."

His starting point, therefore, was the behaviour one can see in the animal's external manifestations. Believing that these offered the safest guide for deepening our knowledge of life, he turned to human behaviour and to child psychology, as if to things we can understand direct. But he quickly found that in the infant there is no trace, of pre-established behaviour. He confirmed, too, the absence of instincts and of psychological heredity, holding that the actions of man are due to a series of "conditioned reflexes," superimposed one upon the other in a series of planes at ever higher levels. Thus arose his *Behaviourism*,[2] which had a great vogue in America, though it was much opposed and criticized by those who thought it premature and superficial.

However, the interest aroused by his proposal stimulated two other American research workers to verify and study behaviour afresh by experimental and laboratory methods.

These were CGoghill and Gesell. The first worked in embryology with a view to clarifying the question of behaviour; while Gesell began a systematic study of child development, founding his famous psychological laboratory to which all the world looks with interest.

Coghill at Philadelphia spent many years studying the embryonic development of a single type of animal. This was *amblyostoma*, at a level of evolution not quite so high as that of amphibia. He chose it for the simplicity of its structure which made it specially convenient for clarity in research.

Coghill's conclusions were not published till 1929[3], and the reasons he spent so long was that the facts he observed seemed to be too inconsistent with the rooted beliefs of biologists. Although he kept on repeating his experiments with more and more exactitude, he constantly found that the nerve centres of the brain develop *before* the organs which they will have to direct. The visual centre, for example, always appeared before the optic nerves. If the embryo were following the presumed order of inheritance by which the structures which come later in the history of the species also develop later in the embryo, then the first thing to be seen should have been the organs, and later—as a result of their use—the centres. How, then, could the visual centres not only take precedence over the eyes, but even over those nerves which put them into communication with the eyes?

Coghill's researches have given a great impetus to the study of real facts in the problems of animal behaviour. Not only that, but they have given rise to a surprising idea, namely, that if the organs develop after the centres, it must be so that they can assume a form corresponding to the services they have to render in the environment. From this, not only does it follow that behaviour is inherited (as already supposed of instinct) but also there is born this new idea, that the organs become shaped in accordance with the creature's cycle of behaviour in its environment.

In fact, we are always meeting in nature with admirable examples of the close correspondence between the forms of the organs and the offices they fulfil, even when these bring no actual benefit to the animal. The insects which suck nectar from flowers of a certain kind, develop probosces adapted to the length of corolla which those flowers possess. But they also develop a coating, quite useless to themselves, by which they collect pollen and this fertilizes the flowers they will visit afterwards. The anteater has a mouth so small that only its long worm-like tongue can emerge from it, a tongue covered with a sticky substance, enabling it to eat ants, etc.

But why should the animal's behaviour have become

restricted like this? Why does one animal crawl, another jump, and another climb? And why does one eat ants, and another so adapt itself that it fertilizes only one particular kind of flower? And why should some eat living creatures and others only putrescent flesh? There are some which live only on grass, others which thrive on nothing but wood, or which spend their time passing through their bodies the humus of the soil. And the immense number of different species: to what is that due? And why should each have its own fixed mode of behaviour, modes which differ so widely from one to another? Why are the instincts of these to be fierce and aggressive, and of those to be timid and shy? The purposes of the living creatures in this world cannot surely be only to live, to survive in the struggle for existence, each trying to get the best it can out of its surroundings for its own benefit in a kind of free for all scramble, as envisaged by the Darwinian explanation of evolution. The "life force"[4] does not seem to go straight ahead to achieve an ever greater perfection in a sequence of improving forms. Perfection in itself does not seem to be the true goal of life.

So here is a great new upheaval in our ideas! From this fresh point of view, the purposes of the living seem to be related rather to the doing of work needed by the environment. It is almost as if the living were agents of creation, charged each with a particular task, like the servants in a large house, or the employees of a business. The harmony of nature on the earth's surface is produced by the efforts of countless living beings, each of which has its own duties. These are the forms of behaviour that we observe, and it follows that such behaviour serves purposes far beyond the mere ministering of each to its own vital needs.

If this be so, what becomes of the evolutionary theories which have for so long held exclusive sway in the world of science? Are they to decay? Not at all. They are merely being extended. Certainly, the idea of evolution can no longer be entertained in its old linear form, which was that of a series of progressive steps towards an indefinite perfection. Today, the vision of evolution has broadened; it has become spread over a bi-dimensional field, wherein are included many functional relationships, near and distant, which link up the activities of different forms of life.

Those links are not to be interpreted just as simple examples of mutual aid, but as being related to a universal end concerning the total world environment—to a kind of oneness of nature. From the order which results, all receive the elements necessary for their own existence.

That life could have a function connected with the earth, had already been recognized by geologists of the last century. There was Lyell,[5] contemporary with Darwin, who showed how the different species had made their appearances on earth at different periods in geological time. From the fossilized remains of animals discovered in the layers of rock at various levels, he was able to prove the antiquity of living things upon the earth. But other geologists, since then, have shown the influence of animal behaviour in the very building up of the world's surface itself. The treatise, *Earth and Life*, by a German geologist, Friedrich Ratzel,[6] became famous in my own land at the beginning of this century, and other publications have followed containing numerous discoveries and deductions.

At first it was with general amazement that the remains of marine animals were found at rock levels so high as those of the Himalayas or the Alps. They were also found in deposits of material washed down by water from the mountain tops. Undoubtedly, these were animals which had helped to construct the land, just as we can still see them doing in a myriad coral islands, springing up like flowers amid the vast waste of the oceans. Such remnants are the "signatures" of an unknown army of builders, who prepared the resurrection of a world in collapse.

Further proofs and studies are always accumulating. The shape of the earth's surface cannot be ascribed to wind and water alone, but the essential parts played by animals, plants and men have had to be included. The Italian geologist,

Antonio Stoppani,[7] after showing how terrestrial conditions depend on living beings, ended by exclaiming: "The animals all form one trained and disciplined army which battles to preserve the harmonies of nature."

But there is no need, nowadays, to quote single and partial observations, for a special science has been founded, the science of ecology, which studies the relationship of living things one to another. This has made the details of behaviour, by which one species interacts with another, so precisely known, that it seems like a science of economics applied to nature. By its aid, one can solve practical local problems of the countryside, as one does in scientific agriculture. For example, to defend an area against imported plants that are proving too invasive for human action to control, one seeks the help of ecology, which may suggest the importation of a destructive insect, so as to restore the needed balance. Examples of this have occurred more particularly in Australia.[8]

Ecology may be called biology in practice, for it deals with the relationships between species, instead of with the characters of each species, considered separately.

The most useful and enlightening parts of modern knowledge are on its practical side, for here the vision of evolution is completed by the action of living things on the environment, and this brings us nearer to the unity of truth. Their functioning in this sense is the most impressive and conclusive thing about them. Life is not present on the earth merely to preserve its own existence, but to carry on a process vital to all creation, and therefore necessary for every thing that lives.

Neither the discoveries nor the theories, derived from the scientific achievements of our day, are enough to explain the mysteries of life, but every fresh detail, which those achievements bring to light, adds something to our understanding of it.

External facts, which can be fully observed, offer practical guidance which it is worthwhile to pursue. And all who, like us, want to help life through education, are under the necessity of regarding the child in the same light as any other living creature in the course of its growth. And this makes us wonder what is the place of human infancy in biology, in the whole world of the living. For the linear concept of evolution, which tries to explain descent by adaptation, by heredity and by the impulse toward perfection, is no longer enough. There exists another force, which is not just an impulse toward survival, but a force for harmony, uniting the efforts of all, so that they work toward a common end.

So, in the child, besides the vital impulse to create himself, and to become perfect, there must be yet another purpose, a duty to fulfil in harmony, something he has to do in the service of a united whole.

You will be asking already, "What, then, is the real purpose of childhood?" And we can hardly proceed with confidence in scientific education without first trying to answer this question.

For the child has a double duty. And if we consider one side of it only, the duty of growing up, there is a danger of suppressing his best energies.

Already we have found it reasonable to suppose that the child, at birth, bears within him constructive possibilities, which must unfold by activity in his environment.

He comes from nothing, in the sense that he has no psychic qualities, nor pre-established powers of movement, but he has in himself potentialities which determine his development, and this will take its characteristics from the world about him.

This "nothingness" of the newborn babe is comparable with the apparent "nothingness" of the germinal cell.

Certainly, it is not an idea easy to accept. Wolff caused great astonishment in his day, simply by showing that the living body constructs itself, and that, previous to this, nothing is already fashioned, as the philosophers of his day used to imagine.

How amazing, is it not, to find that the child also brings

with him into the world none of the acquisitions of his people and race, not even those of his family, but that he himself has to construct all these! And this happens everywhere, not less in the most primitive and widely scattered of races, than in the most civilized; and in all corners of the earth. Every baby has the same appearance; he is motionless, empty, insignificant.

Yet, there exists in this inert being a global power, a "human creative essence," which drives him to form a man of his time, a man of his civilization. And, in this faculty for absorption that he possesses, he follows laws of growth that are universal for the whole of mankind.

His duty is to realize the present stage of an evolving society, a society which comes from an antiquity lost in the hundreds of thousands of years that have gone, and which has a future before it of thousands and perhaps millions of years. Nor is this present level that he has to achieve, without limits in past or future, ever quite the same.

It is difficult to realize the proper division of labour between adult and child in this unique phenomenon, of a progress unaided by any hereditary transmission of acquired characteristics.

Then, there is the child's neutrality, his biological indifference to the taking in, and weaving into his character, of whatever he finds about him. This strikes one as a real proof of unity in the human kind.

Apprehension of this surprising truth, especially in the last few years, has much stimulated the study of backward tribes, wherein it was hoped to find still further proof.

In her recent publication, *Patterns of Culture* (New York 1948), Dr. Ruth Benedict tells how a French missionary party pursuing modern ethnological studies came to Patagonia, where there are races still living thought to be the most primitive on earth. Their level and social habits are those of the Stone Age. These people, who have a terror of the white man, fled at their approach. But in their haste, some of these Patagonians left behind them a newly born little girl. She was rescued by the mission, and today she is an intelligent young woman who speaks two European languages, has Western habits, is a Catholic by religion, and is studying biology at the University. In the space of eighteen years, she has passed in very truth from the Stone Age to the atomic era.

It follows that at the beginning of his life the individual can accomplish wonders—without effort and quite unconsciously.

This absorption of characteristics from the outer world is a vital phenomenon, which reminds one of the facts of biological mimicry. This is rare, but not so unusual as was formerly supposed. Examples are met with more and more often, so much so that a whole wing of the Zoological Museum in Berlin has been adapted to exhibit a rich collection of them. Now, mimicry is a phenomenon of defence, and it consists in absorbing into one's own body the appearance of one's surroundings. Of this nature is the white fur of the polar bear, the leaf-shaped wings of some butterflies, the similarity of certain insects to sticks or to the green stalks of plants, the flatness and sandy appearance of certain fish.

This reproduction of the features of the environment has nothing to do with the history of such features, nor does it depend on knowing them consciously. Many animals only look at the various aspects of their environment; others absorb them.

Though totally different in its nature, this example from other forms of life helps us to realize the psychic phenomena which occur in childhood.

REFERENCES

1. Hugo de Vries, founder of experimental genetics, is best known for the work here quoted: *Die Mutations Theorie*, Leipzig, 2 vols., 1902-3. All his writings have been collected in the volume, *Operate periodicis collata*, Utrecht, 1918-27.
2. John B. Watson, *Psychology from the Standpoint of a Behaviourist* (1919), and *Behaviourism* (1925).

3. G.E. Coghill, *Anatomy and the Problem of Behaviour,* Cambridge University Press, 1929.
4. Bergson's *élan vital.*
5. Charles Lyell, *Principles of Geology* (1836); *Elements of Geology* (1838); *Travels in America* (1845).
6. F. Ratzel, *Earth and Life* (1901-2).
7. Dr. Montessori often spoke with pleasure of the family relationship between her and Stoppani.
8. An immense survey of life in all its aspects can be found in a work by H.G. Wells, Julian Huxley and G.P. Wells, *The Science of Life,* London, (1931).

7

The Spiritual Embryo

It follows that the newborn child has to do a piece of formative work which corresponds in the psychological sphere to the one just done by the embryo in the physical sphere. Before him there is a period of life different from that which he led in the womb; yet still unlike that of the man he is to become. This postnatal work is a constructive activity which is carried on in what may be called the "formative period," and it makes the baby into a kind of "Spiritual Embryo."

Man seems to have two embryonic periods. One is prenatal, like that of the animals; the other is postnatal and only man has this. The prolonged infancy of man separates him entirely from the animals, and this is the meaning we must give to it. It forms a complete barrier, whereby man is seen as a being different from all others. His powers are neither continuations, nor derivations from those of the animals. His appearance on earth was a jump in life: the starting point for new destinies.

What causes us to distinguish between species is always their differences, never their likeness. What constitutes another species is always *something* new. It is not merely derived from the old, but it shows originality. It bears characters that never existed before. A new impulse has appeared in the kingdom of the living.

So it was when mammals and birds came into existence. They bore with them *novelties*. They were not mere copies, or adaptations, or continuations, of the earlier creatures. New features that appeared when dinosaurs became extinct, were, in the birds, the passionate defence of their eggs, the building of nests, the care of the fledglings and their courageous protection. The insensitive reptiles, on the contrary; had always abandoned their eggs. And the mammals surpassed even the birds in their defence of the species. They built no nests, but they let their young grow in their own bodies, and fed them with their blood.

These were quite new biological features.

Then came another new character, that of being human. The human species has a double embryonic life. It is built to a new design, and has a fresh destiny in relation to the other creatures.

This is the point at which we must pause, and make a fresh start in all our studies of child development, and of man on his psychological side. If the work of man on the earth is related to his spirit, to his creative intelligence, then his spirit and his intelligence must be the fulcrum of his existence, and of all the workings of his body. About this fulcrum his behaviour is organized, and even his physical economy. The whole man develops within a kind of spiritual halo.

Today, even our Western ideas have become receptive to this idea, which has ever been prominent in Indian philosophy. Experience itself has forced to our notice that physical disturbances are often caused by psychological states, the spirit no longer exercising proper control.

If the nature of man is to be ruled by a "spiritual halo which enfolds him," if he depends on this and all his behaviour derives from it, then the first care given to the newborn babe—overriding all others—must be a care for his mental life, and not just for his bodily life, which is the rule today.

The developing child not only acquires the faculties of man: strength, intelligence, language; but, at the same time, he adapts the being he is constructing to the conditions of the world about him. And this it is that gives virtue to his particular form of psychology, which is so different from that of adults. The child has a different relation to his environment from ours. Adults admire their environment; they can remember it and think about it; but the child absorbs it. The things he sees are not just remembered; they form part of his soul. He incarnates in himself all in the world about him that his eyes see and his ears hear. In us the same things produce no change, but the child is transformed by them. This vital kind of memory, which does not consciously remember, but absorbs images into the individual's very life, has been given a special name by Sir Percy Nunn, who calls it the "Mneme."[1]

One example of this, as we have seen, is language. The child does not "remember" sounds, but he incarnates them, and can then produce them to perfection. He speaks his language according to its complex rules, with all their exceptions, not because he has studied it, nor by the ordinary use of memory. Perhaps his memory never retains it consciously, and yet this language comes to form part of his psychic life and of himself. Undoubtedly, we are dealing with a phenomenon different from the purely mnemonic activity; we are dealing with one of the strangest aspects of the infant mind. There is in the child a special kind of sensitivity which leads him to absorb everything about him, and it is this work of observing and absorbing that alone enables him to adapt himself to life. He does it in virtue of an unconscious power that only exists in childhood.

The first period of the child's life is one of adaptation. We must understand clearly what is meant by adaptation in this sense and distinguish it from the kind of adaptation made by adults. It is the child's special adaptability that makes the land into which he is born the only one in which he will ever want to live, just as the only language he can speak to perfection will be his mother tongue. A grown-up, who lives abroad, never adapts his life in the same way and to the same degree. Think of the missionaries. These are people who go, of their own free will, to carry on their vocation in distant lands, and, if you ask them, they say, "We sacrifice our lives by living here." It is a confession which shows the limitation in the adult's capacity to adapt.

But, turn to the child. He comes to love the land into which he is born, no matter where it is. However hard the life may be there, he can never find equal happiness elsewhere. One man loves the frozen plains of Finland, another the sand-dunes of Holland. Each has received this adaptation, this love of country, from the child he used to be.

It is the child who brings it about, and the adult finds himself possessed of it. He then feels he belongs to this country; he is obliged to love it, to feel its fascination; nowhere else does he find the same peace and happiness.

At one time in Italy, those born in the villages lived and died there, without ever going far away. After Italy had become a nation, many, for reasons of marriage or work, left their birthplaces; but in later life, these often suffered from a peculiar illness: pallor, depression, weakness, anaemia. Many cures were tried, and, as a last resort, the doctor would advise the sufferer to go back and take the air of his native parts. And nearly always this advice had the best results; the patients regained their colour and health. People used to say that a man's own air was the best cure, even if the climate he went to was far worse than the one he left. But what these sufferers really needed was the peace offered to their subconscious minds by the simple places where they had lived as children.

Nothing has more importance for us than this absorbent form of mind, which shapes the adult and adapts him to any kind of social order, climate, or country. On this, the whole of our study is based. It is opportune to reflect that anyone who says, "I love my country," does not say something superficial or artificial, but reveals a basic part of himself and of his life.

We can therefore understand how the child, thanks to his peculiar psyche, absorbs the customs and habits of the land in which he lives, until he has formed the typical individual of his place and time. The local manner is another of the mysterious formations that a man builds up in childhood. That the customs, and special mentality, of a district are acquisitions is clear enough, since none of these can be natural, or inborn.[2] So we are beginning to gain a much more comprehensive picture of the child's activity. He develops a behaviour not only adapted to this time and region, but also to the local mentality. Thus, the respect for life in India is so great that animals also are included in a veneration firmly rooted in the hearts of the people. So deep a sentiment can never be acquired by people already grown up. Just to say: "Life is worthy of respect," does not make this feeling ours. I might think the Indians were right; that I also should respect animals. But in me this would only be a piece of reasoning; it would not stir my emotions. That kind of veneration which Indians have for the cow, for example, we Europeans can never experience. Nor can the native Indian, reason as he may, ever rid himself of it. These mental characteristics seem to be hereditary, but really they are infantile formations derived from the child's surroundings. Once in a garden attached to the local Montessori school, we saw a small Hindu child of little more than two, who was looking intently at the ground on which he seemed to be tracing a line with his finger. There was an ant there, which had lost two legs and could only walk with difficulty. The child had noticed its predicament, and was trying to be helpful, by making a track for it with his finger. Anyone would have supposed that this Hindu baby must have "inherited" such a fondness for animals.

Another child, attracted by these same doings, now approached, saw the ant, put his foot out and crushed it. This second child was a Moslem. A Christian child would possibly have done the same thing, or would have passed on indifferently. One would be forgiven for thinking that here, too—in this feeling of a barrier separating us from the animals, whereby love and respect are due only to men—we had an example of heredity in the mind.

The nations of the world have different religions, but even when the mind of a people comes to repudiate one of its ancient tenets, the heart feels strangely perturbed. These beliefs and feelings form an integral part of ourselves. As we say in Europe: "They are in our blood." All the social and moral habits that shape a man's personality, the sentiments of caste, and all kinds of other feelings, that make him a typical Indian, a typical Italian, or a typical Englishman, are formed during infancy, in virtue of that mysterious mental power that psychologists have called "Mneme."

This holds good, also, for the habitual tricks of posture, bearing and gait which distinguish so many racial types. There are African natives who acquire a special physique for coping with wild beasts. Others perform instinctively the right exercises for sharpening their hearing, so that auditory acuteness marks all those of their tribe. Every personal trait absorbed by the child becomes fixed forever, and even if reason later disclaims it, something of it remains in the subconscious mind. For nothing that is formed in infancy can ever be wholly eradicated. The "Mneme" (that we may think of as a superior kind of memory), not only creates the individual's special characteristics, but keeps them alive in him. What the child had absorbed, remains, a final ingredient of his personality. And the same thing happens with his limbs and organs, so that every grown-up person has an individuality indelibly stamped upon him in this early period of life.

The hope of altering adults is therefore vain. When we say, "This person is not well-bred," or when we remark on another's slovenly deportment, we can easily hurt or humiliate them; make them conscious of their defects. But the faults remain, for they are ingrained and unchangeable.

The same thing explains man's adaptation—let us call it—to the various historical epochs; for, while an adult of ancient times could not live in the world of our day, the child adapts to civilization at the level it has reached when he enters it. Whatever that level may be, he succeeds in making a man who can live there in conformity with its customs. This shows that the true function of infancy, in the ontogenesis of man, is an adaptive one; to construct a model of behaviour, which renders him free to act in the world about him and to influence it.

Today, therefore, the child must be considered as a point of union, a link joining the different epochs of history, the different levels of civilization. Infancy is a period of true importance, because, when we want to infuse new ideas, to modify or better the habits and customs of a people to breathe new vigour into its national traits, we must use the child as our vehicle; for little can be accomplished with adults. If we really aspire to better things, at spreading the light of civilization more widely in a given populace, it is to the children we must turn to achieve these ends.

Towards the end of the British occupation of India, a family of British diplomats often sent their two children, with an Indian nurse, to have a meal in one of the Indian *hotels de luxe*. There, the nurse, seated on the ground, taught the children to eat rice with their hands, in the Indian manner. The idea was that the children should grow up free from the contempt and repugnance that this national habit of the Indians generally excites in Europeans. For it is these differences of daily life, and the hostile feelings they arouse, that are the main causes of friction between men. If, again, modern customs are felt to be degenerate, and the revival of older ones is desired, nothing effective can be done except through the children.

To influence society we must turn our attention to childhood. Out of this truth comes the importance of nursery schools, for it is the little ones who are building mankind, and they can work only on the materials we give them.

The immense influence that education can exert through children, has the environment for its instrument, for the child absorbs his environment, takes everything from it, and incarnates it in himself. With his unlimited possibilities, he can well be the transformer of humanity, just as he is its creator. The child brings us a great hope and a new vision. There is much that we teachers can do to bring humanity to a deeper understanding, to a higher well-being, and to a greater spirituality.

This means the child, from birth, must be regarded as a being possessed of an important mental life, and we must treat him accordingly. Today the mental life of newly born children is, in fact, receiving much more attention. So interesting has it become to psychologists that it seems likely to give rise to a new science—a thing we have already seen happen for the child's bodily life, in the form of hygiene and pediatrics.

But if a mental life exists even in the newborn babe, this must be already there, otherwise it could not exist. In fact, it must also be present in the embryo, and, when this idea first gained acceptance, the question naturally arose as to when, in the embryonic life, mental life could be said to start. As we know, a child is sometimes born at seven months instead of at nine—and at seven months he is already complete enough to be able to live. So his psyche—like that of the nine-month-old child—must be able to function. This example, on which I need not dwell, serves to show my meaning when I maintain that all life is psychic. Every species of living thing is endowed in some measure with psychic energy, with a certain kind of psychology, however primitive the creature may be. If we observe unicellular creatures, we see that even they give impressions of awareness; they move away from danger, toward food, and so on.

Yet the baby, till quite a short time ago, was credited with having no mental life; and only recently have mental traits of his, previously not noticed, been admitted to the scientific picture.

Certain facts have come to shine out, and these form new points of light in the adult conscience. They indicate responsibilities that lie with us. The event of birth itself has suddenly struck people's imaginations; and we see the results not only in psychotherapy but also in literature.

Psychologists now speak of the "difficult adventure of birth," referring not to the mother but to the child; the child who suffers without being able to protest, who cries out only when his agony and travail are over.

To be forced to adapt suddenly to an environment totally different from the one in which he has been living, to be obliged to assume on the spot functions never before exercised, and to do this in the unspeakably exhausted state in which he finds himself—this is the hardest and most dramatic test in the whole of a man's life. So say modern psychologists, who have coined the phrase, "birth-terror,"[3] to indicate this critical and decisive moment in the child's mental life.

We are not, of course, dealing with a conscious fear, but if the child's mind could speak, it would find words like this to convey the situation: "Why have you thrown me into this dreadful world? What shall I do? How can I live in this new way? How am I to bear all these frightful noises, I, who have never heard so much as a whisper? How can I take over these difficult functions which you, my mother, have been doing for me? How do I digest and breathe? How can I bear these frantic changes in climate, I, who have always enjoyed the moderate and unchanging temperature of your body?"

The child is unaware of what has happened. He could not know he was suffering the pangs of birth. Yet there must remain in his soul some mark even if unconscious; he feels in his subconscious mind, and vents in his cry, something of what I have tried to express.

So, those working in this field find it natural to believe that ways must exist of helping the child to make his first adaptation to the world. Let us never forget that the tiniest babies are able to experience fear. When, in the first hours of life, they are dipped rapidly into a bath, they are seen, very often, to make grasping movements, as if they felt themselves to be falling. This is a typical reaction of fear. How does nature help the newlyborn? She certainly makes some provision: for example, she gives the mother an instinct to press the little one tightly to her bosom. This protects it from the light. And the mother herself is kept helpless for a time. Keeping still for her own benefit, she communicates the necessary calm to her child. Everything happens as if the mother unconsciously realized the damage done to her baby. Holding him tightly, she gives him of her warmth, and protects him from too many sensations.

In human mothers, these protective measures are not so vigorously pursued as in animal mothers. We see, for example, how the mother cat hides her kittens in dark corners, and is restive when anyone comes near. The human mother's protective instinct is not so strong, and is therefore more easily lost. Hardly is the child born than someone else takes it away, washes it, dresses it, holds it to the light the better to see the colour of its eyes, always treating it more like an inanimate object than a living being: It is no longer nature that directs, but human reason, and this acts fallaciously because not illuminated by understanding, and because of the habit we have of thinking the child has no mental life.

It is clear that this period, or, rather, this brief moment of birth, must be considered separately.

It does not concern the child's psychic life in general. It is an episode—his first encounter with the outer world. Natural history shows how cleverly nature provides for this period in mammals. Just before giving her young to the light, the mother isolates herself from the rest of the herd, and she remains apart with her young for some time after their birth. This is most noticeable in animals which live in large herds or packs, such as horses, cows, elephants, wolves, deer and dogs. All these do the same thing. During the period of isolation, the little youngsters have time to adapt themselves to their surroundings. They live alone with their mother, who envelops them in her love, watching over and protecting them. In this phase the little animal comes by degrees to behave like others of its species. During this short period of isolation, there is a continuous psychological reaction, on the part of the little one, to environmental stimuli, and these reactions follow the general plan of behaviour proper to the species. Thus, when the mother rejoins the others, the little one can enter the community already prepared to live as a part of it, and this, not just physically speaking, but also in the psychological sense; the young creature's behaviour is that of a little horse, a little wolf, a little calf, etc.

We may note that, even when domesticated, the mammals keep their old instincts in this respect. In our homes we see dogs and cats hide their young with their bodies. By this they are continuing the instincts of the wild, and an intimacy is preserved which keeps the newborn attached to its mother. The nursling, we may say, has left its mother's body but is still one with it. No more practical help could have been devised for making the first way of life give place gradually to the second.

Today, therefore, we have to interpret this vital phase as follows: the animal's racial instincts awaken in the first days of its life.

It is not that difficult circumstances merely arouse or stimulate instinctive responses suited to the occasion and limited by it, but the acts we see form a part of the very plan of creation itself.

If this happens with animals, something like it must also happen with man. What we are dealing with is not just a difficult moment, but a decisive moment for the whole of the future. What is now taking place is a kind of awakening of potential powers. These will have the task of directing the huge creative work to be done by the child, by this "spiritual embryo." And, because nature puts evident physical signs at each momentous change in the development of the psyche, so we see the umbilical cord, which kept the child attached to its mother, come away a few days after birth. This first phase is of the utmost importance, for during that phase mysterious powers are in preparation.

So what we have to bear in mind, is not only the *trauma* of birth—but the possibility, or otherwise, of setting in train those activities which must necessarily follow it. For, although no definite forms of behaviour are pre-established in the child (as they are in the animals), he must nevertheless possess the power to create a behaviour. There will be no atavistic memories to guide him, but the child will nevertheless experience *nebulous urges without form*, yet charged with potential energy; and these will have the duty of directing, and incarnating in him, the form of human conduct which he finds in his surroundings. We have called these formless urges, "nebulae."[4] When an animal is born, it is equipped by heredity; it will come by nature to have the right kinds of movement, the needed control, the power to select appropriate food, the forms of defence proper to its kind.

But man has to prepare all this during the general unfolding of his social life; and so the child, after he is born, has to incorporate into his life all these practices of his social group. Instead of being born possessed of them, he has to absorb them from outside himself. The vital task of infancy is this work of adaptation, which takes the place of the hereditary "behaviour patterns" present in the animal embryos.

Bearing in mind this special function that he performs, we may now study the development of the child as a "general mechanism" of human life. This is very interesting.

This baby—far from finished even physically—has to build himself up until he becomes the complex being that man is. He has no "awakening of instincts" as the newly-born animals have in the first stage of their contact with the world. But, although he is already born, he continues to carry on an embryonic life, by which he builds up what seems to be no less than a "set of human instincts."

And because, in his case, there is nothing fixed beforehand, he will have to make for himself all man's mental life, and all the motor mechanisms which are its means of expression.

He is an inert being who cannot even support the weight of his own head, but he is about to behave like the child whom Christ resuscitated. First, we are told, this child sat up, then he stood, and then Jesus "gave him back to his mother." In the same way, the motionless baby will eventually be "restored to mankind" in its life of activity on earth.

The child's muscular inertia reminds us of Coghill's discovery—that the organs are formed *after* the nervous centres, in readiness for their work. Also in him, there are psychic patterns of behaviour which have to be laid down *before* he begins to move. Thus, the starting point of infantile mobility is not motor, but mental.

The most important side of human development is the mental side. For man's movements have to be organized according to the guidance and dictation of his mental life. Intelligence is what distinguishes man from the animals, and the building up of his intelligence is the first thing to occur. Everything else waits upon this.

When the child is born, his organs themselves are not finished; the skeleton is far from ossified; the motor nerves are not yet provided with their covering of myelinin which isolates them from one another and enables them to transmit the brain's orders. Therefore, the body remains inert, as if it were the design for a body, roughly sketched in.

Hence the human being grows firstly in intelligence, while the remainder of development takes its form and mode of action entirely from the life of his mind.

Nothing shows better than this the importance of the first year, and how the priority of intelligence in development is characteristic of the sons of men.

Now, the child's growth consists of many parts, all of them following a fixed order, because they obey a common law. A detailed study of postnatal embryonic development shows when the cranium completes its growth, when the fontanelle—due to the meeting of cartilaginous parts—close up by degrees; when certain sutures such as the frontal suture become effaced; and then how the whole bodily structure changes its relative proportions, and final ossification is reached of the limbs and their extremities. It is also known when the spinal nerves are myelinized, and when the cerebellum—the body's organ of equilibrium which is very small at birth—undertakes a sudden and rapid growth till it reaches its normal proportion in relation to the cerebral hemispheres. Finally, how the endocrine glands, and those glands concerned in the digestive processes, come to be modified.

These facts have been well known for some time and they show successive levels of "maturity" in physical development, going side by side with corresponding changes in the physiology of the nervous system. So, for example, if the nerves and little brain or hind brain (cerebellum) have not reached the right level of maturity, it would be impossible for the child to keep his balance, and therefore to sit up or stand.

Never can education, or exercise, set other limits to this possibility. By becoming mature, the motor organs offer themselves, little by little, to the commands of the mind, and this can then make them move in indeterminate ways, so as to gain experience in the environment.

By means of these experiences, and these exercises, the child's movements become coordinated, and finally his will can use them for its purposes.

Man, unlike the animals, is not born with movements already coordinated; he has to shape and coordinate his own movements. Nor has he even a predetermined aim; this, too, he must find for himself. How different from the young of most mammals, who walk, run and jump from birth, according to their species. Almost at once they can execute the most difficult manoeuvres; climb, for example, if that is what their heredity demands of them; jump over obstacles, or take rapidly to flight.

Man, instead, brings no abilities with him into the world, yet his gifts are unsurpassed in the learning of movements. Of skilled movements he can acquire the most varied imaginable: those of the craftsman, the acrobat, the dancer, the musician and of champions in the many fields of sport.

But none of these things come from a mere ripening of

the organs of movement. It is always a matter of experience in action; of practice; in other words, of education. Every person is the author of his own skills, yet the physical constitution with which he starts is the same. It is the man himself who produces his own perfectionment.

Turning, now, to children, it is important to distinguish between the several portions of their make up.

To get our bearings, we must first of all accept the fact that, although they move when the body offers them the physical basis for movement, and although this is due to a sufficient maturity having been reached, nevertheless their mental state is not dependent on this. For in man, as we have seen, the mental side develops first. The organs wait as long as necessary for this development to occur, and then the mind makes use of them. But when the organs come into action, further mental development begins to occur, but always with the aid of movements made in the course of environmental experience. Therefore, it happens that if a child is prevented from using his powers of movement as soon as they are ready, this child's mental development is obstructed. Although mental development has no limits, it depends in great part on being able to use its instruments of action, on overcoming by this means the bonds of its own impotence. But all the time it is developing on its own account.

Mental growth is related to a single mystery, to the invisible secret of its future destiny. Every individual has different powers to bring to fruition, and these cannot be investigated while the child is still in the psycho embryonic stage.

In this period we can only observe the startling uniformity of all the babies in the world. It may well be said, "All children are alike at birth, they unfold in the same way and according to the same laws." Things happen in their minds much as they do in the embryonic body. Here, the segmentation of the cells always passes through the same stages, and this is so true that one can hardly tell the difference between one embryo and another. Yet the cells, as they multiply, are going to produce creatures so different as the lizard, the bird, or the rabbit. Each of these, at first, builds itself up in the same way, though, later on, the profoundest differences appear.

So it is with the "spiritual embryo" from which may later come an artist of genius, a popular leader, a saint, or someone quite ordinary. And these ordinary people may have different tastes which will lead them to different positions in the social fabric. For they are not, it is clear, all destined to "do the same thing," "behave in the same way," as happens among the lower creatures, whose activity is limited by their heredity.

But this later development, these different destinations, we can never predict, nor can we take them into account during the formative embryonic period, the postnatal period in which man's formation occurs.

In the period, there is nothing we can do but help life to unfold, and this happens in the same way for all. For all, there is a first period of adaptation; for all, it is the mental side which initiates the adventure of life. And if this period is helped in conformity with the requirements of human life, to that degree will each one benefit, by being better able, later on, to develop his individual capacities.

Hence, there can be only one way of educating and treating the tiny infant. If education is to begin at birth, there can be only one kind of education at that time. There is no sense in talking about differences of procedure for Indian babies, Chinese babies, or European babies; nor for those belonging to different social classes. We can only speak of one method; that which follows the natural unfolding of man. All babies have the same psychological needs, and follow the same sequence of events, in attaining to human stature. Every one of us has to pass through the same phases of growth.

And, because this is not a matter of opinion, there can be no question of a philosopher, a thinker, or a laboratory experimentalist being able to offer suggestions, to order this or that treatment.

Only nature, which has established certain laws and

determined the needs of the human being in course of development, can dictate the educational method to be followed; for this is settled by its aim—to satisfy the needs and the laws of life.

These laws, and these needs, the child himself must indicate by his spontaneous manifestations, and by his progress. His tranquillity and happiness, the intensity of his efforts and the constancy of his freely chosen responses, bear witness to them.

Our one duty is to learn from him on the spot, and to serve him, as best we can.

Medical psychology, nowadays, singles out a short but decisive period, the moment of birth, from the period of development which follows it. And, while its interpretations are based at present only on the Freudian view, they nevertheless furnish real data and provide a valuable distinction. This is between "symptoms of regression" which are related directly to the birth trauma, and "symptoms of repression" which are connected with circumstances which may occur during the subsequent period of growth. Regressions are not repressions. They signify a kind of unconscious decision in the newborn; a decision to go back, instead of to go forward, in development.

The "trauma of birth," it is now realized, leads to something much worse than the cries and protests of the child; it causes the child to develop in abnormal ways. The result is a psychic change, or rather a deviation of the psychic forces. Instead of taking the path that we call normal, the child's development is deflected in an unfortunate direction.

Instead of making progress, those who suffer from a negative reaction to the shock of being born give the impression of still being attached to the state of affairs before birth. There are several symptoms of regression; but all have this in common: that the sufferer appears to have judged this moment, and said to himself, "I will go back to the place I came from." The tiny baby's long hours of sleep are thought to be normal, but too long a sleep is not normal, even in the newborn, and Freud regarded it as a kind of refuge to which the child retires, an expression of the revulsion he feels towards life and the world.

Besides, is not the kingdom of the subconscious to be found in sleep? When deeply troubled, we turn to sleep; for in sleep there are dreams and not realities; in sleep there is life without the need for struggle. Sleep is a place of refuge, a withdrawal from the world. The position of the body in sleep is also to be noted. The natural position of the newborn babe is to have his hands near his face and his legs drawn up. But in some cases, this position is retained even in grown-up persons, and it shows, one may think, a return to the position of the body in the womb. Still another symptom of regression may be the child's fit of crying when he awakens from sleep. He seems to be frightened, as if he had to live again that terrible moment which brought him into this unpleasant world. Small children often suffer from nightmares and these add not a little to their antipathy towards life.

Later in life, regression may show itself as a tendency to cling to others, as if it were frightening to be left alone. This attachment is not a sign of affection, but of fear. The child is timid and wants to stay always near someone; preferably the mother. He does not like going out, but prefers home and isolation from the world. Everything in the world that ought to make him happy fills him with alarm, and he feels repugnance at the thought of new experiments. His surroundings, instead of proving attractive, as they ought, to a growing creature, seem to repel him, and if—from early infancy—the child feels a revulsion for the surroundings on which he depends for his development, this must necessarily prevent him from growing up normally. Never will this child wish to conquer; not for him will be the absorption of his world to make it part of himself. For him, absorption will always be difficult and never complete. One might call him a living expression of the adage: "Man is born to sorrow." Everything tires him. Even breathing seems to cost him an effort, and whatever he does is contrary to inclination. People of this kind need more rest and sleep than others. Their power of digestion is often poor. One can imagine all too easily what kind of future awaits such children, for these symptoms are not transitory; they will be their companions for life. It is this type of child who cries easily, clamours incessantly for help, seems to be lazy, sad and depressed. When grown up, they still have an aversion to the world, hesitate to meet strangers, are fundamentally timid. We have in these people inferiors in the struggle for existence. In social life they are wanting in joy, courage and happiness.

This is the terrible revenge of the psychological unconscious. With our conscious memory we forget, but the unconscious, although it seems to feel nothing and not to remember, does something worse, for impressions made at this level are handed over to the *mneme*. They become graven on the personality itself.

This is the great danger of mankind. The child who is not protected with a view to his normal formation will later avenge himself on society by means of the adult who is formed by him. Our blindness does not provoke rebellion, as it would among adults, but it forms people who are weaker than they should be.

It produces inner changes which become obstacles to the individual's life, and personalities who impede the progress of the world.

What I have stressed above is the importance which mental specialists are now attributing to the moment of birth in man's psychic life. But, so far, we have only mentioned the earlier observations, those which point to the danger of regression. In conjunction with these, we must now review the protective measures which all mammals take on behalf of their young. Naturalists early concluded that in the first days after birth, the mother's care, which is so detailed and characteristic, is closely connected with an awakening in the newborn of the general instincts of the species, and from this we may derive some very useful contributions to a deeper understanding of the little child's psychology.

We see how necessary it is that we should both give importance to the child's adaptation to his world, and also remember the shock of his birth, for this shows us that he also needs special treatment, just as much as the mother. Mother and child run different risks, but they both undergo grave difficulties. In the child's case, the risk to his bodily life, although so great, is less serious than that to his mental life. If the only cause of regressive symptoms lay in the traumata of birth, all children would present these symptoms. This is why we prefer to follow a more inclusive hypothesis, one which is based both on man and the animals. In the first days of life, it is clear that something of the utmost importance is taking place. To the awakening in mammals of hereditary behaviour, something (as we said above) of a corresponding nature must be happening in the child, for—although he has no hereditary models of behaviour to follow—nevertheless he has "potentialities" able to bring about his development, and these do so by making use of the outer world.

On this basis, we have formulated the concept of "nebulae," likening the creative energies which will guide the child to absorb from his environment, to the starry "nebulae" from which the heavenly bodies take their origin. The particles in the heavenly nebulae are so far apart that the latter have no real consistency, but, all the same, they form something visible which appears from a great enough distance to be one of the company of the stars. Just as this nebula, with the passing of time, changes into something more positive, so we can imagine the slow emergence of something not hereditary, yet produced by an instinctive tendency which is hereditary. For example, the child receives from the nebula of language suitable stimuli and guidance for the formation in himself of his mother tongue, which is not inborn in him, but something he finds in his environment and absorbs according to immutable laws. Thanks to the nebular energy of language, the child becomes able to distinguish the sounds of spoken language from other sounds and noises which reach him, all mixed together. Thanks to this, he can incarnate the language he hears just as perfectly as if it were a racial characteristic. In the same way, he takes on the social characters and customs which make him a man belonging to his particular part of the world.

The nebula of language does not contain the special kind of language which the child is destined to develop, but from it every language which he finds surrounding him at birth can be constructed, and each will develop itself in the same length of time, and following the same procedure, in all children in all the countries of the world.

We see here an essential difference between man and the animals. Whereas the newly born animal produces, almost at once, the special sounds of its race, for which it possesses the model as part of its heredity, the child remains mute for a fairly long time, after which he speaks the language he finds being spoken about him. So will it happen that a Dutch child growing up among Italians will speak Italian and not Dutch, despite the long Dutch lineage of his parents.

So the child, it is clear, does not inherit a pre-established model for his language, but he inherits the power of constructing a language by an unconscious activity of absorption. This potentiality—which may be likened to that of the germ-cell's *genes* in their control of the growing tissues to form a precise and complex organ—is what we have called the "nebula of language."

In the same way, the nebulae which concern the child's power of adaptation to his environment, and the appearance in him of the social behaviour which surrounds him at birth, do not produce by heredity the earlier models of behaviour through which the race has passed on its way to the present level of civilization, but they give the child, after his birth, the power to absorb those particular models that he finds in his surroundings. And this is equally true for all his other mental acquisitions. As Carrel[5] justly writes, "The son of a scientist will not inherit any element of the knowledge of his father. Left alone on a desert island, he will be no better off than our CroMagnon ancestors."

Let me pause here to clarify one point. The reader may have gained the impression that, when we speak of nebulae, we have in mind various instinctive powers, each with an independent existence of its own, and it may be objected that this would obscure the essential unity of the mind. But the nebular analogy is here used only as a vehicle for description, and it does not imply any leaning toward an atomistic conception of the mind. To us, the mental organism is a dynamic whole, which transforms its structure by active experience obtained from its surroundings; it is guided thereto by an energy (*horme*)[6] of which the nebulae are differentiated and specialized kinds or stages.

Let us imagine that the nebula for language did not function, or remained latent for some unknown reason. Then language would not develop. This abnormality, which is not unusual, produces a form of mutism in children who are perfectly normal in the organs of speech and hearing, and whose brains are also normal. I have met several of these cases, before which ear and nerve specialists confessed themselves baffled, as if by a natural enigma. It would be interesting to examine these cases, and to investigate what had taken place in the first days of life of these unfortunates.

These ideas will explain many facts which are still obscure in other fields, for example, those touching adaptability to society. They may even have more practical scientific value than the presumed consequences of the birth trauma. I hold that many regressive tendencies are due to a lack of the vital urge which guides the child to make his social adaptation. In these cases the child, for lack of the proper sensitiveness, does not absorb anything from his environment, or makes an imperfect absorption. Not feeling attraction but revulsion, he fails to develop what is called "love for the environment," from which he should gain his independence by a series of conquests over it.

Then, of course, the characteristic features of the racial type, its customs, religion and so on, are not absorbed in the normal way, and the result is a true moral abnormality, a person out of place, an outcast who presents many of the regressive symptoms mentioned above. Man possesses *creative sensitivities* instead of hereditary models of behaviour, and if it is due to these that adaptation occurs to his surroundings, then it is clear that the whole psychic life of the individual stands upon a foundation which is laid down by them in the earliest years. But now we must ask ourselves, are there any causes to which we may attribute a delayed, or missing, awakening of these creative sensitivities? To this question no answer can yet be made, and everyone must seek it in the lives of these unfortunates, as to whose plight science confesses itself to be at a loss, and speaks of riddles.

At the moment, I have only known one case which may suggest a line of investigation. It was that of a young man incapable of discipline and of application to study: a difficult boy with a bad character which made him intractable and condemned him to isolation. He was good looking, healthy and also intelligent. But he had suffered in his first fifteen days of life a severe malnutrition, cause of a marked loss of weight such as to reduce him to a skeleton, specially about the face. The wet nurse who was sent for to feed him thought him disgusting, and called him, "Skinny." After the first two weeks, and for the rest of his life he developed normally. Also, he was a strong child (or he would have died), but the youth he became was predestined to crime.

But enough of hypotheses which have yet to be confirmed. There is one fact of supreme importance. The nebulae of sensitiveness direct the newborn babe's mental development just as the *genes* condition the fecundated egg in the formation of the body. So let us give to newborn children the same kind of special care as the higher animals give their young during the short period immediately after birth, when the psychic characters of the species are awakening. In this, we are not just speaking of child care in the first year, or early months, of life, still less do we limit it to the field of bodily health alone. But our aim is to establish a principle of special importance to intelligent mothers and to the home in general: there must come into being a special code of rules, exacting, and precise, for the treatment of the child at birth and in the first few days following birth.

REFERENCES

1. The word, *Mneme*, in this order of ideas, was first introduced by the German biologist, Richard Semon, but Sir Percy Nunn developed and extended the idea in his *Hormic Theory*. It is in his sense that we use the word, as with his other concepts: *Horme and Engrams*. For further reference the reader is advised to consult Sir Percy Nunn's excellent book, *Education, its Data and First Principles*, London (1st ed. 1920).
2. A convincing proof of this truth can be found in the book by Ruth Benedict, *Patterns of Culture*, New York, 1948.
3. This phrase was first used in 1923 by Otto Rank, one of the early disciples of Feud, in his theory of "the trauma of birth." Although the whole theory has not been generally accepted, the concept of birth fear, or terror, has an established place today in the field of depth psychology.
4. The awakening of the "nebulae" corresponds to the awakening of what are called "behaviour instincts" in the animals, and it happens in the first days of life, those which mental hygiene is obliged to regard as the most important. See *The Formation of Man: Nebulae and World Illiteracy*, by Dr. Maria Montessori, T.P.H., Adyar, Madras, 1955.
5. Dr. Alexis Carrel, *L'Homme cet Inconnu*, Paris, 1947.
6. The word *horme* (from the Greek *όρμάω* to excite), is used by us to mean a force or vital stimulus. See also footnote opening of Chapter 8.

8

The Child's Conquest of Independence

Except when he has regressive tendencies, the child's nature is to aim directly and energetically at functional independence. Development takes the form of a drive toward an ever greater independence. It is like an arrow released from the bow, which flies straight, swift and sure. The child's conquest of independence begins with his first introduction to life. While he is developing, he perfects himself and overcomes every obstacle that he finds in his path. A vital force is active within him, and this guides his efforts towards their goal. It is the force called "*horme*"[1] by Sir Percy Nunn.

If we tried to find something resembling this *horme* in conscious life, it might be likened to will-power. But this would be an extremely poor analogy. The idea of will is too restricted, too much a part of the individual's awareness. *Horme* belongs to life in general, to what might be called the divine urge, the source of all evolution. This vital force for his growth stimulates the child to perform many actions and, if he is permitted to grow normally, without being hindered, it shows itself in what we call the "joy of life." The child is always enthusiastic, always happy.

The child's conquests of independence are the basic steps in what is called his "natural development." In other words, if we observe natural development with sufficient care, we see that it can be defined as the gaining of successive levels of independence. This is true not only in the mental field, but also in the physical; for the body also has its tendencies toward development, impulses and urges so strong that only death can interrupt them.

So let us study this path and its stages. At birth, the child leaves a prison—his mother's womb—and this makes him independent of her bodily processes. The baby is next endowed with an urge, or need, to face the outer world and to absorb it. We might say that he is born with "the psychology of world conquest." By absorbing what he finds about him, he forms his own personality.

This is the mark of his first period in the world. If the child feels an impulse to conquer his environment, it follows that this must have for him a certain attraction. So, let us say (using words which are not quite appropriate) that the child is "in love" with his world. We could also say with Katz[2] that "the world wears to the child an aspect rich in emotional stimuli."

The first of the child's organs to begin functioning are his senses. But what are these, if not organs for taking in? They are instruments by which we lay hold of impressions, and these, in the child's case, have to become "incarnated," made a part of his personality.

When we look about us, what do we see? We see everything in sight. What do we hear if we listen? We hear every sound within earshot. So it seems that the field on which we can draw is extremely large, almost universal, and this is nature's way. We do not assimilate first this sound and then that, or the various noises, one at a time. But we begin by absorbing all of them at once, an undivided whole. Distinctions between one thing and another thing, between a noise and a note, or between one note or another note, come later, as if evolved from this global accumulation. How well this agrees with Gestalt psychology!

So this is the psychic picture of the normal child. First, he takes in the world as a whole, then he analyses it.

But suppose we have another type of child, who does not feel this irresistible attraction for his environment. In this type his love for it has been thwarted and replaced by fear. It terrifies him.

Clearly, the development of the first type will be different from that of the second. Studies of infant development show that if certain changes make their appearance by six months, the child's growth has been normal. Some of these are physical but invisible, needing tests to determine them. For example, the stomach begins to secrete the hydrochloric acid necessary for digestion. The first tooth appears. So we see gradual perfectionment of the body which develops by certain processes of growth. And the result is that by six months of age the child can live without his mother's milk or at least he can combine this with other kinds of food. If we remember that before this the child was dependent entirely on maternal milk because intolerant of other food which he could not digest, we see the wonderful degree of independence that he has now reached. It is almost as though at six months he said: "I don't want to live any more on my mother. I am now fully alive and can feed myself." Something like this happens at adolescence, when children begin to feel humiliated by dependence on home and try to pay for their keep.

And just about now (which is what makes us think of this as a critical period) the child begins to pronounce his first syllables. These are the first stones in the great edifice of language that he is about to build, and this will be another great step, another gain in his independence. Once the child can speak, he can express himself and no longer depends on others to guess his needs. He finds himself in touch with human society, for people can only communicate by means of language.

Learning to speak, therefore, and the power it brings of intelligent converse with others, is a most impressive further step along the path of independence. The child who is at first almost like a deaf mute being unable to express himself, or to understand what others say—seems to acquire simultaneously both hearing and the power to use words.

Very soon afterwards, at one year of age, the child begins to walk, and this sets him free from yet another prison. Now he can run about, and if you approach he can escape and hide, secure in the feeling that his legs will take him wherever he wishes to go. So man develops by stages, and the freedom he enjoys comes from these steps towards independence taken in turn. It is not just a case of deciding to "set him free," or of wanting him to be free; his independence is a physiological state, a change wrought by the processes of growth. Truly it is nature which affords the child the opportunity to grow; it is nature which bestows independence upon him and guides him to success in achieving his freedom.

Learning to walk is especially significant not only because it is supremely complex, but because it is done in the first year of life, side by side, that is, with the formation of language, of finding one's way about, and so on. Walking, for the child, is a crucial physiological event. No other mammal has to *learn* to walk. Man alone needs to pass through a prolonged and delicate phase of growth to become able to do it. Before he can even stand erect, much less walk, he has to make three distinct physiological conquests. Instead, calves and other animals begin to walk as soon as they are born. Yet these animals are far inferior to us, despite their immense size. It seems as if we are born helpless because our constitution is so much more intricate that it takes longer to build up these powers.

The power to stand upright and to walk on two legs only, requires a most elaborate nervous organization, composed of several parts. One of these is the cerebellum, or hind brain, situated at the base of the brain itself (see drawing).

Exactly at the age of six months, the cerebellum begins to develop at great speed. It continues this rapid growth till the fourteenth or fifteenth month, and then its pace slows down, but it continues growing nonetheless till the child is four and a half. The power to stand up and walk depends on this development. It is easy to follow in the child. In reality

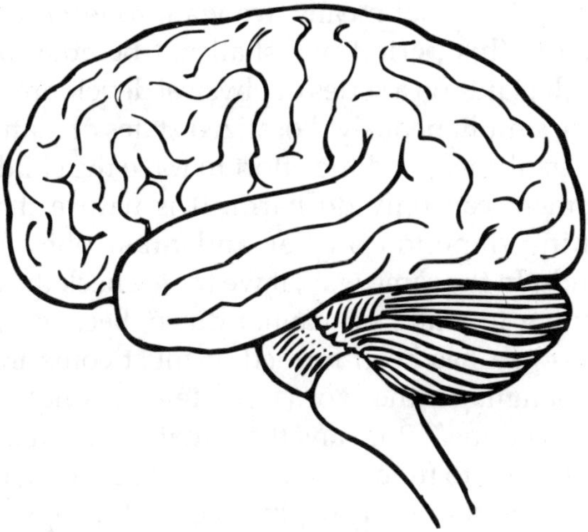

Fig. 6. *The cerebellum at the base of the brain.*

there are two developments which follow one another. The child at six months begins to sit up, and at nine to crawl, or slide himself along, on hands and feet. Then he stands at ten months and walks at twelve to thirteen months. By the fifteenth month he is sure on his legs.

The other part of this complex process is the completion of certain nerves. Unless the spinal nerves were complete, which convey orders to the muscles of the legs, these orders could not be delivered. The completion of these nerves, which takes place in this period, is necessary for the control of those muscles. Thus many elements of a complex piece of development have to be harmonized if walking is to be achieved. A third element is the development of the skeleton. As we have seen, the child's legs at birth are not completely ossified. They are partly cartilaginous, and therefore still soft. How could they support his body like that? The skeleton has to harden before the child begins walking. Still another point must be noted. The bones of the head, which were not joined at the time of his birth, now grow together and become joined. Then, if the child falls, he no longer runs the serious risk of damaging his brain.

If, by educational means, we want to teach the child to walk before this period, we shall not be able to, because walking depends on a series of physical developments which take place simultaneously. Localized states of maturity must first be established, and the effort to force the child's natural development can only do harm. It is nature that directs. Everything depends on her and must obey her exact commands. In the same way, if we try to check the child who is beginning to walk, we cannot do so, because, in nature, once an organ has been formed, it must come into use. In nature's language, the word "create" does not just mean, "make something"; it means that what has been made must also be allowed to function. No sooner has an organ evolved than it must immediately begin to act in its proper sphere. In modern terms, this functional work is called "environmental experience." If such experience be not obtained, the organ fails to develop normally, for at first it is incomplete. It only becomes finished by being used.

It follows that the child can only develop fully by means of experience on his environment. We call such experience "work." No sooner does language appear than the child begins to chatter, and no one can persuade him to stop. One of the hardest things in the world is to make a small child keep silent. And if the child were prevented from walking and talking he could not develop normally. He would suffer an arrest of development. Instead, he walks, runs, jumps, and so develops his legs by use.

So, the child who has extended his independence by acquiring new powers, can only develop normally if left free to exert those powers. The child develops by the exercise of that independence which he has gained. In short, development, as modern psychology puts it, does not occur by itself. "The behaviour of every individual is a product of his environmental experience."

If, therefore, what we mean by education is to help the child's developing life, we can only rejoice each time he shows us that he has reached a new level of independence. What a boundless joy we feel when he speaks his first word, the more so as we realize that we could do nothing to aid this. But a problem of education is posed directly we reflect that this progress of the child—however hard it be to stop—can nevertheless be held back, or slowed down, by any failure to obtain the needed environmental experience.

So the first thing his education demands is the provision of an environment in which he can develop the powers given him by nature. This does not mean just to amuse him and let him do as he likes. But it does mean that we have to adjust our minds to doing a work of collaboration with nature, to being obedient to one of her laws, the law which decrees that development comes from environmental experience.

With his first footstep the child reaches a higher level of experience. Observing him at this time, we see that he tends always to enlarge his independence. He wants to act of his own accord, to carry things, to dress and undress himself; and this is not due to any suggestions from us. His impulses are so energetic that our usual response is to check them. But, in doing this, we are not really checking the child but nature herself, for the child's will is in tune with hers, and he is obeying her laws one by one.

First in one way, and then in another, he becomes ever less dependent on the persons about him; till the time comes when he wants also to be mentally independent. Then he shows a liking to develop his mind by his own experiences, and not by the experiences of others. He begins to seek the reasons for things. And in this way, human individuation comes about in the infantile period. These are not matters of theory or opinion, but of easily observed facts. When we say the child's freedom must be *complete*, that his independence and normal functioning must be *guaranteed* by society, we are not using the language of vague idealism. These are truths revealed by positive observations made upon life and nature. Only through freedom and environmental experience is it practically possible for human development to occur.

All the same, we must not project into the world of

children the same ideas of independence and freedom that we hold to be ideal in the world of adults. If adults were asked to examine themselves, and to give a definition of freedom and independence, they could not succeed with any accuracy, for their idea of freedom is a very sorry one. They lack the breadth of nature's infinite horizons. Only in the child do we see reflected the majesty of nature which, in giving freedom and independence, gives life itself. And she gives it while following unchanging rules concerning the age and needs of the individual. She makes of freedom a law of life: be free or you die!

In this I believe that nature's way offers us a help, a new basis for the interpretation of social life. It is as if the growing child laid bare to our view the whole scene, from which we, in our social life, take only a few minor details. What the child shows is right, inasmuch as it provides us with a guide to reality, to the truth. Whenever a natural truth is discovered, it dispels doubt and for this reason the child's freedom, which he gains by his development and growth, can set us thinking along new lines of the greatest interest.

What, in fact, can be the purpose of this ever growing conquest of independence? Where does it come from? It springs up in the growing personality, which then becomes able to fend for itself. But this happens throughout nature; each living being functions separately, and so we see that the child is following nature's plan. He arrives at that freedom, which is the first rule of life for everything that lives. How does he achieve this independence? He does it by means of a continuous activity. How does he become free? By means of constant effort. The one thing life can never do is to stand still. Independence is not a static condition; it is a continuous conquest, and in order to reach not only freedom, but also strength, and the perfecting of one's powers, it is necessary to follow this path of unremitting toil.

The child's first instinct is to carry out his actions by himself, without anyone helping him, and his first conscious bid for independence is made when he defends himself against those who try to do the action for him. To succeed by himself he intensifies his efforts.

If, as so many people think, the best kind of life would be to do nothing but sit about and be waited on, then what could be more ideal than the life which the child led before he was born? When in the womb, his mother did everything for him. Think of the terrific task of learning to speak, which permits the grown man to converse with his fellows. If "resting" were truly life's ideal, might not the child give up the idea of learning to talk or adapting himself to a normal diet? Might he not spare himself the trouble of walking and using his mind, with all the delight that he feels in becoming acquainted with the world about him?

But this is far from the realities of which children give us proof. They show that nature's teachings differ from the ideals which society fashions for itself. The child seeks for independence by means of work; an independence of body and mind. Little does he care about the knowledge of others; he wants to acquire a knowledge of his own, to have experience of the world, and to perceive it by his own unaided efforts. We must clearly understand that when we give the child freedom and independence, we are giving freedom to a worker already braced for action, who cannot live without working and being active. This he has in common with all other forms of life, and to curb it makes him degenerate.

Everything in the living world is active. Life is activity at its peak, and it is only through activity that the perfectionments of life can be sought and gained. The social aspirations handed down to us by past generations; the ideal of minimum working hours, of having others to work for us, of idleness ever more complete—these betray the marks which nature sets on a degeneracy in childhood. These aspirations are signs of regression in the person who was not helped in the first days of his life to adapt to his environment, and who therefore feels antipathy toward it, towards exertion. His was the type of childhood with a liking for being helped and waited on, carried in someone's arms or in a wheel chair, one timid of companionship and willing to sleep at length. He wears the aspect of a degeneracy now recognized and described by science as a tendency to return to the womb. The child, who was born normally and is growing normally, goes towards independence. One who avoids this is degenerate.

The education of these unfortunates presents quite a different problem. How are we to cure the regression that retards and distorts normal development? The deviated child has no love for his environment because he feels it to contain too many difficulties. For him it is too harsh and resistant. Today it is this deviated child who occupies the centre of the stage in scientific child psychology, which would be better called the psychopathology of childhood. An increasing number of Child Guidance Clinics is being founded and new techniques, such as *play-therapy*, have been worked out to cope with the growing number of disturbed children. Pedagogy teaches that the environment must offer less resistance; so avoidable obstacles which the environment contains are diminished more and more, or perhaps removed entirely. Today, everything about the child is made as attractive as possible, especially for those children who feel repulsion for their environment itself. This is done in the hope of arousing feelings of sympathy and love to overcome those of diffidence and disgust. Pleasant activities are also provided, because we know that development results from activity. The environment must be rich in motives which lend interest to activity and invite the child to conduct his own experiences. These are principles dictated by life and by nature, which help the deviated child who has acquired regressive characteristics, to pass from the tendency to laziness to the desire for work, from lethargy and inertia to activity, from a state of fear (which shows itself sometimes in excessive attachment to people from whom the child cannot be separated) to a joyous freedom, the freedom to begin the conquest of life.

From inertia to work! This is the path of cure, just as from inertia to work is the path of development for the normal child. For a new education this must be the basis. Nature herself indicates and establishes it.

Although I have no wish to engage in long theoretical discussions, I would like, before going on, to make clear something about my use of the word, "maturation." For I think a precise idea of my outlook on this subject is important for the understanding, not only of the chapters which follow, but of other parts of this book. Originally, the word, "maturation," was used, in genetics and embryology, to indicate that period of development of the original germ cell, turning it from an immature cell to a mature cell,[3] before fecundation took place.

But in the psychology of infancy this term has taken on a much wider meaning. It denotes a kind of regulating mechanism for growth, which ensures balance in the organism as a whole, and in the direction of its growth impulses. Arnold Gesell, in particular, has developed this concept, though he has not formulated any very precise definition. But, if I grasp his meaning correctly, he maintains that the individual's growth is subject to fixed laws which must be respected, since a child "has constitutional traits and tendencies, largely inborn, which determine *how, what* and to some extent even *when* he will learn.[4]

In other words, Gesell says that there are functions in the child which cannot be influenced by instruction.[5]

So far as the physical life goes, that is true. In fact, as I have said above, we cannot teach a child to walk before certain localized states of maturity have occurred. In the same way, no child can learn to speak before a certain age (just as no one can stop him once he has begun). Everyone who has followed my work will know that I have always been among the first to defend the idea that children grow according to natural laws; indeed, I regard these laws as the basis of education. Yet Gesell's statements seem to me too biological for strict application to children's mental growth. According to his monistic doctrine he holds that "the child's mind unfolds just like his body as a result of developmental processes."[6] But this can hardly be exact. If we bring a child up in an isolated spot, far from human contacts, giving him nothing more than physical nourishment, his bodily development will be normal but his mental development will be seriously impaired. A convincing example was given by Dr. Itard in the story of his patient efforts to teach the boy who was known to his day as "the Savage of Aveyron."[7]

As I have so often said, it is true that we cannot make a genius. We can only give to each individual the chance to fulfil his potential possibilities. But if we are to speak of a process of "biological maturation," we must also be prepared to recognize a process of "psychological maturation." As we have tried to show in the foregoing chapters, this runs parallel with all the phenomena to be observed in embryology.

In the vital process of forming an organism, we can nowhere discern a totality which grows as a whole; nor does growth proceed regularly and gradually. The development of each organ occurs separately around about points of activity. The activity of these points lasts for a limited time and is extinguished when the organ has appeared. In addition to these points, or active centres, which are concerned in the formation of organs, there are also sensitive periods, which play an important part in guiding the animal's *behaviour* till it can live in the outer world. This has been shown by the Dutch biologist, De Vries, and we find it paralleled precisely in the child's psychological development—a fact which persuades us that human nature is true, throughout, to life's methods.

It follows that "maturation" is far more than "the net sum of the gene effects operating in a self limited time cycle,"[8] for besides the effects of the genes there are also the effects of the environment on which they act. This environment has a dominant part to play in the process of maturation.

As regards psychological maturation, this can only occur by environmental experience, and the latter changes its form at each level of development because the *horme* changes its type, appearing in the individual as an intense interest for repeating certain actions at length for no obvious reason, until because of this repetition—a fresh function suddenly appears with explosive force. Thus, the particular model of the function has been constructed by a ripening not outwardly visible. For these repeated actions do not seem to have any direct relation with the function they produce, and they are abandoned as soon as it appears. Meanwhile, the corresponding interest of the child now passes on to some other activity that will prepare yet another function. If the child is prevented from enjoying these experiences at the very time when nature has planned for him to do so, the special sensitivity which draws him to them will vanish, with a disturbing effect on his development, and consequently on his maturation.

If we look at the broader definition of maturation given in a recent textbook of psychology,[9] we find it said: "Maturation consists of structural changes which are chiefly hereditary, i.e. which have their origin in the chromosomes of the fertilized ovum, but these changes are also produced in part by an interaction between the organism and its surroundings."

Interpreting this in the light of our own findings, we may say that man is born with a vital force (*horme*) already present in the general structure of the *absorbent mind*, with its specializations and differentiations which we have described under the heading of "nebulae."

This structure alters during infancy under the direction of what we have called (following De Vries) the *sensitive periods*.[10] Growth and psychic development are therefore guided by: the absorbent mind, the nebulae and the sensitive periods with their respective mechanisms. It is these that are hereditary and characteristic of the human species. But the promise they hold can only be fulfilled through the experience of free activity conducted on the environment.

REFERENCES

1. This term, which resembles Bergson's *élan vital*, or Freud's *libido*, was first proposed by Nunn and later adopted by Wm. McDougall. See by this author, *An Outline of Psychology*, London, 1948 (1st ed. 1923), p. 71 *et seq*.
2. Prof. D. Katz, *The Psychology of Form* (Italian ed., Einaudi, 1950, p. 188).
3. For a clear account of this process *cf*. H.S. Jennings, *Genetics*, New York, 1935.
4. Arnold Gesell, M.D., *Infant and Child in the Culture of Today*, New York and London, 1948, p. 40.
5. Arnold Gesell, M.D., *Stair Climbing Experiment in Studies in Child Development*, New York and London, 1948, p. 58.
6. Preface to Gesell's book: *The Embryology of Behaviour*, New York and London, 1945.
7. Dr. J.M. Itard, *Rapports et Mémoires sur le Savage de l'Aveyron, l'Idiotie et la Surdi-mutité*, Paris 1807 (English translation by George and Muriel Humphrey, Century, New York, 1932).
8. A. Gesell, *The Embryology of Behaviour*, p. 23.
9. E.G. Boring, H.S. Langfeld and H.P. Weld, *Introduction to Psychology*, New York, 1939.
10. Cf: Dr. Maria Montessori, *The Secret of Childhood*, Orient Longmans, Bombay, Calcutta, Madras, 1951 (1st ed., Longmans Green & Co. Ltd., London, 1936).

9

The First Days of Life

If what we have to do is to help man's mental life, then the first lesson we must learn is that the tiny child's *absorbent mind* finds all its nutriment in its surroundings. Here it has to locate itself, and build itself up from what it takes in. Especially at the beginning of life must we, therefore, make the environment as interesting and attractive as we can.

The child, as we have seen, passes through successive phases of development, and in each of these his surroundings have an important—though different—part to play. In none have they more importance than immediately after birth. Few people, as yet, are alive to this, since only a short while back it was not even suspected that children had mental needs in the first two years of life. Yet these are now known to be so imperious that they cannot be ignored without harmful consequences ever after.

The attention of scientists used to be fixed entirely on the physical side of infant well-being. Especially in this century have medicine and hygiene been evolving a meticulous treatment to reduce the huge mortality which used to prevail. But just because it aimed at reducing mortality, this treatment was limited to physical health alone. The field of mental health is still almost completely unexplored, and those concerned with it find little to guide them outside natural history and the belief that the chief purpose of infancy is to form an individual adapted to the social life of his day.

And natural history, what does that show? It suggests a first period of isolation, and of mental adjustment to the outer world—a thing necessary even for those mammals which are born with their future behaviour already marked out.

But if we remember that man has no behaviour foreordained at birth, and that for a child the question is not one of mental awakening, but of mental creation, we see at once how much greater is the *rôle* which environment must play in his life. Its value and importance are magnified gigantically, just as are the dangers it may contain. Hence the care we must take of all the conditions surrounding the newborn babe, so that he will not be repelled and develop regressive tendencies, but feel attracted to the new world into which he has come. This will aid his great task of absorption, on which his progress, growth and development all depend.

During the first year of life there are various periods, each needing a special kind of care.[1] The first one is very brief, the dramatic episode of the child's birth. Without going into details, we may indicate certain principles. The child must remain (in the first few days) as much as possible in contact with his mother. There must not be too much contrast, as regards warmth, light, noise, with his conditions before birth, where, in his mother's womb, there was perfect silence, darkness, and an even temperature. In modern pediatric clinics, mother and child are kept in a room with glass walls, having a steady temperature under control, so that it can slowly be made the same as the normal temperature outside. The glass is blue, to give a subdued light.

There are also rigid rules for handling and moving the baby. These contrast very much with the practice of earlier days, when the baby was habitually plunged into a bath on the floor, from which he received a severe shock. Nowadays, instead of dressing him rapidly with no thought for his feelings, almost as though he were an insensate object, science holds that the baby should be touched as little as possible and should not be dressed at all, but kept in a room without drafts and sufficiently hot to keep him warm. The way of moving the child has also been changed. He is carried on an eiderdown mattress like a hammock, on which he is placed very gently; he must not be suddenly raised or lowered, and is handled with the same tenderness as we give to the injured. The reasons for this are not just hygienic. The nurses wear a strip of gauze over their noses so that microbes shall not pass from them into the surrounding air, and mother and child are treated as if they were organs of the same body communicating with one another. The child's adaptation to the world is thus favoured on natural lines, because there is a special bond uniting mother and child, almost like a magnetic attraction.

The mother radiates invisible forces to which the child is accustomed, and they are a help to him in the difficult days of adjustment.

We may say that the child has merely changed his position in regard to her: he is now outside her body instead of inside. But everything else remains the same and the communion between them still exists. This is how the mother-child relationship is today conceived, although it is only a few years ago that the mother and her newborn babe were separated at once even in the best of clinics.

What I have described is considered as "the last word" in scientific baby care. But nature shows that these extreme measures are not needed throughout the whole of infancy. After a short time, mother and child can return from isolation and take part in social life.

The child's social problems are not the same as those of an adult. Until now, social inequalities have affected children inversely to their parents. For it is not all paradoxical to say that, while adults suffer among the poor, children suffer among the rich. Apart from the complications of clothing, of social custom, of the crowds of friends and relatives that visit the baby, it happens that in the moneyed class the mother often entrusts her child to a wet nurse, or seeks other means of release, while the mother in poor circumstances follows the path of nature and keeps the child at her side. In a number of small ways we are led to see that things the adult world values can have reversed effects in the world of children.

After this period has passed, the child adapts himself serenely to his surroundings without reluctance. He sets out on the path of independence we have described, and opens his arms to the environment. He absorbs and makes his own the customs of the world around him.

The first of his activities on this path, which may well be called a conquest, is the use of his senses. Because his bony tissues are incomplete, he lies inert and his limbs are motionless. So his life cannot be one of movement. His mind alone is active, absorbing the impressions of his senses.

His eyes are bright and eager, and we must remember, as science has recently shown, that the child's eyes are not only affected by light. He is by no means passive. While undoubtedly receiving impressions, he is an active seeker in his world. He himself is looking for impressions.

Now, if we dissect the eye of an animal, we see a visual apparatus not unlike our own, a kind of *camera obscura*. But the animals are led by their nature to make a more limited use of their eyes. They are more attracted to some things than to others. Thus they do not take in the whole of their environment. They have a guide within themselves that directs their activity into certain channels, and they use their eyes in obedience to this.

The guide within them exists from the first. Their senses are formed and perfected so that they can follow it. Thus, the cat's eyes (like those of other nocturnal hunters) are adapted to the dark, but the cat, though interested in darkness, is attracted by things that move and not by those which keep still. No sooner does something move in the dark than the cat pounces upon it, without paying the smallest attention to the rest of the scene. She has no general interest in her environment, but only an instinctive impulse towards certain aspects of it. In the same way, some insects are attracted to flowers of one particular colour, because in flowers of that colour they find their food. Yet an insect just out of its chrysalis cannot have any experience in this direction. It is guided by its instinct and the eye helps it to act appropriately. It is this guide that controls the behaviour of the species. The individual is by no means mechanically enslaved to its senses. It is not they that drag it along. But the senses exist and render service to their master, and he it is who acts under guidance.

The child is specially favoured. His senses, which also have a guide, are not limited like those of the animals. The cat is limited to the things that move in the environment, and is attracted by these. The child has no such limitation. He observes everything in sight and experience shows that he absorbs it all equally. Furthermore, he does not absorb only by means of the mechanical camera of his eye, but a kind of psychochemical reaction is produced in him, so that these impressions become an integral part of his personality. One may safely say—quite apart from scientific proof—that a person whose life is governed solely by his desires, who stands at their mercy, is suffering from some interior defect. His inner guide may still exist, but its power to influence his conduct has been weakened. This makes him the machine-like victim of his senses, a being lost and abandoned.

To care for, and keep awake, the guide within every child is therefore a matter of the first importance.

The comparison we have already made helps us to understand this power the child has of absorbing from his surroundings. There are some insects which look like leaves and others which look like stalks. They pass their lives on leaves and stalks, which they resemble so perfectly as to seem completely one with them. Something like this happens in the child. He absorbs the life going on about him and becomes one with it, just as these insects become one with the vegetation on which they live. The child's impressions are so profound that a biological or psychochemical change takes place, by which his mind ends by resembling the environment itself. Children become like the things they love.

In every type of life it has been discovered that this power exists, of absorbing the environment and coming to resemble it.

In the insects we have mentioned, and in other animals, it exists physically. In the child it exists *psychologically*.

And we have to count it among the major propensities of living things. The child does not look at the world as we do. We may see something and say, "How beautiful!" then go on to other things and retain this vaguely as just a memory. But the child builds his inmost self out of the deeply felt impressions he receives, and this especially in the first part of his life. It is in babyhood, by means of his infantile powers alone, that the child acquires personal characteristics that will mark him forever—those of his language, his religion, his race, and so on. This is his way of adapting to the world in which he finds himself. In doing so, he is happy and his mind matures.

Not only this, but he makes an adaptation to each form of environment that he may subsequently enter. What is meant by this "making of an adaptation"? We take it to mean a transformation of one's self of such a kind as to make one suited to one's surroundings, which then become a part of one's being. So we have to ask ourselves what we ought to do, and what kind of environment to make, if we want to help the child.

Were we dealing with a child of three, he might himself be able to tell us. We should have to see that he did not lack for flowers and pretty things. We should have to foresee and provide him with motives of activity belonging to his stage of development. We can easily discover what motives of activity should be at hand to permit him to practice his growing powers. But if it is the newborn babe who has to construct his adaptation, what kind of environment can we prepare for him?

In today's thought there is no answer to this question. But actually the baby's natural environment is the world, everything that lies around about him. To learn a language he must live with those who speak it, otherwise he will not be able to. If he is to acquire special mental powers, he must live with people who constantly use those powers. The manners, habits and customs of his group can only be derived from mingling with those who possess them.

Now this, in reality, is a most revolutionary idea, for it opposes all that has been thought and done in recent years. Owing to a piece of reasoning based exclusively on physical hygiene, the conclusion—or mis-conclusion has been reached that the child should be isolated! The result has been a special room, or "nursery," set aside for children, and when this was found to be "unhygienic," the hospital was taken for a model. The child was left alone, and made to sleep as much as possible, as if he were ill.

But we have to realize that if this is a form of progress in bodily hygiene, it has its dangers for the mental life. If the child is shut away in a nursery, with no other companion than a nurse; if no real expression of mother love can reach him; his normal growth and development are arrested. A feeling of retardation, of dissatisfaction, of mental hunger, must affect him harmfully. Instead of living, as he wishes to do, with his mother, with whom he has a special bond of sympathy, his companion is always the nurse who speaks to him seldom. Often he is shut up in a "pram" where he can see nothing of what is going on in the world about him.

These unfavourable conditions are so much the worse, the wealthier the family into which he is born. Luckily, since the war, this state of affairs has become far less common. Impoverishment, and new social ideas, have restored parents to their children in a loving and beneficent companionship.

The treatment of children should really be considered as a matter of social importance. Modern observation and child-study have led us to realize that, as soon as the child can go out of doors, we may take him with us, letting him look about as much as possible. This leads us back to the days of high perambulators, and the design of nurseries has also been transformed. While it conforms rigorously to hygienic standards, its walls are adorned with plenty of pictures, and the child lies on a gently sloping support, so that he can dominate the whole scene—and not have his gaze fixed only on the ceiling.

The problem of language is more difficult, especially when nursemaids are employed, who often belong to a different social class from that of the child. Another side to the question is whether the child should be present when the parents are talking to their friends. Notwithstanding the many objections that can be made, it has to be said that if we want to help the child we must keep him with us, so that he can see what we do and hear what we say. Even if he does not consciously grasp what is going on he will retain a subconscious impression of it. It becomes absorbed and helps his growth. When the child is taken out of doors, where will his preferences turn? No one can say for certain, but we must observe the child. Expert mothers and children's nurses, if they see the child taking a special interest in something, allow him to look at it closely for as long as he wishes. They lift him up to the level at which his gaze is fixed, and see his face light up with interest and love for whatever it was that drew his attention. How can we be the judge of what will interest the little child? We must put ourselves at his disposal. All past ideas are thus reversed, and the knowledge of this revolution must be spread among adults. It is necessary for us all to become convinced that the child constructs in himself a vital adaptation to his environment, and that he must therefore have full and complete contact with it. For if the child fails in this, we shall find ourselves faced by very grave social problems.

How many social questions of today are not known to arise from the individual's failure to adapt himself, either in the moral field or in others? It is a basic problem, and this brings us to see how the science of child care must ultimately become the most permanent and deeply felt concern of every civilized society.

Well may we ask how it is possible that so great and self-evident a truth should have been so long ignored. Those who mistrust novelty will give the well-worn reply that past generations have managed without this knowledge. We shall be told: "The human race is very old; thousands of people have lived already; I myself grew up, and my sons too, without the aid of such theories. The children of my day learned to speak, they even acquired habits so tenacious as to become prejudices!"

But let us think, for a moment, of the many peoples of the world who live at different cultural levels from our own. In the matter of child rearing, almost all of these seem to be more enlightened than ourselves—with all our Western ultramodern ideals. Nowhere else, in fact, do we find children treated in a fashion so opposed to their natural needs. In almost all countries, the baby accompanies his mother wherever she goes. Mother and child are inseparable. All the while they are out together, mother talks and baby listens. If the mother argues about prices with a vendor, it is in the child's presence; he sees and hears all that goes on. And this lasts for the whole period of maternal feeding, which is the reason for this close alliance. For the mother has to feed her child, and therefore she cannot leave him at home when she goes out. In this way, the child's need for nutrition, and the love that unites these two beings, both combine in solving the problem of the child's adaptation to the world, and this happens in the most natural way possible. Mother and child are one.

Except where civilization has broken down this custom, no mother ever entrusts her child to someone else. The child shares the mother's life and is always listening. Mothers are often said to be talkative, but this also must be a help to the child's development and to his work of adaptation. Yet, were he to hear only words addressed to himself, he would gain very little. It is when he hears the full discourse of grown-up people, and can see their actions which make their meaning clear, that he grasps little by little even the construction of sentences. This is far more important than the one-syllabled words that his mother lisps to him. It is the language of living thought clothed in action.

All the great human groups, nations and races, have their individual differences; for example, they have different ways of carrying the baby. The study of this is one of the most interesting in the modern science of ethnology. In most parts of the world, mothers put the baby on a small bed, or in a large bag; they do not carry him in their arms. In some countries the child is attached by means of loops to a piece of wood which is then placed on the mother's shoulders when she goes to work. Some hang the child from their necks, others tie him to their backs, and others again put him in a small basket; but in all countries mothers have found a way of taking their children about with them. To solve the problem of breathing, and prevent risk of suffocation, when the custom is to carry him with his face towards his mother's back, it is usual to take special precautions. The Japanese, for example, carry the child so that its neck is above the shoulder of the person to whom it is tied. This is why the first travellers to Japan called the Japanese a "two-headed race." In India the child is carried on the hip, and the Red Indians strap him to their backs in a kind of cradle which holds him back to back with his mother, but lets him see all that is going on behind her. The idea of abandoning her child is so far from the minds of any of these mothers that, as happened once in an African tribe, when a new queen was about to be crowned, the missionaries attending the ceremony were astonished to see her appear with her baby.

Another point is the custom of prolonging the period of maternal feeding. Sometimes this lasts for a year and a half; sometimes for two, or even three years. This has nothing to do with the child's nutritional needs, because for some time he has been able to assimilate other kinds of food; but prolonged lactation requires the mother to remain with her child, and this satisfies her unconscious need to give her offspring the help of a full social life on which to construct his mind. Because, even if the mother does not speak to the child herself, the mere fact of being with her brings him into contact with the world; he sees and hears the folk in the street and in the market place, carts, animals, and other sights take a place in his mind, even if he does not know their names. Watch how his face lights up when his mother argues at a booth about the price of fruit. You will readily see what a depth of interest the words and gestures arouse in him.

One observes, too, that the little one, going about with his mother, never cries unless he is ill or hurt in some way. Sometimes he may fall sleep, but he does not cry. If you look at photographs taken specially for the purpose of documenting the social life of a country, you will see that none of the children shown with their mothers are ever crying.

Yet the crying of children is a problem in Western countries. How often do we hear parents complain of their children's incessant crying? They discuss what to do to quieten the baby, and how to keep him happy. The reply of modern psychology is this: "The baby cries and becomes disturbed, has screaming fits and rages, because he is suffering from mental hunger." And this is the truth. The child is bored. He is being mentally starved, kept prisoner in a confined space offering nothing but frustration to the exercise of his powers. The only remedy is to release him from solitude, and let him join in social life. This treatment is naturally and unconsciously adopted in many countries. With us, it must become understood and applied deliberately, as a result of conscious thought.

REFERENCE

1. For an exhaustive study of this see Florence Brown Sherbon, *The Child*, New York and London, 1941.

10

Some Thoughts on Language

Let us turn now to the child's development of language. Some reflection on this is necessary, otherwise we may fail to see its connection with social life. Not only does it fuse men into groups and nations, but it is the central point of difference between the human species and all others. Language lies at the root of that transformation of the environment that we call civilization.

Human life is not wholly instinctive like that of the animals. No one can predict what a given baby will do in the world. But without mutual comprehension with others, it is pretty clear that he would not be able to do very much! The power to think is not enough. However intelligent men were, this alone could not produce the deliberations and agreements between them which are necessary for achievement. Language is an instrument of *collective thought*.

Before man's arrival on the earth it did not exist. And what is it? Barely a breath! A few noises strung together.

And the sounds of it in themselves are senseless. Between this vessel and the word, "jug," there is no logical connection. The only thing that gives sense to these sounds is the fact that men have agreed to give them a particular meaning. And so it is with all other words. They are expressions of agreement between the members of a human group, and only those "in the know" can understand them. Other groups may agree on quite different sets of sounds to convey the same ideas.

So it happens that a language is a kind of wall which encloses a given human company, and separates it from all others. And this, perhaps, is why "the word" has always had a mystical value for man's mind; it is something that unites men even more closely than nationality. Words are bonds between men, and the language they use develops and ramifies according to the needs of their minds. Language, we may say, grows with human thought.

A curious thing to note is how few sounds are needed to make up so many words. These can be combined in such an immense number of ways that the words we can make from them are endless. This sound may precede or follow that, some are voiced, others unvoiced, some are spoken with the lips closed, others with the lips open. But more astonishing, even than that, is the power of memory to recollect so vast a quantity of combinations and their meanings. Again, there is the question of thought, which has to be expressed by grouping words together into sentences. The words in these sentences have to be arranged in a particular order. They cannot just be jumbled together like pieces of furniture in a room. There are rules which guide the hearer as to the intentions of the speaker. To express a thought about something, the speaker must use its name and near this put the adjective. The subject, verb and object, all have their proper positions in the sentence. To get the words right is not enough; their order is equally important. We can easily test the truth of this by taking a clearly expressed sentence and writing it on a strip of paper. Then cut out the words separately. When mixed, their meaning vanishes. In a different order, the same words have no meaning. It follows that the order of the words must also be agreed upon by men.[1]

Hence, language is truly the expression of a kind of superintelligence. As a matter of history, languages have sometimes grown so cumbersome that, on the break up of the civilization they served, they have fallen into disuse; and, being so hard to remember, have disappeared. At first sight, one would think that language was something given us by nature, but we are forced to conclude that it is something over and above nature. It is a creation superimposed on nature, an intelligent product of the mass mind. It spreads in all directions, like an unlimited network by which everything can be expressed. With a language like Sanskrit, or Latin, we may study it for years and still not master it completely. It is a mystery impossible to fathom. To carry out any of their projects, men must agree, and for this they need a common tongue. Speech is a real thing; yet of all the instruments that man uses it is the least substantial.

The attention we have given to this problem—how this instrument becomes acquired by man—leads us to believe that it is the child who "absorbs" language. The reality of this absorption is something deep and puzzling, to which not enough attention has yet been given. All we usually say is that, "Children live with people who speak, so naturally they come to speak themselves." But, considering the innumerable complications of most languages, this idea is very superficial. Nonetheless, it has held the field for thousands of years without the slightest advance being made on it.

Study of the problem suggests still another observation: it is that a language, however difficult we may find it, was at one time spoken by the uneducated classes in the land of its origin. Latin, for example, which is hard even for those of us who speak one of its modern derivatives, was originally spoken by the slaves of Imperial Rome. Its complications then were just as great as they are now. And did not untaught labourers in the fields use the same language as three-year-old children in the Roman palaces?

And what of India where, many years ago, any tiller of the soil, any wanderer in the jungle, expressed himself naturally in Sanskrit?

The curiosity which these questions awaken has led to the making of careful studies of language development as it can be observed in actual children. I say, development, not teaching, for the mother does not teach her child language. It develops naturally, like a spontaneous creation. Also, its development follows fixed laws which are the same in all children. The various periods of the child's life show the same stages in the level reached—a thing repeated for children all over the world, regardless of whether the language be simple or complex. There are still many tongues of extreme simplicity spoken by primitive peoples, and the children reach the same level in these as in the much more difficult ones. All children pass through a period in which they can only pronounce syllables; then they pronounce whole words, and, finally, they use to perfection all the rules of syntax and grammar.[2]

The differences between masculine and feminine, singular and plural, between tenses and moods, prefixes and suffixes, are all applied in the children's speech. The tongue may be complex, have many exceptions to the rules, and yet the child who absorbs it learns it as a whole and can use it at the same age as the African child, who uses only the few words of his primitive vocabulary.

If we watch the production of the different sounds, we find that they also follow laws. All the sounds that occur in words are produced by the use of certain mechanisms. Sometimes the nose acts in unison with the throat, at others the muscles of the tongue and of the cheeks have to be co-ordinated. Various parts of the body take part in the construction of this mechanism, which functions perfectly for the mother tongue, the tongue learned by the child. Yet, in a foreign country, we adults cannot even detect all the sounds we hear, far less reproduce them vocally. We can only use the machinery of our own language; no one but a child can construct his own machinery and so learn to perfection as many languages as he hears spoken about him.

This is not the result of conscious work. It is something done at an unconscious level in the mind. It begins and unfolds in the darkest depths of the unconscious, and when it emerges it is as a fixed acquisition. We adults can only imagine what it is like to want to learn a language consciously. We then apply ourselves deliberately to this task. But we must try to cultivate another idea. It is the idea of natural mechanisms, or rather of mechanisms superimposed upon nature, which act apart from consciousness, and these wonderful mechanisms or series of them, develop at depths not directly accessible to our observation. The only evidence we have of them is external, but this is fully visible, being common to all mankind.

Striking as the whole picture is, some of its details are even more impressive. One is that in the speech of all peoples there is continuity of pronunciation from one generation to the next. Another is that complex languages are absorbed with the same ease as simple ones. No child finds it tiring to learn his mother tongue; "his mechanism" brings it into being as a single whole no matter what it may be.

This absorption of language by the child makes me think of an analogy which, though not very close, may provide us with some inkling of what goes on in the child's mind.

Suppose we are needing a picture of something. Either we can make this ourselves, using pencil and paints, or we can take a photograph, which depends on quite a different principle. The picture, in that case, becomes recorded on a sensitized plate which can receive the image of ten people just as readily as one. It all happens in a flash, and to take a thousand people gives it no more trouble. The work is the same whether we apply it to the title page of a book, or to a page of closely set print in foreign characters. The chemicals react to anything, simple or complex, in the fraction of a second. But for us to draw a human figure takes time, and the more figures we draw the longer it takes. If it takes us so long to copy the title page of a book, it will take far longer to do a page of it, in very small type.

Not only that, but the photographic image becomes imprinted on the plate in total darkness; the developing process is also done in the dark; it is fixed in the dark, and then only can it be shown in the open. But by that time, it has become unalterable.

So with the child's psychic mechanism of learning a

language. Its work begins in the deepest shadows of the unconscious mind; there it is developed and the product becomes fixed. Then only does it appear in the open. Beyond question, there is some mechanism at work causing all this to happen.

Once we are convinced of this, it is natural to wonder what exactly takes place, and today there is much enthusiasm for technical researches into this problem. But one side of the work, which is purely observational, we can do for ourselves. This is to watch the visible events—these, after all, being the only ones of which we can be sure. Such studies must be very exact. They are carried on today with the utmost care, from birth to two or more years. What happens every day is noted, and also the periods in which development remains stationary. From such notes, certain facts stand out like milestones. The quantity of inner work may be immense, yet the outer signs of it are often small. This means there is a great disproportion between the powers of expression and the inner work the child is doing. It is also found that visible progress does not go gradually, but in jumps. At a certain time, for example, the power to pronounce syllables appears, and then for months the child utters only syllables. Externally, he seems to be making no progress, but all of a sudden, he says a word. Then, for a long time, he uses only one or two words, and seems discouragingly slow to go any further. Nevertheless, other forms of activity show that his inner life is undergoing a steady and remarkable expansion.

Yet, are things very different in our own experience? We read in history of primitive peoples who live for centuries at a very low level, seemingly incapable of progress; but this is only the outer appearance, visible to the historian. The truth is that a continuous inner growth is taking place, which suddenly appears in a series of discoveries leading to rapid change. Then there follows another period of calm and slow development, before the next vigorous outburst.

Just the same thing happens with man's language in childhood. There is no smooth and slow advance, word by word, but here also we find explosive phenomena—as psychologists call them—which are not provoked by any teacher's action, but occur of themselves for no apparent reason. Every child, at a particular period of his life, bursts out with a number of words all perfectly pronounced. Within a space of three months, the child who was almost dumb, learns to use easily all the varied forms of the noun, suffixes, prefixes and verbs. And, in every child, all this occurs at the end of the second year of his life.

So, we ourselves may take courage from the child's example, and be willing to wait. From the stagnant periods of history we may always hope that progress will come. Perhaps the foolishness of man is less than it seems. Wonderful things for the future may lie waiting for explosions in the inner life which is hidden from us.

These explosive happenings and eruptions in his powers of expression continue in the child well after the age of two. There is the use of sentences simple and complex, the use of verbs in their tenses and moods, including the subjunctive. Coordinate and subordinate clauses appear in the same unexpected way. So become established the mental structures and the language mechanisms of expression peculiar to the race, or social class, to which the child belongs. This is a treasure prepared in the unconscious, which is then handed over to consciousness, and the child, in full possession of his new power, talks and talks without cessation.

Beyond this age of two and a half, which marks a border line in man's mental formation, there begins a new period in the organization of language, which continues to develop without explosions, but with a great deal of liveliness and spontaneity. This second period lasts till somewhere about the fifth or sixth year, and during it the child learns many new words and perfects his sentence formation. It is true that if the child's circumstances are such that he hears very few words, or nothing but dialect, he will come to speak like this. But if he lives among cultured people with a wide vocabulary, he takes it all in equally well. Circumstances, therefore, are very important, yet the child's language, at this time, becomes richer no matter what his surroundings.

Some Belgian psychologists have found that the child of two and a half has only two or three hundred words, but at six he knows thousands. And this all happens without a teacher. It is a spontaneous acquisition. And we, after he has done all this by himself, send him to school and offer as a great treat, to teach him the alphabet.

We must be careful to bear in mind the double path which is always followed. There is an unconscious activity that prepares speech, succeeded by a conscious process which slowly awakens and takes from the unconscious what it can offer.

And the final result? It is *man*. The child of six who has learned to speak correctly, knowing and using the rules of his native tongue, could never describe the unconscious work from which all this has come. Nevertheless, it is he, *man*, who is the creator of speech. He does it entirely by himself, but if he lacked this power, and could not spontaneously master his language, no effective work would ever have been done by the world of men. There would be no such thing as civilization.

This is the true perspective in which we must see the child. This is his importance. He makes everything possible. On his work stands civilization. This is why we must offer the child the help he needs, and be at his service so that he does not have to walk alone.

REFERENCES

1. See also G. Revesz, *Ursprung and Vorgeschichte der Sprache*, Berne, 1946.
2. For a concise picture of the different phases of language development in the child, see W. Stern, *Psychology of Early Childhood*.

11

How Language Calls to the Child

Let me try to illustrate the many wonders of the language mechanism itself. It is well known that the central nervous system provides the living being with machinery for adjusting itself to the outside world, and that the various sense organs, the nerves and nerve centres, and the muscular organs of movement or locomotion, all have parts to play in this. But the existence of a language mechanism implies—in a way—something more than the presence of purely material factors. Areas of nerve cells, or "centres," in the brain cortex were shown to be connected with language toward the end of the last century. Two of these are primarily involved, one being concerned with the *hearing* of speech (an auditory receptive centre), and the other with the *production* of speech, of the movements required for vocalizing words. One of these is therefore a sensorial centre, the other a motor centre.

In its visible aspects, the language apparatus has organs in which the same division can be seen. The organic centre of the ear receives the sounds of speech, and that of the mouth, throat, nose, etc., produces them. These two centres develop separately, both on the physiological and the psychological side. In some way, the hearing organs are connected to the mysterious seat of mental life where the child's language is evolved in the depths of his unconscious mind. As for the motor side its activities can be inferred from the astonishing complexity and precision of the movements needed to produce spoken words.

It is very clear that this latter part develops more slowly and shows itself later than the other. One asks why? It can only be because the sounds heard by the child *provoke* the delicate movements necessary to reproduce them.

That, of course, is supremely logical, because if man is not blessed with a pre-established language (but has in fact to create one for himself), the child must naturally hear the sounds in use among his own people before he can repeat them. Hence the movements for reproducing the words must be based on a substratum of sounds registered in the mind, because the movements he will make depend on the sounds he has heard and which the mind has retained. That much we can readily understand, but we have to remember that speech is produced by a natural mechanism, and not by logical reasoning. It is really nature which is being logical. What happens in studying nature is that the facts first of all come to our notice, and then, when we have understood them, we say how logical they are. And this leads naturally to the thought: "There must be some intelligent force directing these events!" The apparent influence of such an intelligent direction, acting creatively, is often more marked when the phenomena are psychological than when they are purely physical, though even then it is striking enough; one thinks of flowers, in all the beauty of their colouring and form. What is clear is that when the child is born, he has neither hearing nor speech. So what exists? Nothing, yet all is ready to appear.

There are these two centres, innocent of every sound and of all hereditary influences, so far as a particular language is concerned. They have the power, nevertheless, to seize upon a language, and to work up the movements needed to produce the words of it. They are parts of the machinery which nature uses to develop language in all its fullness.

Probing still more deeply, it becomes apparent that, as well as these two nerve centres, there must exist a special sensitiveness, and a readiness to act, which are centralized too. The child's activity therefore follows his sensations of hearing; all is stupendously well arranged so that directly the child is born he can begin his work of adaptation and of preparation for speech.

The organs themselves form just one more part of these complex preparations. Observing them we see a mechanism no less wondrous than the events which occur on the psychological side. The ear (organ of the heard side of language) which is formed by nature in the mysterious conditions of intra-uterine life, is so delicate and complex an instrument that it seems like the contrivance of a musical genius. The central part of the ear reminds one of a harp, with strings that can vibrate in response to various sounds, according to their length. The harp of our ear has sixty-four strings arranged in gradation, and, because the space is so restricted, they are arranged spirally, as in a sea shell. Despite the limited space, nature has been clever enough to provide everything needful for the reception of musical notes. But what is to make these strings vibrate? For if nothing strikes them, they will remain silent for years, like a disused piano. But in front of the harp there is a resonating membrane, like the stretched surface of a drum, and whenever a noise strikes this tympanic membrane, the strings of the harp vibrate and our hearing picks up the music of speech.

The ear does not respond to every sound in the universe, because it has not enough strings, but those it has can resonate to complex music, and a whole language can be transmitted in all its delicacy and refinement. The instrument of the ear is made in the wondrous prenatal life. If a child is born at the seventh month, the ear is already complete, and is ready to begin its work. How does this instrument transmit the sounds which reach it, sending them along the tiny nerve fibrils to that point in the brain where the special centres are located for their reception? Again, we are facing one of nature's mysteries.

But how is speech formed after birth? Psychologists who have made special studies of the newborn say that the slowest sense to develop is hearing. This is so torpid that many maintain that children are born deaf. To any kind of noise—unless accompanied by violence—they make no response whatever. To my mind, this could have a mystical meaning. I find no reason to suspect insensitiveness, but rather a deep gathering in of the sound; a concentration of sensitiveness in the centres for language, especially in that which accumulates words. I reason that these centres are specially designed for the capture of language, of words; so it may be that this powerful hearing mechanism only responds and acts in relation to sounds of a particular kind—those of speech. The result is that words heard by the child set in motion the complicated mechanism by which he makes the movements needed to reproduce them. If there were no special isolation of the sensitivity which directs this—if the centres were free to welcome every kind of sound—the child would start making the most astonishing noises. He would imitate all those peculiar to the place where he happened to be, including the nonhuman ones. It is only because nature has constructed and isolated these centres for the purpose of language, that the child ever learns to speak at all. There have been "wolf children" abandoned in the forest, from which later they have made miraculous escapes, and these children—although they have lived amid the cries of animals and birds, the murmuring of water and the rustling of leaves—remain completely dumb. They emit no sound of any kind, since they have never heard the human tongue which alone has the power to activate the machinery of speech.[1]

I emphasize this because I want to show that a special mechanism exists for language. Not the possession of language in itself, but the possession of this mechanism which enables men to make languages of their own, is what distinguishes the human species. Words, therefore, are a kind of fabrication which the child produces, thanks to the machinery which he finds at his disposal. In the mysterious period which follows immediately after birth, the child—

who is a psychic entity endowed with a specially refined form of sensitiveness—might be regarded as an *ego* asleep. But all of a sudden he wakes up and hears delicious music; all his fibres begin to vibrate. The baby might think that no other sound had ever reached his ears, but really it was because his soul was not responsive to other sounds. Only human speech had any power to stir him.

If we remember the great compelling forces that create and conserve life, we can understand how it is that formations due to this music must remain forever, and why the means for preserving the continuity of a language are the new beings who keep on arriving in the world. Whatever is formed at that time in the child's *mneme* has the power to become eternal.

So it is, also, with rhythmic songs and dances. Every human group loves music. Each creates its own music, just as it does its own language. Each group responds to its own music by bodily movements and accompanies it by words. The human voice is music and words are its notes, meaning nothing in themselves but to which every group attributes its own special meaning. In India hundreds of languages separate the groups but music unites them all—proof once again of the retentivity of childhood. Let us think what this means; none of the animals have music and dancing, but the whole of mankind, in all parts of the world, knows and makes up dances and songs. These sounds of speech become fixed in the unconscious. We cannot see what goes on within the living being, but the external happenings offer us a guide. First to become fixed in the little one's unconscious are the single sounds of language, and this is the basic part of the mother tongue: we might call it the alphabet. Syllables follow, and then words, but these are used without understanding —as happens sometimes when the child reads aloud from his primer. But how wisely is all this work conducted! Within the child is a tiny teacher who works like one of those old-fashioned teachers who used to make the children first of all recite the alphabet, then pronounce syllables and then words.

Except that *she* did it at the wrong time, when the child had already done it for himself and was in full possession of his language! The inner teacher, instead, does it at the right time. The child first fixes the sounds and then the syllables, following a gradual process as logical as the language itself. Words follow and finally we enter the field of grammar. Here, the first words to be learned are the names of things, substantives. We see how greatly nature's teaching illuminates our own thought. She is the teacher, and at her behest the child learns what to us adults seem the dullest parts of language. Yet the child shows the keenest interest, and this lasts well into the next period of his development, from three to five years of age. Methodically, she teaches nouns and adjectives, conjunctions and adverbs, verbs in the infinitive, then the conjugation of verbs and declension of nouns; prefixes, and suffixes, and all the exceptions. It is like a school, and we have at the end an examination, in which the child shows in practice that he can use every part of speech. Only then do we notice what a good teacher has been at work in him, what a diligent pupil he has been, and how clever he was to learn all this correctly. But no one pauses to admire this marvellous work, and only when the child has begun going to school do we take an interest and pride in what he learns. Yet if we older people are sincere in our profession of love for the young, it is the miracle of their triumphs that should dazzle our eyes and not their so-called defects.

The child is truly a miraculous being and this should be felt deeply by the educator. In two years this mite has learned everything. In these two years we see a consciousness gradually awakening within him, at an ever faster rhythm, until suddenly it seems to be taken by a fair wind and begins to dominate everything. At four months (some put it earlier and I am inclined to agree) the babe becomes aware that this mysterious music which surrounds him and touches him so deeply, comes from the human mouth. The mouth and its lips produce it by their movement. Seldom does anyone notice how closely the baby watches the lips of a person speaking; he looks at them most intently and tries to imitate the movements.

Then his consciousness intervenes to play an active part in the work. The movements, of course, have been unconsciously prepared. Not all the exact co-ordinations of the very minute muscular fibres needed for the production of speech are yet complete, but conscious interest has now been awakened and this reinforces his attention, leading to a series of lively and intelligent trials.

After watching the speaker's mouth for two months, the child produces syllabic sounds, by then being six months old. Unable, before this, to make a single sound of speech, he wakes up one morning before you do and you hear him saying, "pa... pa ... ma . . . ma." He has produced the words "papa" and "mama." For some time he will go on pronouncing only these two syllables, and that is when we say, "This is all a baby can do." But we must bear in mind that he has reached this point only after very great efforts. It is the end proposed by his *ego* which has made a discovery, and is now aware of its power. We have a little man, no longer a machine; a person who can use the machinery at his disposal.

This brings us to the end of the first year of life; but earlier, at ten months, the child has made another discovery. This is that the music coming from a person's mouth has a purpose. It is not merely music. When we talk to him fondly, the baby realizes that these words are meant for him, and he begins to grasp that we are saying them intentionally. So, two things have happened by the end of the first year: in the depths of his unconscious he has understood and at the level he has reached of consciousness, he has created speech—even though, for the moment, this is nothing but babbling, a simple repeating and combining of sounds.

At one year of age the child says his first *intentional* word. He babbles as before, but his babbling has a purpose, and this intention is a proof of conscious intelligence. What has happened within him? Close study convinces us that in his inmost being there is much more than is shown by these modest expressions of his ability. He becomes ever more aware that language refers to his surroundings, and his wish to master it consciously becomes also greater. And, just here, a great war springs up within him. It is the struggle of consciousness against the machine. This is the first conflict in man, the first warfare between his parts! Let me use my own experiences to illustrate what happens. I am a person with many ideas to express, and I want—as often happens in a foreign land—to convey them in a language not my own; so as to reach the heart of my audience. But, in a foreign tongue, my words are a useless babbling. I know my audience to be intelligent, and my wish is to exchange views with them, but this privilege is denied me because I lack the means of expression.

The time in which the mind has many ideas which it would like to communicate to others, but cannot express them for lack of language, is a very dramatic one in the child's life, and brings him his first disappointments. Subconsciously and unaided, he strains himself to learn, and this effort makes his success all the more astonishing.

A person trying to express himself is badly in need of a teacher to enunciate the words for him very distinctly. Why cannot the home do this? Our usual habit, instead, is to do nothing. We just imitate the child's babbling ourselves and, were it not that he has an inner teacher of his own, he would be unable to learn. It is this teacher who makes him listen to grown-ups talking to one another, even when they are not thinking about him. It urges him to master his language with that exactness which we make no effort to give him.

Yet one might arrange, as we do in our schools, for children of a year old to find intelligent persons who would talk to them intelligently. The difficulties the child meets with between one and two are not sufficiently realized, nor do we see how important it is to give him the chance of learning perfectly. We must come to understand that the child reaches his knowledge of grammar by himself; but this is no reason for our not speaking to him grammatically or for not helping him to construct his sentences.

The new "Helpers in the Home"[2] for children from birth to two years of age must have a scientific knowledge of the development of language. By helping the child, we become servers and collaborators with that nature which is creating him, and we find that his whole programme of studies has already been laid down.

Returning to my illustration, how should I behave myself if—babbling in a foreign tongue—I wanted to say something specially important? I might well lose my temper, get angry and even shout. The same thing happens with the child of one or two. When he tries to tell us something with a single word, and we fail to understand him, he gets furious. He goes into paroxysms of rage that seem to us senseless. In fact, we often say, "There! Now you can see for yourself the inborn depravity of human nature!"

But this is a little man, misunderstood and battling towards his independence. Being possessed of no language, all he can do is to show his exasperation. Yet he has the power to construct a language, and his anger is due to his frustrated efforts to produce the right word, which he has to frame as best he can. All the same, neither disappointments nor misunderstanding cause him to stop trying, and words somewhat resembling those in use, begin gradually to appear.

At about a year and a half, the child discovers another fact, and that is that each thing has its own name. This shows that, from all the words he has heard, he has been able to single out the nouns, and especially the concrete nouns. What a wonderful new step to have taken! He was aware of being in a world of things, and now each of these is indicated by a special word. It is true that one cannot say everything with nouns, and at first he has to use the one word to express a whole thought. Psychologists give much attention to these words the children use in place of sentences. They are called "fusive" words, or sometimes "portemanteau" words—

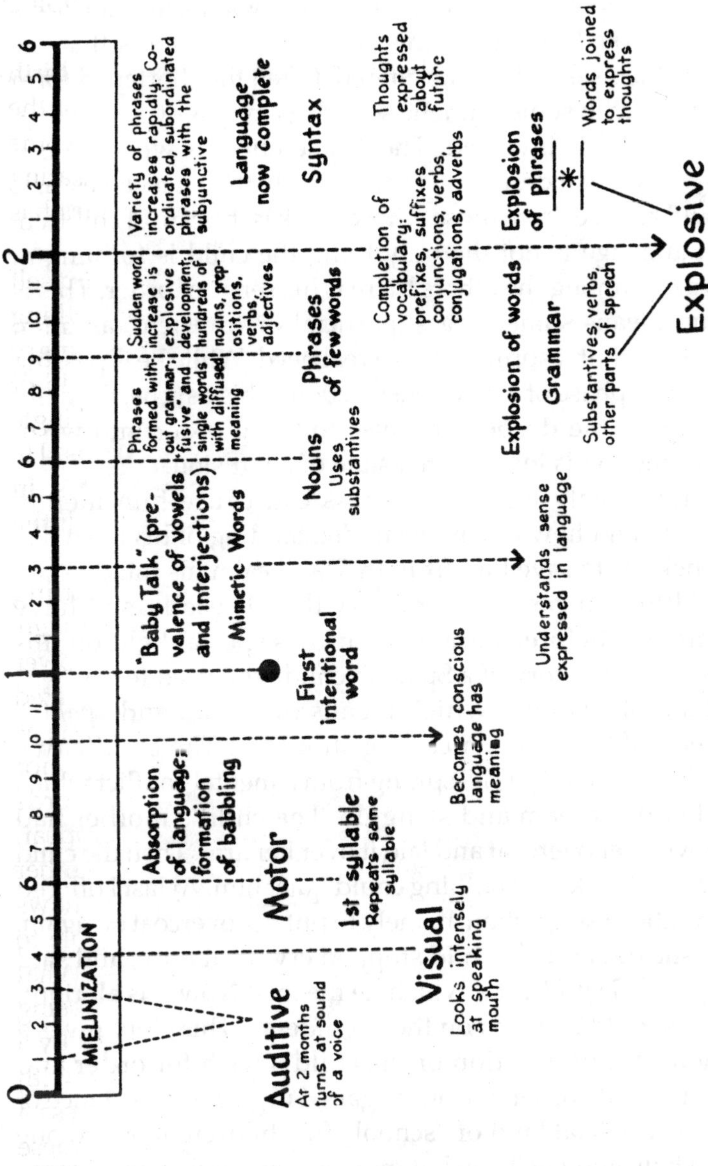

Fig. 7. The development of language.

"one-word sentences." Seeing his supper prepared, the child says, "Mupper," meaning "Mummie, I want some supper."

A marked feature of this condensed speech is that the words themselves become altered. Often the shortened form is united with some mimetic sound, as in bow-wow for dog, or the word is invented. The whole effect is what we call baby-talk, but it deserves far more study than it receives, and should receive, from those whose work is the care of children.

Language is not the only thing the child is forming at this age. Among the others there is his sense of order. This is by no means something superficial or transient, as often supposed, but it springs from a real need. While he is passing through a phase of active construction of his psyche, the child often feels the deepest impulse to bring order into what, according to his logic, is in a state of confusion.

How easily his helplessness can cause him mental anguish, and how much our understanding of his language can help us to save him from this, and calm his mind!

Although cases occur every day, I recall one I have mentioned before,[3] because it throws special light on this point. It is the story of a Spanish child who used to say "*go*" instead of "*abrigo*," which means overcoat, and "*palda*" instead of "*espalda*", meaning shoulder. The child's two words, "*go*" and "*palda*" sprang from a mental conflict which made him scream and struggle. The child's mother had removed her overcoat and laid it over her arm. Then the child began to shriek, and nothing could quiet him. At last I offered the mother a suggestion, namely to put her overcoat on again. This she did and the child stopped crying at once, and said happily, "*Go palda*," by which he meant, "Now it is all right, a coat should be worn on the shoulders." This story gives a very useful illustration of the child's wish for order and aversion to disorder. So, once again, I urge the importance of having a special kind of "school" for children of one to one and a half, and I believe that mothers, and society in general, far from keeping babies in isolation, should let them live in contact with grown ups and frequently hear the best speech clearly pronounced.

REFERENCES

1. An interesting example is that of the Savage of Aveyron. See note at the end of Chapter 8.
2. The Montessori Society in Rome conducts special training courses for these "Helpers" who specialize in the care of children at this age. (Scuola. Assistenti Infanzia Montessoriane, 116 Corso Vittorio Emanuele, Rome.)
3. This and other examples of the kind, which show the child can even understand whole conversations before being able to express himself, can be found in my book, *The Secret of Childhood*, Orient Longmans, 1950.

12

The Effect of Obstacles on Development

It will, I think, help to give a clearer idea of children's hidden tendencies if I pause to speak of certain profound forms of sensitiveness which their minds possess. We come to something like a psychoanalysis of the infant mind. In Fig. 8, I have used symbols to show the child's development of language. This will help to make our ideas clear.

Black triangles are chosen to represent substantives (the names of things), black circles stand for verbs, and the remaining parts of speech are as in the key—Fig. 8. If, now, we know that the child uses some two or three hundred words at a particular age, the method I offer enables us to show this pictorially, and so we are enabled to see at a glance how language develops, for whether the child's language be English, Tamil, Gujarati, Italian or Spanish, the parts of speech are always represented by the same symbols.

On the extreme left of our diagram are some nebulous patches which show the baby's first efforts to speak: exclamations, interjections, etc. Then comes the stage when two sounds are joined to produce a syllable; then three sounds leading to words. Later still, towards the right hand side of the diagram, we see various groups of words. These consist of certain nouns often used by the child, then come phrases of two words each—phrases which have a diffused meaning, each word standing for many.[1] Soon after this an immense "explosion" occurs, in which a multitude of new words comes into use. I have shown the actual number estimated by psychologists.

Just before this we see in the diagram a group of words, mostly nouns, and near them various other parts of speech scattered about at random; but immediately after the age of two, a second phase is shown in which the words form orderly groups. This is an explosion into sentences. The first explosion is therefore one of words, the second explosion is one of thought.

But, before these explosions can occur, there must have been some kind of preparation. This may be hidden and secret, but the fact of its existence is no mere guess or hypothesis, for we can see by their results the efforts the child has been making to express his thoughts! It is because the adult cannot always understand what the little child is trying to say that the child's bouts of irritation and anger occur just in this period of his life. We have hinted at this already. Vexation, at this age, is a part of the child's life. All his efforts, when not crowned with success, provoke him to rage. It is a well-known fact that deaf mutes are often extremely quarrelsome, and this we may attribute to their inability to express themselves. There is a great inner wealth waiting to be externalized, and the normal child finds ways of doing it, but only with the greatest difficulty.

This is a difficult period for the child because his obstacles are all environmental, or due to limitations in his own powers. It is the second time that he finds adaptation difficult. The first was when, immediately after birth, he was called upon to function on his own account, while up till then his mother had done everything for him. We saw, then, how the child's shock at birth, the mental traumata and regressions due to it, threaten him in the absence of adequate care and understanding. We saw, too, how some children are stronger than others, or more fortunate in their circumstances, and how these go straight on towards independence, which is the basis of normal development. To all this the present situation has parallel features. The quest of language is a laborious journey to that greater independence which speech gives, and dangers of regression lurk here also.

For there is another feature of this creative period which the reader will remember. It is that both the impressions the child's mind receives, and the emotional consequences they provoke, tend to remain permanently registered in it. This happens usefully in the case of spoken sounds and grammar, but, just as children in this period retain what they learn for the rest of their lives, so do they retain the unfortunate effects of obstacles. Every phase of the creative life has this dual nature. A struggle, a dread, a reverse of some kind, can have incalculable consequences, since the reaction to these obstacles becomes absorbed, just as much as the positive effects of progress. One thinks of the mark on a photographic plate resulting from a light leakage, which appears in every subsequent print. So, in this period, we not only have the development of character to be normally expected, but certain malformations, or "deviations" of personality, may also be formed, which become serious at later stages of growth.

Both walking and talking are established in this very formative period. It extends beyond two and a half, but its intensity and fertility then begin to diminish. But just as these powers continue to grow and develop, so also do the defects and difficulties which have had their origin in the same period. In fact, it is a commonplace of psychoanalysis that most of the mental disturbances of adult life are traceable to these early years.

Difficulties bound up with normal development fall within the general orbit of "repression," a term used in general psychology but associated particularly with psychoanalysis. "Repressions," of which everyone has now heard, are rooted in infancy. Speech furnishes numerous examples, although they occur plentifully in all fields of human activity. When the "word explosion" begins, this mass of words must have an outlet. So must the sentences when —in the next stage—the child starts putting his thoughts into grammatical form. Educational theory, nowadays, gives much importance to freedom of expression, connecting this not only with the immediate needs of the speech mechanism, but also with the future life of the individual. There are cases in which the normal explosion does not happen at the right age. For instance, the child of three, or three and a half, may use only the few words customary at a much younger age. Or he may seem completely dumb; yet his organs of speech are normal. This is called "mental dumbness," because the causes of it are wholly in the mind; it is a psychopathological condition.

Other types of mental disturbance studied by psychoanalysis (which is a true branch of modern medicine) begin at this time. The dumbness may depart all of a sudden, as if by a miracle. The child unexpectedly starts talking, well and composedly, and with a perfect regard for grammar. It is plain that everything was already prepared in his inmost being, but that some obstacle prevented it from showing.

In our schools we have had children of three and four who had never been heard to speak. They had never even used the "fusive" words uttered by children of two. But, thanks to the freedom they found, and to the stimuli of their surroundings, they showed suddenly that they could have talked all the time. How was this? Some grave mental injury, or a persistent impediment of some kind, must have been at work, preventing free outlet to the wealth of language really possessed.

How many adults find difficulty in speaking! They do it only with great effort and as if wondering all the time what to say. This hesitancy takes various forms:

(a) lack of courage to speak at all,
(b) lack of courage in forming words,
(c) difficulty in the use of sentences,
(d) the speech is slower than normal, and interspersed with ejaculations like—*er–ah–um*—etc.

These difficulties which lie within have now become

invincible. They are forms of a permanent inferiority, and have to be endured for life.

Other obstacles of psychological origin prevent clear articulation; the victim stammers or has defects in his powers of pronunciation. These failings proceed from that period of life in which the speech mechanism was being formed. So it is clear that each different period of acquisition has its own kind of regression.

First Period. The mechanisms are being acquired for word-formation.

Corresponding regression: poor pronunciation, stammering.

Second Period. The mechanisms of sentence formation are being acquired (thoughts are being expressed).

Corresponding regression: hesitancy in framing sentences.

These forms of regression are connected with the child's sensitiveness. Just as he is specially receptive for the purposes of creation and to increase his powers, so he is to overmuch opposition, and the results of this frustrated creativeness become fixed in the form of defects for the rest of his life. For we must always remember that the child's sensitiveness is greater than anything we can imagine.

It is often we who obstruct the child, and so become responsible for anomalies that last a lifetime. Always must our treatment be as gentle as possible, avoiding violence, for we easily fail to realize how violent and hard we are being. We have to watch ourselves most carefully. The real preparation for education is a study of one's self. The training of the teacher who is to help life is something far more than a learning of ideas. It includes the training of character; it is a preparation of the spirit.

Children have many kinds of sensitiveness, but they are all alike in their sensitiveness to *trauma*. How easy it is to wound them! Yet they feel just as keenly the adult's cold and ruthless calm, "Now darling, remember what mummy told you." Parents who are still in the habit of leaving their children to a nanny, should be especially cautious of the coldly authoritarian manner in which the nanny so often speaks. It is often to this that upper class people owe their troubles when, although they have plenty of physical courage, they are timid in speech, hesitate or stammer.

I have myself, sometimes, been too severe with a child, and the following example appears in one of my other books.[2] A child had put his outdoor shoes on the beautiful silk coverlet of his bed. I removed them in a somewhat determined manner, and brushed the coverlet energetically with my hand to show him that this was no place in which to leave one's shoes. For two or three months, whenever the child saw a pair of shoes, he first put them somewhere else, then looked for a coverlet, or cushion, that he could dust. In other words, the response to my overdone lesson was not that of a resentful or rebellious spirit. The child did not say, "Don't treat me like that, I shall put my shoes where I like!" but his rejoinder to my faulty conduct was an abnormality of behaviour. It often happens that children do not react violently. It might be better if they did, because the child who gets angry has discovered how to defend himself, and may then develop normally. But when he replies by a change of character, or by taking refuge in abnormality, his whole life has been damaged. Adults are unaware of this, and think there is nothing to worry about unless the child gets angry.

Another group of anomalies found among grown-ups takes the form of senseless fears and "tics." Most of these can also be traced to violence done to the little child's extreme sensitivity. Some reflect unfortunate experiences with animals, such as cats or chickens; others originate with the child's fright at being locked in a room. Neither reasoning nor persuasion can help the victims of these fears, which are known to medicine as *phobias*. Some are so common as to have special names; for example, "claustrophobia," the fear of locked doors, or of closed-in spaces.

Many more cases could be cited from medical experience, but I mention these just to show the child's kind of mentality at this age, and to insist that all our handling of him will bear fruit, not only at the moment, but in the man he is destined to become.

To understand the baby's mind, it is absolutely essential to take the path of observation and discovery. We have to do something like what is done by psychoanalysis when it reaches down to unconscious levels in the adult's mind. This is by no means easy, for our knowledge of "baby talk" is seldom sufficiently good, or we may fail to grasp the special implications which the child wants us to attach to his words. Sometimes we need to know the baby's whole life, or at least we must investigate his immediate past, before we can pacify this tiny creature in the difficulty he is facing. How often do we long for an interpreter to tell us his meaning!

I have worked for a long time on this myself, trying to make myself into the child's interpreter, and I have noted with surprise how, if you try to do this for them, they come running to look for you, as if understanding that here is someone who can help them.

Children's affection for those who merely pet and caress them is not on the same plane with this high enthusiasm. The child's one hope lies in his interpreter. Here is someone who will unlock the garden of discovery to which the world has shut the door. The child's helper is admitted to an intimacy which exceeds affection, because help is a greater gift than consolation.

In a house where I used to live, I had the habit of rising to start work very early in the morning. One day a little boy, who cannot have been more than a year and a half old, came into my room at that unheard-of hour. I questioned him affectionately, wondering if he wanted something to eat. He answered, "Worms." Showing my surprise, I answered, "Worms, worms?" Finding I did not understand, he tried to help me by adding another word, "Egg." I said to myself, "It can't be the early morning drink that he wants. Whatever can he mean?" Then he said, "Nina, egg, worms," and I understood, because I remembered (and here I repeat how important it is to know the whole framework of the child's life) that on the day before, his sister, Nina, had been shading an egg-shaped outline with a coloured crayon. He had wanted the crayon, but she had become angry and sent him away. And now, see how the child's mind works. Instead of opposing his will to hers, he had waited his opportunity—and with what constancy and patience—to try again. I gave him a crayon and the oval-shaped metal inset, and his face lit up, but he could not draw the egg-shaped outline, and I had to do it for him. Then he began to shade it with wavy lines. His sister had done it with the usual straight lines, but he had a better idea and used wavy lines, like worms. So this baby had waited till all were asleep, except his interpreter, and had then gone to her, confident that she would help.

Not anger and violence, but patience, marks this period in children's lives; the patience to wait for the right moment. It is when the child cannot express himself, finds inner obstacles to his wish, that he shows violence and rage (tantrums). The above example also shows how these tiny tots try to behave like older children. If a child of three starts on a piece of work, the little one of a year and a half will want to do it too. He may find it difficult, but he tries.

A baby boy in our house wanted to imitate his sister of three who was learning the steps of a new dance. The teacher had already asked us how she could be expected to teach the steps of ballet to such a tiny girl. We begged her not to worry about how much the child learned, but just to try. Knowing that our idea was to help the child in her development, the teacher condescended to do this, and began. At once the little boy of a year and a half ran forward, crying, "Me too!"

At this the teacher took a definite stand, protesting that it was absolutely impossible, and contrary to her dignity as a teacher of ballet, to take on anyone so young. However, we persuaded her to pocket her pride and to humour us .in our whim; so she sat down to play a march. Immediately, the baby flew into a rage and refused to move. This, she thought, confirmed her opinion. But he was not worrying about the dance. The cause of his rage lay in the teacher's hat which was lying on the sofa. Without saying either "hat," or "teacher," he repeated two words with concentrated fury. They were "hall" and "peg." What he meant was, "This hat is all wrong here. It should be on a peg in the hall." All his pleasure in the dance was forgotten, as if he felt a paramount call to bring order out of confusion. Directly the hat was placed on the peg, his temper cooled and he got ready to dance. It seems clear that the tiny child's basic need for order takes priority over all other social claims that the world may make upon him.

The study of words, and of children's sensitivity, enables us to penetrate to a depth in their souls seldom reached by psychologists.

The child's patience in our first example, and his passion for order in our second, give us much to think about of the greatest interest. If to these we add the story of the child who understood a whole conversation, but disagreed with the last speaker's conclusion about the happy ending of a narrative under discussion,[3] we see that besides the facts shown in our diagram (Fig. 7) there is going on in the child's mind a whole life, a whole mental drama from which we are excluded.

Every discovery made about the child's mind at this age ought to be published, because of the light it throws on helping babies to adapt better to their conditions. However tiresome we may find it, anything that helps human life has an ultimate importance of the greatest value. The child's helper in early infancy has a noble task. It is to begin, and to collaborate in developing, a future science on which mental development and the formation of character must eventually come to rest. Meanwhile, it behoves us to shoulder this burden, so as to prevent deviations and defects from marring the infantile personality, and so producing inferior adults. To this end we must remember:

1. that the first two years of life affect all the rest.

2. that the baby has great mental powers to which little attention has been given.
3. that he is supremely sensitive and for that reason any kind of violence produces not only an immediate reaction but defects which may be permanent.

REFERENCES

1. See Chapter 11.
2. *The Secret of Childhood.*
3. See *The Secret of Childhood.*

13

The Importance of Movement in General Development

It is high time that movement came to be regarded from a new point of view in educational theory. Especially in childhood we misunderstand its nature, and a number of mistaken ideas make us think of it as something less noble than it actually is. As a part of school life, which gives priority to the intellect, the role of movement has always been sadly neglected. When accepted there at all, it has only been under the heading of "exercise," "physical education" or "games." But this is to overlook its close connection with the developing mind.

Let us review man's nervous system in all its amazing complexity. In the first place, we have the brain (or "centre"). Then there are the various sense organs, which collect impressions and pass them on to the brain. Thirdly, there are the muscles. And nerves, what do they do? These are like cables for transmitting nervous energy to the muscles. And this energy is what controls the movements of the muscles. So the organization has three main parts, brain, senses and muscles. Movement is the final result to which the working of all these delicate mechanisms leads up. In fact, it is only by movement that the personality can express itself. The greatest of philosophers must use speech or writing to convey his ideas, and this involves muscular movement. What would be the value of his thoughts if he gave them no expression? And this he can only do by making use of his muscles.

If we take up animal observation, the first thing that strikes us is that animals can only express themselves through their movements. So it hardly seems logical, in the case of man, to ignore the whole of this side of his existence.

Physiologists regard the muscles as a part of the central nervous system, saying that this works as a whole to put man in relationship with his surroundings. In fact, this whole apparatus of brain, senses and muscles, is often called the *system of relationship*, meaning that it puts man in touch with his world, living and nonliving, and therefore with other people. Without its help a man could have no contact with his surroundings or his fellows.

Compared with this, all the other arrangements of the human body are—so to speak—selfish, because they serve only the person himself. They enable him to keep alive, or (as we say) to "vegetate," and therefore they are called "organs and systems of the vegetative life." The vegetative systems only help their owner to grow and exist. It is the system of relationship which puts him into contact with the world.

The vegetative system provides for a man's physical well-being and enables him to enjoy the best of health. But we have to think quite differently about the nervous system. This gives us the beauty of our impressions, the perfections of our thought. It is the source of all inspiration. So it is wrong for it to be lowered to the vegetative level. If the standards to which we cling are solely connected with our own self-perfection, with the raising of ourselves to spiritual heights, this brings us into the region of spiritual pride. It is a grave error, perhaps the greatest that man can make. The behaviour of animals does not lead them just to have beautiful bodies and to make graceful movements, but it has other and far more distant ends. In the same way, man's life is purposive: It is not enough to be always reaching out to higher levels of spiritual refinement and inward beauty. Naturally, a man may aim, and ought always to aim, at the highest levels of physical and mental perfection, but his life would be a vain and worthless thing if his wishes ended at this point. Indeed, what would be the use of his having a brain or muscles? There is nothing in the world which plays no part in the universal economy, and if we are endowed with spiritual riches, with aesthetic feelings and a refined conscience, it is not for ourselves, but so that these gifts shall be used for the benefit of all, and take their place in the universal economy of the spiritual life.

Spiritual powers are a form of wealth. They must go into circulation so that others can enjoy them; they must be expressed, utilized, to complete the cycle of human relations. Even the heights of spirituality, if pursued for their own sake, have no value, and if we aim at these alone; we shall be neglecting the greater part of life and its purposes. Were we believers in reincarnation, and said to ourselves, "By living well now, I shall be better off in my next life," this would be only selfishness speaking in us. We should have reduced the spiritual level to the vegetative level. If we are always thinking about ourselves, and of ourselves even in eternity, we shall be eternally selfish. Instead, we must take the other point of view, and this not only in everyday life but also in education. Nature has endowed us with many abilities: these must be developed, and not only developed but used.

The following analogy may be helpful. We know that for the enjoyment of good health, heart, lungs and stomach must all work together. Why not apply the same rule to the system of relationship, the central nervous system? If we have a brain, sense organs and muscles, all these must cooperate. The system must exert itself in all its parts, none of them being neglected. We want, let us say, to excel in brain power, but to succeed in this we must include the other sides also. To perfect any given activity movement will be needed as the last stage of the cycle. In other words, a higher spirituality can only be reached through action. This is the point of view from which movement has to be judged. It belongs to the total activity of the central nervous system, and as such it cannot be ignored. The system of relations is a single whole, even though it has three parts. Being a unit, it can only become perfect when set to work as a unit.

One of the greatest mistakes of our day is to think of movement by itself, as something apart from the higher functions. We think of our muscles as organs to be used only for health purposes. We "take exercise," or do gymnastics, to keep ourselves "fit," to make us breathe, or eat or sleep better. It is an error which has been taken over by the schools. In the world of physiology, it is just as though a great prince were being made the servant of a shepherd. The prince—the muscular system—is only being used to help the vegetative life.

Such a grave error cannot but lead to injury: there comes about a separation between the life of movement and the life of thought. Since the child has a body as well as a mind, we feel we must include games in his curriculum, so as to avoid neglecting any part of nature's provisions. But to be always thinking of the mind, on the one hand, and the body, on the other, is to break the continuity that should reign between them. This keeps action away from thought. But the true purpose of movement is far higher than to produce an appetite or strengthen the lungs; it is to serve the ends of existence, the universal and spiritual economies of nature.

To give them their right place, man's movements must be coordinated with the centre with the brain. Not only are thought and action two parts of the same occurrence, but it is through movement that the higher life expresses itself. To suppose otherwise is to make of man's body a mass of muscles without a brain. Development may occur on the vegetative side, but the interconnection between mind and muscle does not keep pace. The power of decision lacks the muscular control by which alone it can be expressed. Not thus is independence achieved, but only the breakup of what nature, in her wisdom, intended to be one.

When mental development is under discussion, there are

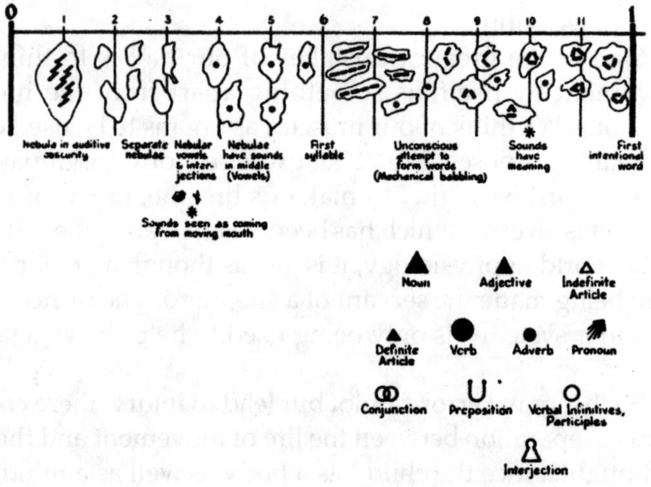

Grammar symbols.

Fig. 8. The development of language from its nebulous

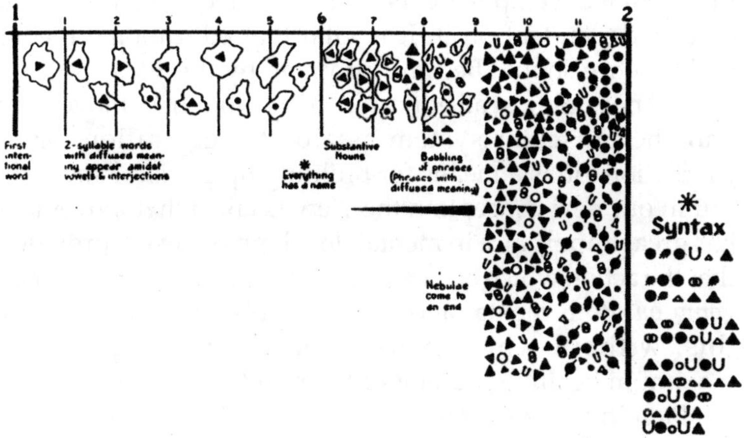

stage to conscious expression in grammatical form.

many who say, "How does movement come into it? We are talking about the mind." And when we think of intellectual activity, we always imagine people sitting still, motionless. But mental development *must* be connected with movement and be dependent on it. It is vital that educational theory and practice should become informed by this idea.

Till now, almost all educators have thought of movement and the muscular system as aids to respiration, or to circulation, or as a means for building up physical strength. But in our new conception the view is taken that movement has great importance in mental development itself, provided that the action which occurs *is connected with the mental activity going on*. Both mental and spiritual growth are fostered by this, without which neither maximum progress nor maximum health (speaking of the mind) can exist.

Plentiful proofs of this are to be found in nature, and it becomes indisputable if we follow children's development with care and attention. Watching a child makes it obvious that the development of his mind comes about *through* his movements. In the development of speech, for example, we see a growing power of understanding go side by side with an extended use of those muscles by which he forms sounds and words. Observations made on children the world over confirm that the child uses his movements to extend his understanding. Movement helps the development of mind, and this finds renewed expression in further movement and activity. It follows that we are dealing with a cycle, because mind and movement are parts of the same entity. The senses also take part, and the child who has less opportunity for sensorial activity remains at a lower mental level.

Now, the muscles directed by the brain are called voluntary muscles, meaning that they are under the control of the will, and will power is one of the highest expressions of the mind. Without the energy of volition, mental life could hardly be said to exist. Hence if the voluntary muscles are directed by the will they must form a kind of organ of the mind.

The muscles, which are the flesh of the body, make up the greater part of it. Skeleton and bones merely act as supports for the muscles. Yet for this reason they, also, must form a part of the same system. The outer form that we contemplate in man and the animals is given by the bones and muscles. From the voluntary muscles comes the shape that most strikes the eye. The number of these is almost beyond computation, and great interest is to be found in the differences between them. Some are massive, others supremely delicate; some are quite short, others long and strip-like, and all have different purposes. If one pulls in a given direction, there will always be another which pulls the opposite way, and the more vigorous and precise this play between opposed forces, the more delicate will be the movements performed. If we repeat at length, or "practise" a new movement, with the idea of making it as perfectly as possible, this will be an exercise directed towards bringing into being a wonderful harmony between opposing forces. The result is not so much an agreement as a harmonized opposition, an agreed disagreement.

We are not all aware of these opposing forces. Nevertheless we are indebted to them for all the control of our movements that we consciously exert. In animals this inner harmony is given them by nature: the grace of the tiger's bound, or the squirrel's leap, is due to a wealth of opposites so perfectly balanced as to bring about these exquisite effects. One is reminded of a complicated piece of machinery working to perfection, such as a clock, with wheels turning in opposite directions, which keeps perfect time because of the accuracy with which it has been adjusted.

All movement thus has a most intricate and delicate machinery. But in man none of it is established at birth. It has to be formed and perfected by the child's activity in the world. Unlike the animals, man finds himself so richly endowed with muscles that there are hardly any movements he cannot learn to make, and while he is doing this we do not talk about strengthening his muscles, but of coordinating them, which is a very different thing. The point is that, in man's case, he finds all his muscles unco-ordinated, and the nervous arrangements for all the movements he learns have to be built up and perfected by actions initiated by his mind. In other words, the child has an internal power to bring about coordinations, which he thus creates himself, and once these have begun to exist he goes on perfecting them by practice. He himself is clearly one of the principal creative factors in their production.

The wonderful thing is that man's movements are not fixed and limited like those of the animals, but he can decide upon and choose those he will learn. There are animals with special gifts for climbing, running or swimming, but man has no such gifts. Instead, he has one gift only, that he can learn them all, and do them better than the animals!

But such versatility depends on work. They cost him the effort of much repetition, of "practising," and in the course of this the muscles come to act in unison, because the nervous interconnections have an unconscious way of finding the needed harmony, given an initiative provided by the will.

In reality, no one ever acquires all the muscular powers of which they are capable. Man is like a person born to enormous wealth, so rich that he can only use a part of his inheritance, but he can choose which part he will use at his pleasure. A man may become a gymnast by profession, but it does not follow that he was born with muscles of any special kind. Neither is the professional dancer endowed with muscles suited specially for dancing. The gymnast and the ballerina develop themselves by force of will. Everyone, whatever he may want to do, has such a wide range of muscular powers that he can choose and set himself a course. His mind can propose and direct his development. Nothing is preordained but everything is possible. It is only necessary for his will to collaborate.

It is not in human nature for all men to tread the same path of development, as animals do of a single species. Even if many people cultivate the same art, each goes about it in a slightly different way. We see this in writing. Though we can all write, each has his own handwriting. Every human personality has its own way of doing things.

The nature of a person's work is betrayed by his movements. For his work is the expression of his mind—it is his mental life—and this has access to a whole treasury of movements which develop in the service of this—the central and directive—part of his inner being. Should a man fail to develop his whole musculature, or—as sometimes happens—should he develop only those muscles needed for heavy physical work, his mind also will stay at this low level at which his movements have remained. Thus a person's mental life may be restricted by the type of work open to him, or preferred by him. The mental life of anyone who does not work at all is in grave peril, because—although it is true that all the muscular powers cannot be used—there is a limit beneath which it is dangerous for those in use to fall. When reduced below this, a person's whole life is weakened. This is why gymnastics and games have been made a compulsory part of the school curriculum. It prevents too great a part of the muscular system from falling out of use.

We also, in this method, would have to follow the ordinary schools in planning an alternation of mental and physical activities, were it not that the mental life shown by our children brings the whole of their musculature into constant use. This has nothing to do with the learning of particular skills. It differs completely from some modern educational trends in which the child learns to write nicely so as to become a clerk, or others are set to pick-and-shovel work to make them better labourers. Professional training of this kind does not serve the true purposes of movement in education as we understand it. The concept we have in mind is quite different. It is a question of the child coordinating those movements which play a necessary part in his mental life, so as to enrich the practical and executive sides of it.

Without this companionship of movement the brain develops on its own account, as if estranged from the results of its work. Movements not directed by the mind occur haphazardly, and do harm. But movement is so essential to the life of any individual in touch with his surroundings and forming relationships with other people, that it must be developed on this plane.

Its place is to serve the whole man and his life in relation to the outside world.[1]

Today's principles and ideas are too much set on *self*-perfection and *self*-realization. Directly we understand the true purposes of movement, this self-centredness is bound to disappear. We are obliged to extend the concept to include all realizable potentialities. In short we must ever cling firmly to what may be called the "philosophy of movement." Movement is that which distinguishes the living from the non-living. Yet living things never move at random. They go towards goals, and their lives follow natural laws. Let us (to make this quite clear to ourselves) try to imagine what it would be like if everything became quite motionless. If, within the plants, all movement ceased, there would be no more flowers and fruit. The percentage of poisonous gases in the air would increase disastrously. If all motion stopped, if the birds stayed still on the trees and all insects fell to the ground, if beasts of prey no longer roamed the wilds and fish no longer swam in the waters, what a frightful place this world of ours would become!

Immobility is impossible. The world would become chaotic if all movement stopped, or even if living things moved about aimlessly, without the guidance of that useful end which all creatures have assigned to them. Every living being has its own characteristic movements, and its own pre-established goals, and in creation there is a harmonious balance between all these different activities which are co-ordinated to achieve some purpose.

Work is inseparable from movement. The life of man, and of the great human society, is bound up with movement. If everyone stopped working for a single month, mankind would perish. So movement has a social side also; it is not just a matter of hygiene. If all human capacity for movement went into the "taking of exercise," mankind's total energy would be consumed and nothing produced. The very existence of the social order depends on movement directed to constructive ends. The individual in the womb of social life performs his actions for ends which are both individual and social. When we speak of "behaviour," the behaviour of men and animals, we are thinking of purposive movements of this kind. Such behaviour is the core of their activities, and it is not limited to actions which serve only a personal need; for example, cleanliness, or work about the house. But the doing of it may serve far distant ends whereby it acts for the benefit of others. But for this, man's work would count for nothing more than a gymnastic exercise. Dancing is the most individual of all movements but even dancing would be pointless without an audience; in other words without some social or transcendental aim.

To have a vision of the cosmic plan, in which every form of life depends on directed movements which have effects beyond their conscious aim, is to understand the child's work and be able to guide it better.

REFERENCE

1. For a clear and convincing exposition of this necessity, see Prof. Dr. J. J. Buytendijk, *Erziehung durch lebendiges Tun*.

14

Intelligence and the Hand

It is very interesting to study the mechanical development of movement, not only because of its intricacy but because each of the phases it passes through is clearly visible.

In Figure 9, I have shown the development of movement by two horizontal lines, with various lines standing on them. The heavier lines mark six-monthly intervals. The lower line stands for development of the hands, and the upper line for that of equilibrium and walking. So the diagram shows the development of all four limbs, two at a time.

In lower animals the four limbs develop and work together, but in man one pair develops apart from the other, a thing which shows clearly that they serve different functions. The power to walk and to keep one's balance develops so regularly in all men that we may think of it as a biological event. It is safe to say that once a man is born he will surely walk, and that all men will resemble one another in the way they use their feet. But no one can tell what any given man will do with his hands. Who knows what special skills the babies of today will develop? Those of past generations developed quite different ones. Our two lines, therefore, will have different meanings, according as we are studying hands or feet.

The functioning of the feet undoubtedly has a biological basis, and it is even connected with an inner development of the brain. On the other hand, man is the only mammal to

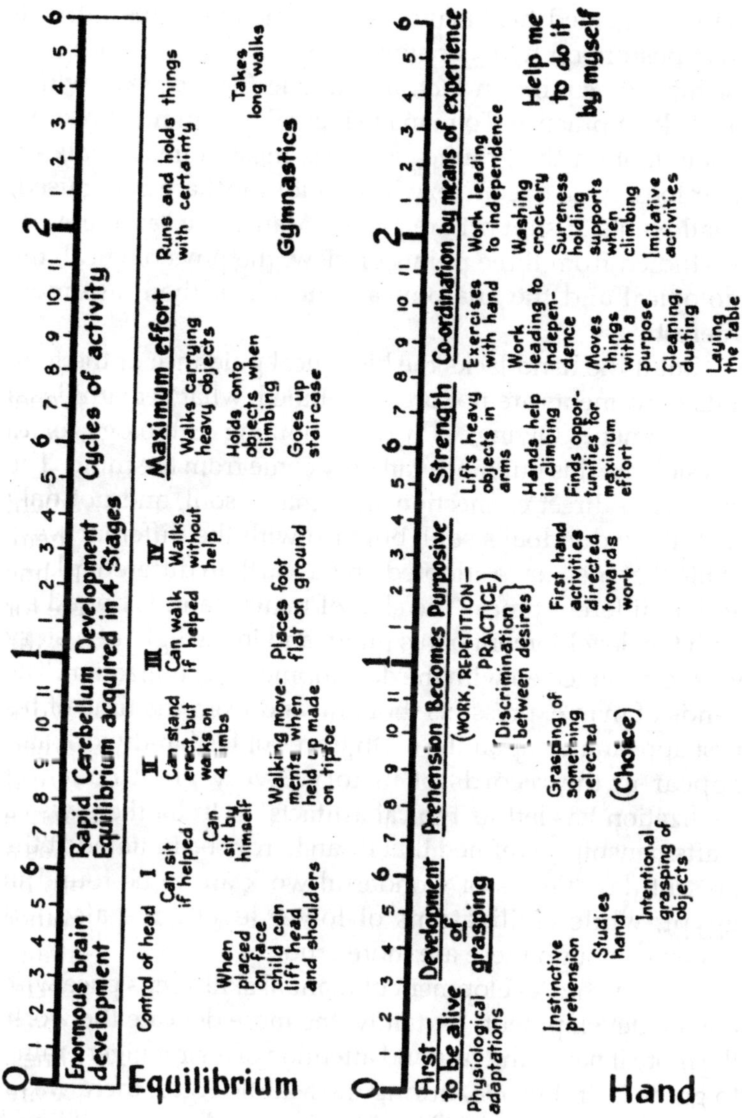

Fig. 9. The development of movement.

walk on two feet, while all the others walk on four. Once man has gained his balance he can maintain this difficult erect posture on two feet alone. But this balance is not easy for him to acquire; in fact, it is a true form of skill which needs long practice. To manage it at all, a man must rest his whole foot on the ground, whereas most animals walk on their toes. And, of course, when all four feet are being used, small points of support are plenty. Man's foot can therefore be studied from three points of view: the physiological, the biological and the anatomical, and all of them are most interesting.

But if the hand lacks the biological guidance of the foot, if its movements are not predetermined, what is to guide its development? Owing, as it does, nothing to biology, or to physiology, this guidance can only come from the mind. The hand is in direct connection with man's soul, and not only with the individual's soul, but also with the different ways of life that men have adopted on the earth in different places and at different times. The skill of man's hand is bound up with the development of his mind, and in the light of history we see it connected with the development of civilization. The hands of man express his thought, and from the time of his first appearance upon the earth traces of his handiwork also appear in the records of history. Every great epoch of civilization has left its typical artifacts. In India there was a craftsmanship so refined that it can hardly be imitated at the present day. Proofs of wonderful work are to be found in Egypt, while civilizations of lower level have also left remains, though these are more crude.

Hence, the development of manual skill keeps pace with mental development. Certainly, the more delicate the work, the more it needs the care and attention of an intelligent mind to guide it. In Europe, during the Middle Ages, there was a period of great mental awakening, and the books and manuscripts which reflected the new ideas, were beautifully illuminated. Even the spiritual life, which seems so far removed from earthly things, had its splendours of this kind, and we admire the miracles of building wrought in the temples which drew men to common worship—temples which have always sprung up wherever there was spiritual life.

We are told that St. Francis of Assisi—perhaps the simplest and purest of human souls—used to say:

"Look at these great hills! They are the walls of our temple and the aspiration of our hearts!"

Yet one day he and his spiritual brethren were invited to build a church, and both he and they, being poor, made use of the uncut rocks ready to hand, and carried them on their shoulders to build the chapel. The truth is that when a free spirit exists, it has to materialize itself in some form of work, and for this the hands are needed. Everywhere we find traces of men's handiwork, and through these we can catch a glimpse of his spirit and the thoughts of his time.

If we try to think back to the dim and distant past, so remote that not even bones remain, what is it that helps us to reconstruct those times, and to picture the lives of those who lived in them? It is their art. In some of these prehistoric ages there are signs of a primitive civilization based on physical strength. The monuments and artifacts are formed from huge blocks of stone, and we ask in amazement how they came to be set up. Elsewhere more refined art shows an indisputably higher level of civilization. So we may say that man's hand has followed his intellect, his spiritual life and his emotions and the marks it has left betray his presence. But even without this psychological view of things we can see that all the changes in man's environment are brought about by his hands. Really, it might seem as if the whole business of intelligence is to guide their work. For if men had only used speech to communicate their thought, if their wisdom had been expressed in words alone, no traces would remain of past generations. It is thanks to the hand, the companion of the mind, that civilization has arisen. The hand has been the organ of this great gift that we inherit.

The hands, therefore, are connected with mental life.

Indeed, does not the ancient art of palmistry maintain that racial history is imprinted on the hand and that this is a spiritual organ? Hence, the study of a child's psychological development must be closely bound up with the study of his hand's activities, which are stimulated by his mind. Nothing shows better than this how closely the two are entwined.

We may put it like this: the child's intelligence can develop to a certain level without the help of his hand. But if it develops with his hand, then the level it reaches is higher, and the child's character is stronger. So even here, in what we tend to think of as a purely psychological matter, the facts are that a child's character remains rudimentary unless he finds opportunities for applying his powers of movement to his surroundings. In my experience, if—for special reasons—a child has been unable to use his hands, his character remains at a low stage in its formation: he is incapable of obedience, has no initiative, and seems lazy and sad. But those children who have been able to work with their hands make headway in their development, and reach a strength of character which is conspicuous.

This brings to mind an interesting moment in the history of Egypt, when skilled manual work was to be seen on all sides; in art, architecture and religion. Inscriptions on the tombs of that epoch show that the highest praise a man could be given was to say that he was a person of character. So the development of character must have seemed very important to these people, whose manual achievements were on the grandest scale. This illustrates once again how the movements of the hand keep pace all through history with the development of character and civilization, and of how the hand is related to personality.

And if, against this, we set the way in which all these people walked, it was, as one might expect, always on two legs, erect, and keeping their balance. They probably danced and ran somewhat differently from ourselves, but always they used their legs alone for just moving about.

The development of movement is therefore duplex; partly it is tied to biological law; partly it is connected with the inner life; though both kinds are dependent on the use of muscles. Studying the child, we therefore have to follow two lines of development: the development of the hand, and that of walking and keeping one's balance. From Figure 9 we observe that only at the age of one and a half does any linkage come about between the two. This is when the child wishes to carry heavy objects with his hands, and his legs have to support him. Man's legs, which are his natural means of transport, carry him to the places where he can work, but this work he does with his hands. He may walk for great distances, and men have come in fact to occupy the whole of the earth's surface, and while this conquest of the land was going on they lived and died. But what they left behind them, as a sign of their passing, was the work of their hands.

In our study of language we saw that speech goes primarily with hearing. But action is connected with sight, for we need to see where we are setting our feet, and when our hands are at work we need to see what they are doing. These two senses, hearing and sight, are the ones most concerned in the child's psychophysical development. In his mental life, the first thing to awaken is his power to observe what lies about him, and it is clear that he must come to know the world in which he is about to move. A work of observation precedes his first movements, and when he begins to move he will be guided by what he already knows and has become able to perceive. Getting one's bearings and moving are both dependent on a previous degree of mental development. This is why the newborn child starts by lying motionless. When, later, he moves, he will be able to follow the guidance of his mind.

The first sign of movement is the child's effort to grasp, or take something. Not till grasping has occurred is the baby's attention drawn to the hand which enabled him to do it. Prehension which at first was unconscious, now becomes conscious, and, as we see by watching the child, it is his hand

and not his foot which first claims his attention. Once this has happened, grasping goes on apace, and instead of being instinctive, as it was at first, it becomes intentional. At ten months the child's observation of the world about him has awakened his interest in it, and he desires to master it. Intentional grasping, impelled by his wishes, then ceases to be grasping pure and simple. It gives way to true exercises of the hand expressed particularly in the moving of objects here and there. Possessor of a clear vision of his surroundings, and full of desires in regard to them, the child begins to act. Before the year is out his hands become busy in various ways which to him, one may say, are so many kinds of work: the opening and closing of cupboards, of boxes with lids, the sliding of drawers in a cabinet, taking corks and stoppers out of bottles and replacing them, removing oddments from a basket, and putting them back. It is by dint of these efforts that he comes to acquire more and more control over his hands.

Meanwhile, what has been happening to the other pair of limbs? Here, neither intelligence nor consciousness has to intervene. What occurs is anatomical in the shape of a rapid development of the cerebellum, the special organ for controlling the muscles which keep us in equilibrium.

It is as if a bell were to ring, calling on an inert body to get up and keep its balance. The environment, here, plays no part. The orders come from the brain. The child, with effort and some assistance, first sits up and then staggers to his feet.

Psychologists now say that man's rise to the erect posture has four stages. In the first he sits, in the second he rolls on to his belly and crawls, and if, during this phase, one offers two fingers for him to cling to, he may move his feet in turn but with only his toes touching the ground. When at last he stands alone, it is with his whole foot resting on the ground. Having thus reached man's normal erect position, he can walk provided he holds on to something, for example, his mother's dress. And very soon after this, he reaches the fourth stage which is to walk by himself.

All this has come about purely from an internal process of maturation. The child's next tendency is to say,

"Now that I've got my legs, I'm off Goodbye!"

He has now reached another level of independence, for the essence of independence is to be able to do something for one's self. The philosophical concept which underlies these successive conquests of independence is this: that man achieves his independence by making efforts. To be able to do a thing without any help from others: this is independence. If it exists, the child can progress rapidly; if it does not, his progress will be slow. With these ideas in mind, we can see how the child must be treated: they give us a useful guide in our handling of him. Although our natural inclinations are all toward helping him in his endeavours, this philosophy teaches us never to give more help than is absolutely necessary. The child who wants to walk by himself, must be allowed to try, because what strengthens any developing power is practice, and practice is still needed after the basic power has been attained. If a child is always carried in someone's arms even to the age of three (a thing I have often seen happen), his development is not being helped but hindered. Directly independence has been reached, the adult who keeps on helping becomes an obstacle.

Therefore, it is clear that we must not carry the child about, but let him walk, and if his hand wishes to work we must provide him with things on which he can exercise an intelligent activity. His own actions are what take the little one along the road to independence.

Observation shows that at the age of one and a half a new factor appears of great importance to the development of both arms and feet. This is the factor of strength. The child who has become active and skilful feels himself to be strong. His main idea, in whatever he does, is not merely to practice, but to exert the maximum of effort (how different from us)!

Nature seems to be telling him, "You have agility and skill, and now you must become strong. Otherwise all will be useless."

And this is where the skill of the hands, and the power to keep balanced on the feet, make common cause. Instead of merely walking, the child likes to take very long walks and to carry quite heavy things: Men, in fact, are not meant only to walk but also to carry burdens. The hand which has learned to grasp must train itself to lift weights and to move them. Here is a child of one and a half clutching in his arms a huge jar of water which he manages to support, but keeping his balance with difficulty and walking very slowly. There is also a liking to defy the laws of gravity and overcome them. The child loves to climb and, in doing so, to cling with his hands and pull himself up. No longer is he clasping in order to possess but gripping in order to clamber. These are all trials of strength and there is a whole period of life dedicated to them. So here, again, we see the logic of nature, for the grown man must be physically strong.

It is after this that the child, who can now walk and feels confident of his strength, begins to notice the actions of those about him, and tries to do the same things. In this period he imitates not because someone has told him to do so, but because of a deep inner need which he feels. It is something we only perceive when the child is free. So here we may set out the logic of nature:

1. To give the child the upright posture.
2. To make him walk and become strong.
3. To enable him to take part in the life going on about him.

We see from this how preparatory phases follow one another. The child must first prepare himself and his bodily instruments, then become strong, then observe others and finally begin to do things himself. Nature urges him and even suggests gymnastic exercises, like climbing on to chairs and up ladders. Only after this does a new phase set in when he feels the need to start doing things himself. "I am ready and now I want to be free."

No psychologist has yet taken sufficient account of the

fact that the child becomes a great walker and has the need to go for very long walks. Usually, we either carry him or put him in a gocart. According to us, he cannot walk so we provide him with transport; he cannot work so we work for him. At the very moment of his entry into life, we give him an inferiority complex.

15

Development and Imitation

We left the child in the last chapter at the age of one and a half. This age has become a centre of interest, and it may well be a turning point in education. It is the moment in which the preparation of the upper limbs joins with that of the lower limbs. The child's personality is also about to expand, because with the "explosion into language" at two he will shortly reach a stage of real completeness. On the threshold of this event at a year and a half, he is already making efforts to express what he has in mind. It is a time of great effort and constructive work.

In the presence of this phase of the child's development, we must be specially careful not to destroy any of life's natural tendencies. If nature shows so clearly that this is a period of intense effort, we must be prepared to help this effort. To say that is to make a very general assertion, but there are many students of childhood who would express it in greater detail. They say that in this period of life the child begins to imitate. This, in itself, is no new idea, for children have always been said to imitate their elders. But this was a very superficial way of putting it. Today one realizes that, before he can imitate, the child must first of all *understand*. The old idea was that all we grown-ups had to do was to behave in our usual ways, and the children, by imitation, would grow up to do likewise. This ended our responsibilities. Naturally, we included the idea of "setting a good example," and stressed the importance of all adults doing this, especially teachers. On their example depended the good of humanity. And mothers, too, had to be perfect. But nature does not reason like this. She is not concerned with the perfection of adults. The important thing is that before the child can imitate, he must be prepared for doing so, and this preparation derives from the efforts he has been making. This is true of every single human being. The example set by adults only provides the aim, or motive, for imitation. It does not produce a successful result. As a matter of fact, the child, once launched on his attempts, often improves on the examples set him. He does more perfectly and exactly everything to which he has been inspired. In some kinds of action this truth is self-evident. Everyone knows that, for a child to become a pianist, he has to do far more than merely imitate those who can play already. He has to practise interminably to give his fingers the skill, that is needed. Yet, how often do we apply this *naive* belief in imitation to fields which are higher still. We read to the child, or tell him stories, about heroes and saints, thinking that this will influence him to become heroic, or saintly, too. But this is impossible without a far deeper preparation of the spirit. No one can ever become great just by imitation. The example may arouse a hope, awaken an interest. The desire to imitate may stimulate effort; but training on a vast scale is needed before the heights can be attained. In the educational field, nature herself teaches that imitation requires preparation. The first efforts the child makes are not aimed at imitating, but at *forming in himself the capacity to imitate;* they are aimed at changing *himself* into the thing desired. This shows the universal importance of indirect preparation. Nature gives us not merely the power to imitate, but also the power to transform ourselves, to become what the example typifies. And if, as educators, we believe we can help the child's life-powers to achieve their ends, then it is important for us to know at what points our help can be usefully given.

If we watch a child of this age, we shall see that he is

trying to do something definite. What he tries to do may seem absurd to us, but this does not matter. He has to finish it. It is the urge of life within him that commands this. If his cycle of activity be interrupted, the results are a deviation of personality, aimlessness and loss of interest. Nowadays, it is held to be highly important to let these cycles of activity run their course. No less important are indirect forms of preparation; in fact all these are forms of it. Our whole life prepares us indirectly for the future. In all those who have done something of fundamental importance, you will find there has always been a strenuous period in their lives which preceded the doing of this actual piece of work. It was not necessarily work of the same kind, but there must have been an intense effort made along some line or other, and this acted as a spiritual preparation, provided it was able to exhaust itself fully. The cycle must have been completed. So, whatever intelligent activity we chance to witness in a child—even if it seems absurd to us, or contrary to our wishes (provided, of course, that it does him no harm)—we must not interfere; for the child must always be able to finish the cycle of activity on which his heart is set.

As said in the last chapter, infants of this age show interesting ways of carrying out their intentions. We see mites under two who seem to be carrying weights far beyond their strength for no apparent reason. In the home of one of my friends there were some heavy stools, and I saw a child of one and a half who took it on himself to move them with visible effort from one end of the room to the other. Children like helping to lay the table and will carry loaves of bread in their arms so large that they cannot even see their feet. They will go on doing this, carrying things back and forth, till tired out. The adult's usual anxiety is to relieve the child of the weight, but psychologists in these days are convinced that help of this kind, interrupting, as it does; the child's self-chosen activity, is one of the most harmful forms of repressive action we can take. The nervous troubles of many "difficult" children can be traced back to this kind of interference.

Another kind of effort which children feel called on to make, is that of going upstairs. When we do this, it is for some purpose, but the child does it without any purpose. Having reached the top he is not content, but comes down in order to climb up again, and so completes his cycle many times over. The slides, or "chutes" made of wood or cement, that we often see in school playgrounds, lend themselves very well to this purpose; but to the little child it is not the sliding down that matters, but the climbing up, the joy of making an effort.

So difficult is it to find adults who will not interfere with infantile activities, that all psychologists agree in asking for places to be set aside for children to work in, where they can be free from interruption. For this purpose, day nurseries and infant schools are very important, especially for tiny tots of one and a half upwards. All kinds of things are being specially made for these schools. There may be a little house on a treetop, with a ladder for going up and down. But this house is not a place to live, or rest, in; it is a point to arrive at. The aim is the effort needed to get there; the house is incidental. If the toddler wants to carry something, he will always choose the heaviest things he can find. Even the instinct for climbing, which is so noticeable, is nothing but a desire to make the needed effort. He tries to find something "difficult" on which to clamber, perhaps a chair. But staircases give the greatest joy, because children have in themselves an innate tendency to go upwards.[1]

This kind of activity, which serves no external purpose, gives children the practice they need for co-ordinating their movements. It is the possession of co-ordinated movements (movements in which many muscles have to co-operate) that enables the child to imitate actions of ours. The ostensible aim of the child's work is not its ultimate purpose; all the child does is to obey an inner impulse. It is only after he is prepared that he can imitate adults. Only then can his surroundings inspire him. If he sees someone sweeping the floor, or making pastry, he is now able to join in; the new idea can stimulate a successful action.

Let us now turn to the child of two and his need to walk. It is natural for him to feel this need, for he has to prepare the future man, and must therefore build up in himself all the essential human abilities. The child of two is well able to walk for a mile or two, and also to climb, if he is in the mood for it. The difficult parts of the walk appeal to him most. We must remember that the child's idea of walking is quite different from ours. Our belief that a long walk is beyond him, comes from making him walk at our pace. This is as stupid as it would be for us to go out on foot with a horse, and expect to keep up with it. The latter, seeing we were out of breath, would then say (as we do to the child): "This is no good. Jump on my back and we will both get there together." But the child is not trying to "get there." All he wants is to walk. And because his legs are shorter than ours, we must not try to make him keep up with us. It is we who must go at his pace. This necessity we are under of taking our time from the child is clear enough in this case, but we ought to note that this rule applies whenever we are educating little children, no matter in what field. The child has his own laws of development, and if we want to help him to grow, it is a question of following these, not of imposing ourselves upon him. The child does not walk only with his legs, he also walks with his eyes. What urges him on are the interesting things that he sees. Here is a sheep grazing. He sits down near it to watch. Presently he gets up and goes a fair distance—sees a flower—smells it—sees a tree—goes up to it, walks around it several times, then sits down to look at it. In this way, he may wander for miles. His walks are broken by periods of rest and at the same time full of interesting discoveries. If some obstacle lies across his path, for example, some fallen rocks, or a tree-trunk, then his happiness is complete. Water he loves. Sitting down by the side of a brooklet, he murmurs happily, "Water, water!" His grown-up companion, wanting to get somewhere as soon as possible, has quite different ideas on the subject of what walking is for.

The child's way is like that of the first tribesmen to wander the earth. No one said, "Let's go to Paris," for there was no Paris. "Let's take a train"... there were no trains. Men walked till they came to something useful or interesting; a forest where wood could be gathered; an open plain for fodder. Children are like this. The instinct to move about, to pass from one discovery to another, is a part of their nature, and it must also form a part of their education. To the educator, the child who goes for a walk is an explorer. The idea of exploration, or scouting, which is used today as a kind of relief, or change, from school work, ought to be a regular part of education, and come much earlier in life. All children should be able to go for walks like this, guided by what appeals to them. The school, in that event, would be able to offer preparatory help in the classroom; teaching, for example, the names of colours, the shapes of leaves and their veining, the habits of insects, birds and other animals. All this opens fields full of interest: the more the children know the more they will see and then the further they will walk. To explore, one needs to be filled with intellectual interests and these it is *our* business to give.

Walking is an exercise complete in itself. Other muscular exertions need not be added to it. A man who walks, breathes and digests better, enjoys all the benefits to health that we pursue in sport. It is a form of exercise which brings beauty to the body, and if, by the wayside, we find something of interest to collect and classify, a ditch to jump, wood to gather for the fire, these movements—of extending the arms and bending the body—make it the perfect gymnastic. Little by little, as man's knowledge increases, his intellectual interests widen and with these the activities of his body. The path of education should follow the path of evolution, to walk and to enjoy ever wider horizons. In this way, the child's life becomes increasingly rich.

To make this principle a part of education is especially

important in these days, when people are walking less, and using all kinds of vehicles to carry them about. It is not a good thing to cut life in two, using the limbs for games and the head for books. Life should be a single whole, especially in the earliest years, when the child is forming himself in accordance with the laws of his growth.

REFERENCE

1. In my book *The Secret of Childhood* the reader will find many examples of this cycle of activity.

16

From Unconscious Creator to Conscious Worker

So far, we have been discussing a period in the child's development which we find to have much in common with his life in the womb. This kind of development continues till the child is three, and during that period—which is a highly creative one—many important changes take place. Yet, in spite of this, we have to think of it as a part of life which falls into oblivion. It is as though nature had drawn a dividing line; on the one side are happenings we can no longer remember: on the other side is the beginning of memory. The forgotten part is the one we have called *psycho*embryonic, that is to say, the part inviting comparison with the *physico*-embryonic, or prenatal, life which no one can remember.

In this psychoembryonic period various powers develop separately and independently of one another; for example, language, arm movements and leg movements. Certain sensory powers also take shape. And this is what reminds us of the prenatal period, when the physical organs are developing each on its oven account, regardless of the others. For, in this psychoembryonic period we see the mental powers of control coming into existence separately. And it is not surprising that we fail to recall what happens, for there is still no unity in the personality—this being a unity which can only be brought about when the parts are complete.

Thus it happens that at the age of three, life seems to begin again; for now consciousness shines forth in all its fullness and glory. Between these two periods, the unconscious period and the one which follows it of conscious development, there seems to be a well marked boundary. In the first, there is no possibility of conscious memory. Only with the advent of consciousness do we have unity of the personality, and therefore the power to remember.

Before three the functions are being created: after three they develop. The line of demarcation between these two periods reminds one of the Waters of Lethe—the River of Forgetfulness in Greek mythology. We find it very hard to recollect anything that happened to us before the age of three, and still more before we were two. Psychoanalysis tries by every means to draw the mind back to its past, but no one in a general way can push their memories further back than the third year of life. Could any situation be more dramatic, for just at the time when creation was bringing us forth out of nothing, not even the person concerned can tell us anything about it!

The unconscious creator, this forgotten being, seems to be wiped out from human memory, and the child who comes to greet us at the age of three is a person we find it impossible to understand. The bonds which link us to him have been cut by nature. That is why there is so much danger of the adult destroying what nature is trying to do. For we have to remember that in this first section of his life, the child is entirely dependant on us. He cannot fend for himself, and unless we adults are enlightened—either by nature or by science—as to the way in which his mind develops, we are likely to become the greatest obstacles to his progress.

But, by the end of this period, the child has acquired powers which permit him to defend himself. If he feels oppressed by the adult, he can protest in words, he can run away or play pranks. Not that the child's real aim is to defend himself. What he wants to do is to master his environment, finding therein the means for his development. And what is it (to be exact) that he has to develop? It is all those powers which, up till now, he has been creating. So, from the age of three till six, being able now to tackle his environment deliberately and consciously, he begins a period of real constructiveness. The hidden powers he was previously creating are now able to show themselves, thanks to the opportunities for conscious experience which he finds in the world about him. Such experience is not just play, or a series of random activities, but it is work that he has to do in order to grow up. His hand guided by his intelligence begins to do jobs of definitely human type. If, at first, the child was an almost contemplative being—gazing at his world with apparent passivity and using it to construct the basis of his mind—in this new world he exercises his will. At first he was guided by an impersonal force seeming to be hidden within him; now he is guided by his conscious "I," by his own personal self, and we see that his hands are busy. It is as if the child, having absorbed the world by an unconscious kind of intelligence, now "lays his hand" to it.

The other kind of development which begins just now consists in the perfecting of the acquisitions already made. Language is a very clear example, for its spontaneous development goes on till five or so. Already it has existed since the child was two and a half, and it was then complete, for the child could not only form words but use sentences grammatically correct. But there still remains this special sensitiveness (the sensitive period for language, as we have called it) that goes on urging the child to fix its sounds ever more accurately, and above all to enrich it with an ever greater *repertoire* of words.

Hence there are two tendencies: one is the extension of consciousness by activities performed on the environment, the other is for the perfecting and enrichment of those powers already formed. These show us that the period from three to six is one of "constructive perfectionment" by means of activity.

The mind's power to absorb tirelessly from the world is

still there, but absorption is now helped and enriched by active experience. No longer is it a matter purely of the senses, but the hand also takes part. This hand becomes a "prehensile organ of the mind." Whereas the child used to absorb by gazing at the world while people carried him about, now he shows an irresistible tendency to touch everything, and to pause a while on separate things. He is continuously busy, happy, always doing something with his hands. His intelligence no longer develops merely by existing: it needs a world of things which provide him with motives for his activity, for in this formative period there are further psychological developments which still have to take place.

It has been called "the blessed age of play"—something people have always been aware of, but only recently has it been subjected to scientific study.

In Europe and America, where the speed of civilized life causes an ever greater cleavage between man and nature, people try to meet this need by offering the children an immense quantity of toys, when their real needs are for stimuli of quite a different kind. At that age children need to touch and handle all kinds of things, yet hardly any real articles are placed at their disposal, and most of those they can see they are forbidden to touch. There is only one substance that the modern child is allowed to handle quite freely, and that is sand. Letting children play with sand has now become universal. Water is sometimes allowed, but not too much, for the child gets wet and water mixed with sand makes a mess. Grown-ups take little pleasure in repairing the consequences!

But in those countries where the toy making industry is less advanced, you will find children with quite different tastes. They are also calmer, more sensible and happy. Their one idea is to take part in the activities going on about them. They are more like ordinary folk, using and handling the same things as the grown-ups. When the mother washes out some linen, or makes some bread and little cakes, the child joins in. Though his action is imitative, it is a selective and intelligent imitation, through which the child prepares himself to play his part in the world. There is no doubt whatever that the child needs to do these things to serve ends of his own, interior ends connected with self-development. In our schools we give everything needed so that the child can imitate the actions he sees in his home, or in the country in which he lives. But we have implements specially made for him, of the right size to suit his diminutive proportions and strength. The room is dedicated to him, and he is free to move about in it, talk and apply himself to intelligent and formative kinds of work.

Nowadays, all this seems very obvious, but when I first propounded the idea people were much astonished. When I and my helpers prepared for children of three to six a world with furnishings of their own size, so that they could live in it as though it were their own home, this was thought to be absolutely wonderful. The little chairs and tables, the tiny plates and bowls for washing up, the "real life" activities of laying the table for meals, of cleaning out the fireplace, sweeping and dusting—beside the frames for learning to dress one's self—were hailed as wondrous innovations in the field of educational ideas.

The social life which these children then came to lead brought out in them unexpected tendencies and tastes. It was the children themselves who showed that they preferred one another's company to dolls, and the small "real life" utensils to toys.

Professor John Dewey, the well-known American educator, narrates how he had the idea that in New York—that great centre of American life—he would be able to buy some small utensils made specially for the use of children. So he made a personal search in the New York shops for little brooms, stools, plates, and so on. He could find nothing of that kind whatever: the very idea of making them was absent. All that existed were numberless toys of every description. He exclaimed in astonishment: "But the children have been forgotten!"

Alas, the child is forgotten in many more ways than this. He is the Forgotten Citizen, who lives in a world where there is plenty of everything for everyone else, but nothing for him. In this empty world he wanders aimlessly getting constantly into mischief, breaking his toys, vainly seeking satisfaction for his spirit, while the adult fails completely to realize what are his real needs.

Having in our schools broken this barrier, and torn aside the veils which hide the truth, having given the child real things in a real world, we expected to see his joy and delight in using them. But actually we saw far more than that. The child's whole personality changed and the first sign of this was an assertion of independence. It was as though he were saying: "I want to do everything myself. Now, please don't help me."

All at once he became a man seeking for self-sufficiency, scorning every help. Who would have expected this to be his response, and that the adult would have to limit his *rôle* to that of an observer? No sooner was the child placed in this world of his own size than he took possession of it. Social life and the formation of character followed automatically.

So, what resulted was not just the child's happiness, but the child began his work of making a man. Happiness is not the whole aim of education. A man must be independent in his powers and character, able to work and assert his mastery over all that depends on him. *This was the light in which childhood revealed itself to us, once consciousness had come to birth and begun to take control.*

17

Further Elaboration Through Culture and Imagination

Children of this age are urged by the laws of their nature to find active experiences in the world about them. For this they use their hands and not only for practical purposes, but also for acquiring knowledge. If we leave children free in this new kind of environment that we have provided, they give us quite an unexpected impression of their nature and abilities. They seem to be happier, and they have such deep interests that they can work for long periods of time without fatigue. As a result, their minds seem to open out and they become eager for knowledge.

It was this that lay behind the "explosion into writing," the occurrence which first drew widespread attention to this unknown mental life of little children.

But the explosion into writing was really nothing but "smoke from the fire." The real explosion takes place within the inner personality. One thinks of those mountains which contain an inward furnace. Outwardly they seem solid and unchangeable, but one day there is a bang and flames come bursting out through the massive rock. And from the nature of these flames, from the smoke and unfamiliar solids that emerge, experts can determine the nature of the earth's contents.

Directly these children found themselves under

conditions of real life, with serious implements for their own use, of a size proportionate to theirs, unexpected activities seemed to awaken within them. These were as unmistakable as they were surprising and it was our effort to follow them and interpret their meaning, helping others like them to appear also, that brought this method of education into being.

No educational method, in the accepted sense, had caused these happenings. On the contrary, it was they—as they progressively unfolded—that became our guide and taught us how to treat the children. All began with our efforts to give satisfactory conditions of life, wherein the children should find no obstacles to their development, and in leaving them free to choose the various means of activity that we had provided. Hence it was true to say that what we had made was a discovery in infant psychology. In fact, Peary the explorer, who was then just back from his North Pole expedition, called our work, "The discovery of the human soul." He thought this would give a better idea of its nature than to call it a method of education.

From the very beginning, there were two groups of facts which stood out clearly. One was that the child's mind can acquire culture at a much earlier age than is generally supposed, but his way of taking in knowledge is by certain kinds of activity which involve movement. Only by action can the child learn at this age. He has to do something which develops his unfolding self. Now that we know how great his receptivity is between three and six, there can no longer be any doubt about this.

The second group of facts relate to character formation, but I shall deal with these in a later chapter. Here I shall confine myself to the first group, the taking in of culture by means of spontaneous activity.

Children feel a special interest for those things already rendered familiar to them (by absorption) in the earlier period. On these they can focus their minds with great ease. For example, the child's explosion into writing is closely connected with his special sensitivity for language, and this was operative at the time when he began to speak. By the age of five and a half or six, this sensitivity has ceased to exist; so it is clear that writing can be learned with joy and enthusiasm only before that age. Children older than this have lost the special opportunity which nature grants them of learning to write without making special and conscious efforts of application and will.

All the same, we know from other experiences that this easy writing does not come from our use of the sensitive period alone: it also depends on certain preparatory exercises which the child does at an earlier stage still, when his hand is busy with our carefully designed apparatus for practicing his powers of sensorial discrimination. For this reason a new principle has found its way into our method, the principle of "indirect preparation."

Nature herself works on this principle. Even in the embryo, she builds organs in anticipation of the need which the individual will have for them, and only when the machinery exists does she call it into action.

It follows that if the child tends to elaborate in the second period those inner formations which he has built in the first, we may take the last-named as guides to those that will follow. In acquiring speech, for example, we have seen that the child in the first period passes through a series of phases as precisely ordered as those in the grammar book. In turn, he enunciates separate sounds, syllables, nouns, verbs, adjectives, adverbs, prepositions, conjunctions and the rest. We therefore know that we can help him in the second period by following the same sequence. Yes, we shall teach him grammar from the first! And truly, it sounds absurd, in today's way of thinking, that we should start our first direct teaching of language with grammar, and that the child can begin learning this *before* he begins to read and write.

But let us think more carefully. What is the basis of meaningful speech. Is it not grammar? Whenever we (and the children) talk, we talk grammatically. If, then, we give him some grammatical help when he is four years old, while he is perfecting his language mechanisms and enriching his vocabulary, we provide conditions favourable to his work. By teaching grammar, we help him to master perfectly the spoken language that he is absorbing. Experience has shown us that little children take the liveliest interest in grammar, and that this is the right time to put them in touch with it. In the first period (from 0 to 3) the acquisition of grammatical form was unconscious; now it can be perfected consciously. And we notice something else: that the child of this age learns many new words. He has a special sensitiveness for words; they attract his interest, and he spontaneously accumulates a very great number.

Many experiments have been made which show conclusively that this is the age in which vocabulary is most rapidly enriched. It is as if the child were hungry for new words. If he is not helped, he will obtain them with effort and at random. So we try to facilitate his work by collecting those he will need and offering them systematically.

Incidentally, this has led us to another point of procedure which we have permanently adopted. The teachers who helped me in the first stages of my work had no higher education. They wrote many words for the children to read, each word on a separate card. But before long they came to tell me they had used up all the words referring to clothing, to things in the house, the street, the names of trees, and so on. But the children still wanted more. So I began choosing words from the higher learning; for example, the names of the geometric figures which the children handle when using our sensorial apparatus: polygons, trapezia, triangles of various kinds, etc. The children learned them all! So we wrote the names of scientific instruments: thermometer, barometer, etc., then passed on to botanical terms: sepal, petal, stamen, pistil, etc. These also they learned with enthusiasm, and still asked for more. When taking the children out for a walk, these teachers found it difficult not to feel resentful when the children taught them the names of every kind of automobile, to the disclosure of their own ignorance!

Insatiable at this age is the child's thirst for words, and inexhaustible his capacity for learning them. But this is not true of the next period. Other faculties are then being born, and the child learns new words with much greater difficulty. We saw that the children who had learned these words early in life, retained them, and could use them fluently, after going on to the ordinary schools when they were eight or nine, and in the years which followed. But the results were much inferior when children of eight and older, were taught these same words for the first time. We have to conclude that scientific words are best taught to children between the ages of three and six; not in a mechanical way, of course, but in conjunction with the objects concerned, or in the course of their explorations, so that their vocabulary keeps pace with their experiences. For example, we show the actual parts of a leaf or flower, or point out the geographical units (cape, bay, island, etc.), on the globe. It is easy to have solid models, or pictures and diagrams to which the children have access. For them there are no difficulties here, but teachers often do not know the words, or find them hard to remember and get them confused.

At Kodaikanal I saw some fourteen-year-old schoolboys from the ordinary schools who were hesitating about the names they should give to the parts of a flower. A mite of three came over to help them. He said, "Pistil," and then ran back to his work.

On another occasion, after we had explained the textbook classification of plant roots and illustrated them by pictures hung on the walls, one of the tinies came in and asked what these pictures were. We told him and shortly afterwards we found that many plants in the garden had been uprooted. The little ones had become enamoured of the idea, and wanted to see what kinds of root all these plants had! So we thought it advisable to give them some direct lessons, but this only led to protests from their parents who said that the children, when they reached home, had pulled up all the plants in the garden; then they had washed the roots to see their forms.

Is the child's mental horizon limited to what he sees? No. He has a type of mind that goes beyond the concrete. He has the great power of imagination.

The picturing, or conjuring up, of things not physically present depends on a special mental ability of high order. If man's mind were limited to what he actually saw, his outlook would be dreary indeed. We do not see only with our eyes, and culture is not made up of what we see alone. Take our knowledge of the world, for example, if, within sight, there are no lakes and no snow, we can nevertheless bring them into our "mind's eye." Only the possession of a certain kind of mental activity enables us to do this.

Up to what point can children imagine? Not knowing the answer, we began to experiment with children of six, but instead of starting with the lesser geographical units (river, bay, island, etc.), we tried the effect of presenting the whole world at once: that is to say, we showed a land and water terrestrial globe—"the world."

Now, the world is something for which there is no sensorial image drawn from the child's surroundings. If, therefore, he has formed an idea of it, this can be only in virtue of an intangible power of his mind, an imaginative power. We provided the children with a small terrestrial globe in which the sea was depicted as a smooth surface of deep indigo blue and the land as a surface, rough to the touch, of a fine sparkling powder.[1] The globe had none of the ordinary markings, names or places, yet the children began at once to say:

> "Here is the land"
> "That is the sea"
> "Look, here is America"
> "This is India," etc.

They loved the globe so much that it became the most popular feature of their room. The child's mind between three and six can not only see by intelligence the relations between things, but it has the higher power still, of mentally imagining those things that are not directly visible. Imagination has always been given a predominant place in the psychology of childhood, and all over the world people tell their children fairy stories which are enjoyed immensely as if the children wanted to exercise this great gift, as imagination undoubtedly is. Yet, when all are agreed that the child loves to imagine, why do we give him only fairy tales and toys on which to practise this gift? If a child can imagine a fairy and fairyland, it will not be difficult for him to imagine America. Instead of hearing it referred to vaguely in conversation, he can help to clarify his own ideas of it by looking at the globe on which it is shown. We often forget that imagination is a force for the discovery of truth. The mind is not a passive thing, but a devouring flame, never in repose, always in action.

Some children of six were once standing around the globe discussing it, when a little one of three and a half pushed his way forward and said,

"Let me look. Is this the world?"

"Yes," said the others, somewhat surprised. And the little one said:

"Now, I understand. My uncle has been around the world three times!" Yet he had not failed to grasp that this was a model, for he knew the world to be immense. This he must have gathered from conversations overheard.

Another of our children, a boy of four and a half, also asked to see the globe. After looking at it closely and listening to some older children who were talking about America without noticing his presence, he suddenly interposed:

"And where is New York?" The others were evidently surprised, but nevertheless showed him. Then he asked, "And where is Holland?" This caused still more astonishment, but when he was shown, he said:

"So this is the sea!" At this they all began to question him with eager curiosity, and he told the following story.

"My father goes to America twice a year and stays in

New York. After he has gone, Mummy says, 'Daddy is on the sea.' She says this for many days. Then she says, 'Daddy has arrived in New York.' And after another few days, she says, 'Daddy is on the sea again.' Then there comes a lovely day when she says, 'Now he is in Holland and we are going to meet him at Amsterdam.' "

This child had heard so much about America that when he heard it mentioned in connection with the globe, he stopped at once to look, and his expression seemed to say, "I have found America!"

To visualize what was meant must have been a great comfort to him after having sought in vain to get his bearings in the world of thought as he had done previously in the material world. Till then he had only been able to clothe the words he had heard in faulty fantasy, which is what the child usually has to do.

People have always thought that to play with bricks and exercise the imagination on fairy tales, were two of the child's primary needs at this age. The first was supposed to set up a direct relationship between the child's mind and his environment, so that he could know it and master it, thus achieving much mental development. The second was held to give proof of a wealth of imagery which the child poured out in his games. But by having in his hands something real on which to exercise this powerful force, one may reasonably suppose that he is greatly helped, for his mind is then also brought into contact with the outer world.

Children of this age are always asking us to explain things. Everyone knows how curious they are, and we feel we are being bombarded by questions. But if we do not regard these as a torment, but as the expressions of a mind longing to know, we may find them illuminating. The child of this age cannot follow long explanations, and usually we try to be far too exhaustive.

A small boy once asked his father why leaves were green. Thinking this a sign of very high intelligence, the father gave him a long talk about chlorophyll and how it utilizes the sun's rays. But later he overheard the child muttering to himself, "All I wanted to know was why leaves were green: not all that stuff' about chlorophyll and the sun!"

Play, imagination and questions are the features of this age, and this is known to all. But often there are misunderstandings. Sometimes the questions are difficult.

"Mummy," says the child, "where did I come from?" He has been puzzling about this. An intelligent mother who was expecting this question from one day to the next had decided to tell the truth. So, as soon as the little one, aged four, put his question, she replied, "Child of mine, it was I who made you."

This answer was rapid and brief, and the child was pacified at once. After about a year, she said to him, "Now I am making another child," and when she went to the nursing home she announced that on her return she would bring the baby back with her.

On reaching home, she showed him the child and said, "Here is your baby brother. I have made him as I made you."

But by this time the boy was close on six and he protested vigorously. "Why don't you tell me how we really come into the world? I am now big enough to know. So why don't you tell me the truth? Ever since you told me that you were making another child, I have been watching you closely, but you have not done anything!"

Even to tell the truth is not so easy as it seems. Parents and teachers need a special wisdom to know how to satisfy the infant imagination.

Teachers require training, because it is not our logic that can solve these problems. We must know how children develop and give up all preconceived ideas. It needs great tact and delicacy to follow the mind of a child from three to six, and grown-ups seldom have enough. Luckily the child learns more from his surroundings than he does from us, but we need psychological insight to help him as much as we can.

The child's way of doing things has been for us an inexhaustible fountain of revelations.

It has shown the magnitude of the prejudice that has hitherto blinded us to the true nature of the child's psychology, and shown how impossible it is to guide him by means of a *priori* principles, because he is an unknown quantity. Only the child himself can teach us to know him, and that by his behaviour.

In thousands of cases we have seen that the child not only needs something interesting to do but also likes to be shown exactly how to do it. Precision is found to attract him deeply, and this it is that keeps him at work. From this we must infer that his attraction towards these manipulative tasks has an unconscious aim. The child has an instinct to coordinate his movements and to bring them under control.

Another observation of supreme importance is that the child, when captivated by a piece of work, repeats the same series of movements time after time. Nothing is more astonishing than to see one of our children engaged in a so-called "exercise of practical life": completely absorbed, for example, in polishing a brass vessel and carefully following his instructions till it shines brilliantly; then without pause beginning all over again, and repeating every detail till he has polished the already shining pot several times over! This proves that the external aim was only a stimulus. The real aim was to satisfy an unconscious need, and this is why the operation is formative, for the child's repetition was laying down in his nervous system an entirely new system of controls, in other words, establishing fresh coordinations between his muscles, coordinations not given by nature, but having to be acquired. It happens no differently with ourselves in sport, in all games that we repeat with enthusiasm. Tennis, football, and the like, do not have for their sole purpose the accurate moving of a ball, but they challenge us to acquire a new skill—something lacking before —and this feeling of enhancing our abilities is the real source of our delight in the game.

It is true that in all these activities, the child may be said to be playing. But this kind of play is effortful, and it leads him to acquire the new powers which will be needed for his future.

His instinct has been awakened to adapt himself to the needs of his day, and it takes the form of a laborious effort of inner construction, as if someone were to have told him: "Not just anyhow, but thus and thus must you build, because it is these movements, and not others, which will be required of you." But this kind of effort is proper to childhood, and that is why I say that imitativeness in children is a kind of inspiration which leads them to self-constructive work.

Here, then, we see a true dynamism for the building up of the child's powers. Actions which the child sees performed by those about him become stimuli for activities which he conducts in such a way as to fix the power to do them in himself. And what is it that becomes fixed? As in the learning of a language, it is like the weaver's warp that is placed first on the loom—not the cloth which is going to be woven, but the basis for it. This warp corresponds to the sounds of words, with their rhythms and vocal cadences, and the order of their arrangement in grammatical form. So it is with these exercises of practical life that the warp of general behaviour is laid down for a particular nation or race. In the period from three to six, the cloth itself is woven and perfected. Hence the period under six is decisive. Whatever abilities the child constructs then will remain incarnate in him for life. His ways of moving and of doing things, become fixed and permanent features of his personality, and they will mark him as a person belonging to the lower strata of society, or to a higher social level, for these are the differences which separate the classes, in almost the same way as differences in language separate the nations.

Because of this, a man of lowly birth, should altered circumstances cause him to move in a higher sphere, will be unable to throw off the stigma of his origin. And if an aristocrat wishes to disguise himself as a working man, something in his manner and habits is sure to betray him.

As for language, this is the age at which dialects are fixed.

Even a university professor, accustomed to use a highly technical vocabulary, will unfailingly show by his accent the province from which he came.

No amount of higher education can cancel what has once been formed in infancy. Hence we can see the importance of social education at this age. During it there is still the chance of correcting such deviations of the personality as have been produced by obstacles encountered in the first three years, because this is nature's time for completing her work. At the same time, if education be conducted on scientific lines, we can effectively reduce the differences that divide men of diverse race and country, and this would lead to a greater harmony of life upon the earth. In other words, civilization can produce changes in man himself, just as it has produced changes in the surroundings offered him by nature. Magic powers are thus conferred upon the human race.

That part of the child's personality which is actively concerned in guiding his development shows itself in all his activities. One sees it at work just as clearly in the exercises which he does with our sensorial apparatus.

What ought we to think about sensorial education?

The senses are points of contact with the environment, and the mind, in what it takes from these, can become extremely skilled, just as a pianist can learn to draw the loveliest melodies from the same set of keys. Silk workers, for example, may attain to such delicacy of touch that they can tell whether the strand beneath their fingers is composed of one thread or two. A savage tribesman may hear the hardly perceptible rustling of a snake.

These are acuities which ordinary daily life brings into being, though they are subject to wide individual differences. But no sensorial education can ever occur except as a part of some total activity in which both intelligence and movement are involved.

Individual differences depend on inner tendencies productive of interest, and this is something which people come to possess in differing degree. In other words, we all have inborn attractions which cause us to grow and to develop, in accordance with that nature which is ours alone.

The child who has worked with our sensorial apparatus has not only acquired greater skill in the use of his hands, but has also achieved a higher degree of perceptiveness towards those stimuli which come to him from the outside world. To this extent the outside world has become enriched for him, because he is able to appreciate delicate differences which to a less perceptive person might as well not exist.

Our sensorial material provides a kind of guide to observation, for it classifies the impressions that each sense can receive: the colours, notes, noises, forms and sizes, touch-sensations, odours and tastes. This undoubtedly is also a form of culture, for it leads us to pay attention both to ourselves and to our surroundings. No less than speech and writing, it is one of the forms of culture which bring perfection to the personality and enrich its natural powers.

The senses, being explorers of the world, open the way to knowledge. Our apparatus for educating the senses offers the child a key to guide his explorations of the world, they cast a light upon it which makes visible to him more things in greater detail than he could see in the dark, or uneducated state.

Simultaneously, everything appertaining to the child's higher energies becomes a stimulus, setting his creative powers to work and extending the interests of his exploring mind.

In the ordinary schools of today, teachers often give what are called "object lessons" in which the child has to enumerate the various qualities of a given object: for example, its colour, form, texture, etc. But the number of different objects in the world is infinite, while the qualities they possess are limited. These qualities are therefore like the letters of the alphabet which can make up an indefinite number of words.

If we present the children with objects exhibiting each of these qualities separately, this is like giving them an alphabet for their explorations, a key to the doors of knowledge.

Anyone who has beheld not only the qualities of things classified in an orderly way, but also the gradations of each, is able to read everything that their environment and the world of nature contains.

This "alphabet" of the outer world has an incalculable value. In fact, culture, as we have said above, is not just a matter of accumulating information, but it implies an extension of the personality. To teach a child whose senses have been educated is quite a different thing from teaching one who has not had this help. Any object presented, any idea given, any invitation to observe, is greeted with interest, because the child is already sensitive to such tiny differences as those which occur between the forms of leaves, the colours of flowers, or the bodies of insects. Everything depends on being able to see and on taking an interest. It matters much more to have a prepared mind than to have a good teacher.

Now, in the apparatus we have devised, there is—as I have said—a classification of the qualities of things, and from this the child derives one of the most effective helps to the ordering of his mind.

It is natural to distinguish between things and their qualities. Everyone sees differences between colours, notes, shapes, etc., without any special education. Indeed, this is something connected with the form itself of the human mind. Of its nature, the mind not only has the power to imagine (i.e. to think of things not immediately present), but it can also assemble and rearrange its mental content, extract—let us say an "alphabet of qualities" from all those numberless things that we meet in the outside world. This it does by the power it possesses of abstract thought. The inventors of the alphabet used this power: for they selected and spoke separately the few sounds of which all words were composed. The alphabet is therefore an abstract system, for the only spoken sounds having real existence are words. Unless man could imagine and make abstractions, he would not be intelligent; or his intelligence would resemble that of the higher animals, that is to say, it would be rigid and restricted to some particular form of behaviour, and this would prevent its expansion.

Now, abstract ideas are always limited in number, while the real things we encounter are innumerable. These limited abstractions increase in value with their precision. In the world of the mind, they come to have the value of a special organ, an instrument of thought which serves to give us our bearings in space, just as a watch gives us our bearings in time.

These two powers of the mind (imagination and abstraction), which go beyond the simple perception of things actually present, play a mutual part in the construction of the mind's content. Both are necessary for the building up of language. A precise alphabet, on the one hand, and grammatical rules on the other, permit an indefinite accumulation of the wealth of words. For words, if they are to be utilized and enrich the language, must be capable of taking their place in the groundwork of sounds and of grammatical order. And what happens in the construction of a language happens also in the construction of the mind.

When you say, "There goes a man of vague mentality. He is clever but indefinite," you are hinting at a mind with plenty of ideas, but lacking in the clarity which comes from order. Of another you may say, "He has a mind like a map. His judgments will be sound."

In our work, therefore, we have given a name to this part of the mind which is built up with exactitude, and we call it "the mathematical mind." I take the term from Pascal, the French philosopher, physicist and mathematician, who said that man's mind was mathematical by nature, and that knowledge and progress came from accurate observation.

Just as the form of a language is given by its alphabetical sounds and by the rules for arranging its words, so the form of man's mind, the warp into which can be worked all the riches of perception and imagination, is fundamentally a matter of order. And if we study the works of all who have left their marks on the world in the form of inventions useful to mankind, we see that the starting point was always something orderly and exact in their minds, and that this was what enabled them to create something new.[2] Even in the imaginative worlds of poetry and music, there is a basic order so exact as to be called "metrical" or measured.

In education it therefore seems clear that we have to keep in mind these two mental powers, and although one usually prevails over the other in any given personality, they must nevertheless both exist, and work together in a harmonious fashion. The effort to cultivate imagination alone, must lead to a lack of balance which becomes an obstacle to success in the practical things of life.

In our tiny children the evidence of a mathematical bent shows itself in many striking and spontaneous ways.

In fact, if we showed them exactly how to do something, this precision itself seemed to hold their interest. To have a real purpose to which the action was directed, this was the first condition, but the exact way of doing it acted like a support which rendered the child stable in his efforts, and therefore brought him to make progress in his development. Order and precision, we found, were the keys to spontaneous work in the school.

And if we look now at the sensorial apparatus which is able to evoke such deep concentration (remarkable in very small children between the ages of three and four), there is no doubt that this apparatus may be regarded not only as a help to exploring the environment, but also to the development of the mathematical mind.[3]

The results we obtain with our little ones contrast oddly with the fact that mathematics is so often held to be a scourge rather than a pleasure in school programmes. Most people have developed "mental barriers" against it. Yet all is easy if only its roots can be implanted in the *absorbent mind*.

Articles of mathematical precision do not occur in the little child's ordinary environment. Nature provides him with trees, flowers and animals, but not with these. Hence the child's mathematical tendencies may suffer from lack of opportunity, with detriment to his later progress. Therefore, we think of our sensorial material as a system of *materialized abstractions*, or of basic mathematics: My ways of providing for mathematical education are fully described in two of my other books, which are also treatises on the special psychology of this field of learning.[4]

The child, in the first stages of his development, lays down a kind of weaver's warp composed of triumphs he has made over his material surroundings. This is truly an event of embryonic type, because an embryo is the product of pre-existing patterns, and this is true whether the patterns be those of his future bodily organs, laid down in the genes, or those of his behaviour, as Coghill discovered.

Again in regard to language, the child lays down another kind of warp—a warp which is fixed and precise because it is composed of particular sounds and of fixed rules for the arrangement of words. Those sounds, and that ordering of words, had no previous existence in nature. They were evolved by a human group. For words and meanings arise, as we have seen, by the mutual consent of people wishing to understand one another.

Other things also are established by social groups. For example, habits and customs which finally become imbued with the force of morals. It is interesting to note that these customs seldom arise merely to make life easier, as used to be maintained in evolutionary theory. Social rules have aspects which are more contradictory than otherwise to this idea. The "instinct of self-preservation" does not merely seek out the best conditions of life. On the contrary, restrictions of life appear which make one think rather of an inborn instinct of sacrifice, although it is true that to give form to a shapeless block, one has to model it, in other words, some parts have to be cut away or sacrificed. The facts are that studies of the customs or primitive peoples show that restrictive practices (prohibitions—taboos, etc.), and even bodily mutilations, occur in all of them.

Beauty itself is sometimes sought in the shape of

unnatural distortions, which are often inflicted at the cost of heavy sacrifice (one remembers the famous stunting of Chinese women's feet, or the more common perforations of ear and nose for the wearing of jewels, and the deformations that such jewels often produce).

But the most important restrictions occur in diet. Those millions of Indians, who recently died of famine, lived in a land of flocks and herds as prolific as anywhere in the world. But so deeply ingrained was their custom of not slaughtering animals for food, that this habit was stronger than death.

Now, morals are a superstructure of social life, which fixes them in a determinate form. And it must not be forgotten that these forms have also to be established by common consent in the measure to which their influence is able to extend.

And the same thing must be said of religions: even the idol has to receive social assent. Religions are not only agreements between men based on certain ideas, but they are born unquestionably of spiritual needs of the human species—needs which give rise to adoration, and not just to an intellectual acceptance of certain beliefs. Primitive man, struck by the wonders of nature, adores it in some of its more impressive aspects, adding gratitude and fear to his wonder. The process ends with an attachment, by common consent, of these deep emotional responses to certain events and things which become sacred to the group.

It is not just that they stimulate the imagination, but the mind itself seizes upon them, drawing therefrom its own syntheses (much as happens with sensorial impressions from which the mind derives its abstract ideas); the qualities of things become discerned by a basic mental activity. But here, where the unconscious operates (as it does in the experiences leading to worship), we reach the point of abstract expression of them, and this is done by using symbols for their personification. To become social emblems, these symbols must be accepted by common consent. As forms of symbolic expression, we thus find acts of worship, and therefore rites, which play fixed parts in the life of the group.

All this becomes established during the passing of the centuries. Not only does there arise a fixed system, like the system of morals, but it becomes a source of unity among the people. It combines them in a way which differentiates their group from other groups. These social differences between the human groups resemble the biological differences between species, and just as the latter are transmitted by heredity, so do these psychological formations become passed on from generation to generation.

But these features of the group are not outlined, accepted and fixed solely by imagination. It is imagination, accompanied by the spiritual need that collects the material for them, just as the senses do on another plane, but abstraction then supervenes to simplify and unite, so that the mind can succeed in expressing infinite immensities in a determinate form.

Precise and stable as these forms are, they become embodied in simplified symbols to which all can cling. From these symbols is derived a stability of behaviour almost mathematical in its precision. Imaginative and spiritual impressions are therefore captured and crystallized by the mathematical powers of the directing mind.

When, therefore, the child absorbs the customs, morals and religion of a people, what does he really absorb?

By analogy with what happens in language, he takes in a pattern; that is to say, he accepts a stability and a precision derived from abstractions, and ordered according to the mathematical mind. This pattern becomes part of him, in much the same fashion as biological configurations form part of an embryo. The pattern is something potent and creative, giving form to the personality in just the same way as hereditary features of the body are shaped by the genes, or modes of behaviour by patterns graven on the nerve centres.

The child in the postnatal (or psychological) period of his embryonic life, absorbs from the world about him the distinctive patterns to which the social life of his group conforms. That is to say, he does not at first absorb the actual mental riches of his race, but only the patterns which result from them. He absorbs, therefore, the basic or summarized part, the precise part, which—for that very reason—is repeated in the habitual life of the people. He absorbs, in short, the mathematical part. And, once the patterns have become established within him, they remain as fixed characters, just like his mother tongue.

Later on, a man may develop himself indefinitely, but it will always be on this foundation. In the same way, his mother tongue can be enriched indefinitely, but it will always be on the basic pattern of those sounds and grammatical rules which were laid down in the embryonic period.

That the mathematical mind is active from the first, becomes apparent not only (as we have hinted) from the attraction that exactitude exerts on every action the child performs, but we see it also in the fact that the little child's need for order is one of the most powerful incentives to dominate his early life. A sensitiveness to the orderly arrangement of things, to their relative positions, is contemporaneous with simple perception, i.e. with the first taking in of impressions from the environment. Also, in his purposive actions, the child can only sustain them if there is an exact procedure to be followed, and in no other way can he arrive at concentration and constancy in his work.

These things taken together have brought to us the idea of a basic formation on the mental side of the child's personality. A psychic organism is forming itself, and it does so on a pre-established pattern. If it were not for this, the child's mental horizon would have to be fashioned by his reasoning and his will, that is to say by powers that are not acquired till later on. But that we must dismiss as absurd.

Just as a man does not create his body by logical reasoning, so he does not follow a line of argument when creating the form of his mind. Creation, here, means that mysterious primordial occurrence which gives rise to something which at first did not exist, something which is later destined to grow in accordance with vital laws. But, indeed, everything begins with a creation of sorts: *Omne vivum ex ovo*! All life comes from an egg.

Hence, the human mind is built up on a basis which is itself creative, but in the period which follows birth; for the mind of man has to fashion itself on what it takes from the outer world. This it incarnates to form a basis, and so makes every individual into the type of person constituting his racial group. This is how differential continuity is kept going between the various human communities which have evolved each its own civilization down the ages.

The continuity of anything which nature has not fixed, but which evolves gradually as a social pattern must do, is only possible if the new individuals born into it have a creative power, one which can adapt them to the circumstances into which they are born. This is the child's true biological function, and it is this which permits of social progress. But, just because it is a creative operation which may come under our control, it has for us an incalculable importance.

REFERENCES

1. Such as silver sand. This may be sprinkled over a sticky surface of gum, or paint, and then allowed to dry.
2. See my book, *The Advanced Montessori Method* (Vol. I)—Chapter on Imagination. Heinemann, London.
3. For a full account of this apparatus the reader is referred to my book, *The Discovery of the Child* (Kalakshetra, Madras).
4. Maria Montessori: *Psico-aritmetica and Psico-geometrica* (Casa Editorial, Araluce, Barcelona, 1934).

18

Character and its Defects in Childhood

We must now turn to the second group of facts which have importance during the first years of life, those concerning the child's character and its formation.

Old time pedagogy has always given a prominent place to character training, though it failed to say what was meant by character or to indicate how it should be trained. All it stated was that the intellectual and practical sides of education were not enough, but that this unknown factor, this "X," which the word character denoted, must also be included. None the less, this showed a certain insight because it meant that educators were trying to bring out the important elements of human personality. Certain virtues have always been highly valued: courage, perseverance, the sense of duty, good moral relationships with others, and a high place has always been given to moral education.

But, this notwithstanding, ideas remain vague in all parts of the world as to what character really is.

Philosophers and biologists have debated the matter from early times but always failed to reach a precise definition. From the Greeks to ourselves, from Theophrastus to Freud and Jung, many have tackled the problem, but, as Rümke rightly says "We are always in the tentative stage."[1]

There is no ultimate concept acceptable to all. Yet, intuitively, everyone knows the importance of that sum total of qualities that goes universally under the name.

The most recent studies of character detect in it physical, moral, and intellectual elements, will-power, personality, and heredity. Since Bahnsen in 1876 first introduced the word, "characterology," there has been growing up what is almost a new branch of science for the study of character. And it is mainly within this field of somewhat speculative elaboration —rather than in one of precise knowledge—that the majority of modern students and innovators have made their contributions. But the curious thing is that all of them start with grown-ups, with adult man, either in the abstract, or regarded as a living being. Even those who refer to education (and this regardless of whether they adopt an empirical or religious point of view) generally overlook the little child, though they speak much of heredity, that is to say, of prenatal influences. The result is a jump from heredity to adulthood, and an unexplored gap is left which very few have tried to fill.

However, it is just with this gap that our own studies have been concerned, and it was a contribution made spontaneously by our children that showed us fresh ways of thinking about this ill-defined problem. It allows us to visualize the development of character as a natural sequence of events resulting from the child's own individual efforts, which have no reference to any extraneous factors, but depend on his vital creative energy, and on the obstacles he meets with in daily life. Our interest is therefore turned towards the observation and interpretation of the work that nature does in the construction of man on his psychological side. We must do this from birth, when character and personality are zero, till the age in which they begin to disclose themselves. For, rooted in the unconscious mind, natural laws undoubtedly exist which determine psychological development and are common to all men. Differences, instead, depend largely on the vicissitudes of life: on the accidents, setbacks and regressions produced in the mental field by those obstacles the individual has had to encounter in his path.

No doubt a theory such as this must be able to interpret

character at every stage from childhood to maturity, but for the moment let us take the child's unfolding life as the basic factor, and make this our guide to the infinite variations among individuals which are caused by their efforts to adapt.

From this point of view, we may regard everything concerning character under the guise of human behaviour. As I have said above, the life of the individual from 0 to 18 may be divided into three periods: 0-6 (which forms the subject of this book); 6-12, and 12-18; each of these being subdivided into two secondary phases. If these periods be considered separately, the typical mentality of the children in each appears so different that they might almost belong to different individuals.

As we have seen, the first period is one of creativeness. The roots of character lie here, even though at birth the child has no character. From 0 to 6 is the most important part of life, and this applies to character development also. All know that the infant in arms cannot be influenced, either by example or external pressure; so it must be nature herself who lays the foundations of character. The small child has no sense of right and wrong; he lives outside our notions of morality. In fact, we do not call him bad or wicked, but naughty, meaning that his behaviour is infantile. So the terms "good," "bad," or "moral," will not be used in this book. It is in the second period, from 6 to 12, that the child begins to become conscious of right and wrong, this not only as regards his own actions, but also the actions of others. Problems of right and wrong are characteristic of this age; moral consciousness is being formed, and this leads later to the social sense. In the third period, from 12 to 18, the love of country is born, the feeling of belonging to a national group, and of concern for the honour of that group.

Although as I have hinted, each period is basically different from the other two, nevertheless each lays the foundation for the one following it. To develop normally in the second period a person must have developed well in the first. In the same way, the caterpillar and the butterfly are two creatures very different to look at and in the way they behave, yet the beauty of the butterfly comes from its life in the larval form, and not through any efforts it may make to imitate another butterfly. *We serve the future by protecting the present*. The more fully the needs of one period are met, the greater will be the success of the next.

Life springs from the act of conception. If conception follows the union of two healthy people, not alcoholic or degenerate, the person who is born will be free from certain taints. So the way in which the embryo develops is dependent on the conditions operative at conception. Later, the foetus can be influenced, but only by its surroundings, that is to say, by the mother's circumstances during gestation. If the embryo's conditions are favourable, the child at birth will be strong and healthy. Hence, gestation and conception both affect postnatal life.

We have mentioned the *trauma* of birth and the danger of this giving rise to regressions. The nature of these regressions may be serious, but they are not so grave as the prenatal effects of alcoholism or of hereditary disease (epilepsy, etc.).

After birth begin the critical years that we have just been studying. In the first two or three, the child may undergo influences that will alter his whole future. If he has been injured, or suffered violence, or met with severe obstacles during this period, deviations of personality may ensue. It follows that the child's character develops in accordance with the obstacles he has encountered or the freedom favouring his development that he has enjoyed. If, at conception and during gestation, at birth and the period following birth, the child has been scientifically treated, he should at three be a model individual. This ideal is never reached because apart from other reasons, many obstacles intervene. Children, by the age of three, differ from one another, and the differences vary in importance not only according to the severity of the experiences that have caused them, but also, and especially, according to the age at which these occurred. Changes due to difficulties after birth will be less severe than those caused during gestation, and these again will not be so serious as those deriving from nocuous influences operative at conception.

As to prognosis, or the hopes we may entertain of correcting children's defects, we may place those acquired in the postnatal period, from 0 to 3, as being curable in practice during the period from 3 to 6, when nature is still busy in the perfecting of many newly formed powers.

Our schools have brought a noteworthy contribution of experience and results obtained in this period, and in the light of these we can give positive help; in other words, we can act educationally. But if (owing to negligence or wrong treatment) the defects caused between 0 and 3 be not then corrected, not only do they remain but they get worse. Thus at six one may have a child with deviations produced before three and other defects acquired since. After six, these in their turn will have an influence on the second main period of life, and on the developing awareness of right and wrong.

All these defects have their repercussions on mental life and on intelligence. Children find it harder to learn, if circumstances in their previous period have been inimical to the unfolding of their powers. Hence, a child of six may show an accumulation of characteristics which are not really his own, but are the result of earlier misfortunes. He may, for example, be unable to develop that moral awareness that should appear between 6 and 12, or his intellectual capacity may be subnormal. Then we have a child devoid of character and unable to learn. In the final period, his inferiority will cause other failings to add themselves to these, and he will become a wastrel through no fault of his own.

In our schools (as in many others, today) a biological chart is kept of the physical and psychological characteristics of each child. This can be a guide to the staff, for if we know what upsets have occurred at each period of the child's life, we can estimate their gravity and probable response to treatment. On this chart we enter any hereditary diseases disclosed to us from which the parents suffer, their respective ages when the child was born, and also information (tactfully obtained) about the mother's life during her pregnancy, whether she had any accidents, falls, etc. Also, whether the child's birth took place normally, with the baby in good health, or whether there was a period of suspended animation. Other questions concern the child's life at home. Are the parents over-anxious or severe? Has the child had any frights, or other kinds of shock? If a child is difficult or capricious, we seek for possible causes of this in the life he has led hitherto. At three, when they come to us, almost all of them are suffering from some kind of abnormality which is nevertheless correctible. Let us review, very briefly, the common types of deviation that we now see.

It is usual to discuss children's defects one at a time, with a view to counteracting each by some separate and direct form of treatment. But, numerous though they are, we find it better to classify all of them under two simple headings, viz: those shown by strong children (who resist and overcome the obstacles they meet) and those shown by *weak* children (who succumb to unfavourable conditions).

In the first group are capriciousness and tendencies to violence, fits of rage, insubordination and aggression. Disobedience is marked, and a so-called "destructive instinct." Possessiveness is common, which leads to selfishness and envy (the latter not being passively shown, but in efforts to seize other people's things). Instability of purpose (very common in the youngest); inability to focus the attention or to concentrate; difficulty in coordinating the movements of the hand, so that objects are readily dropped and broken; mental confusion; extravagant imaginings. These children may shout, scream and be generally noisy. They disturb and tease the others; are often unkind to weaker children and animals. At table they are inclined to be greedy.

Children of the *weak* type are passive by nature and their defects are negative. Indolent and idle, they cry for what they want and try to get others to wait on them. They are always wishing to be entertained and are easily bored. They find everything frightening and cling to grown-ups. They are often untruthful (a passive form of defence) or steal things (another form of psychological compensation), and so on.

It may also happen that they appear to suffer from physical defects which are really of psychological origin. For example, they refuse to eat, having apparently no appetite, or else a senseless overeating brings on digestive troubles. Nightmares, fear of the dark, disturbed sleep, do physical harm and provoke anaemia: (Certain forms of anaemia and liver troubles are definitely of psychological origin.) There are also nervous complaints, and all these maladies which proceed from psychological states are usually incurable by the ordinary measures known to medicine.

It follows that the general picture of moral behaviour, and consequently of character, is complicated by the presence of all these ailments and distortions, defects and shortcomings, which have been produced in the personality by conditions adverse to its normal and healthy development.

Many of these children—especially those of the "strong" type—are not felt to be blessings about the house. Their parents try to get rid of them, willingly entrust them to nannies, or send them to school. They become orphans with living parents. They are ill, yet live in healthy bodies, and this inevitably leads to bad behaviour. The parents wonder what to do with them. Some seek advice, others try to solve the problem alone. Sometimes they decide on severity, thinking this will settle everything. They use all kinds of means, smacking, shouting, sending to bed hungry . . . but the children only get worse and become more troublesome, or adopt a passive form of the same defect. Tactful persuasion is then tried; they are reasoned with, or appeal is made to their affections: "Why do you make mummy so unhappy?"

Finally, the parents are defeated and stop worrying.

Children of the more passive, or recessive, type seldom attract all this attention. Their behaviour is not a problem. The mother thinks her child is good and obedient because he does nothing wrong. His clinging to her she takes to be affection. He loves her so much, she says, that he won't go to bed without her. But later on she notices that his movements and speech are backward. He is uncertain on his feet. "His health," she says, "is good, but he is so sensitive. Everything frightens him. He is not even interested in food: truly a most spiritual child! To get him to eat I always have to tell him a story. Surely he is going to be a saint or a poet!" But in the end she decides he is ill, and sends for the doctor. Child specialists make fortunes from these maladies of the mind.

All these problems become soluble if we understand the cycle of constructive activities which every child ought by nature to traverse. It is now apparent that every defect of character is due to some wrong treatment sustained by the child during his early years. If children have been neglected at this time, their minds are empty because they have had no chance to build up their contents. This starved mind (to which psychologists are now devoting much attention) is a basic cause of many evils. Another cause is the lack of spontaneous activities directed by the creative impulse. Few of these children have been able to find the necessary conditions for a full development. Often they have been left entirely alone, with little to do but sleep. Or grown-ups may have done everything for them, thus preventing them from carrying out their own cycles of activity. The result is passivity and inertia. Unable to look at anything without having it snatched out of their hands, there was nothing they could handle, although they had seen and desired plenty of things. When at last they succeeded in possessing themselves of a flower or an insect, they had no idea what to do with it, so reduced it to pieces.

Irrational fears also have causes traceable to this early period.

One of the chief reasons for the spread of our schools has been the visible disappearance of these defects in children as soon as they found themselves in a place where active experience upon their surroundings was permitted, and where free exercise of their powers could nourish their minds.

Surrounded by interesting things to do, they could repeat the exercises at will, and went from one spell of concentration to another. Once the children had reached this stage, and could work and focus their minds on something of real interest to them, their defects disappeared. The disorderly became orderly, the passive became active, and the troublesome disturbing child became a help in the classroom. This result made us understand that their former defects had been acquired and were not innate. Nor did they differ greatly from one another, just because one told lies and another was disobedient. But all these disturbances came from a single cause, which was insufficient nourishment for the life of the mind.

What advice can we give to mothers? Their children need to work at an interesting occupation: they should not be helped unnecessarily, nor interrupted, once they have begun to do something intelligent. Sweetness, severity, medicine, do not help if the child is mentally hungry. If a man is starving for lack of food, we do not call him a fool, nor give him a beating, nor do we appeal to his better feelings. He needs a meal, and nothing else will do. The same thing applies here. Neither severity nor kindness will solve the problem. Man is an intelligent being, and needs mental food almost more than physical food. Unlike the animals, he has to build up his own behaviour. If the child is placed upon a path in which he can organize his conduct and construct his mental life, all will be well. His troubles will disappear, his nightmares vanish, his digestion will become normal, and his greediness subside. His health is restored because his mind is normalized.

So these are not problems of moral education, but of character formation. Lack of character, or defects in character, disappear of themselves, without any need for preaching by grown-ups or for grown-up examples. One does not need to threaten or cajole, but only to "normalize the conditions" under which the child lives.

REFERENCE

1. H.C. Rümke, *Introduction to Characterology*, Haarlem, 1937.

19

The Child's Contribution to Society—Normalization

Children's defects of character (as described in the last chapter in which we differentiated between the defects of strong children and those of weak children) are not always regarded as bad by public opinion. Some are even valued. Passive children are thought to be good. Noisy and exuberant children with vivid imaginations are thought to be specially brilliant or even superior.

We may say that society groups them like this:

1. Those whose defects need correction;
2. Those who are good (passive) and to be taken as models;
3. Those thought to be superior.

The last two belong to the so-called desirable types and the parents are very proud of them, even when (as happens with the last type) their company is none too agreeable.

I have stressed this point and drawn attention to this classification, because it has existed for centuries. Yet I saw in my first school, and in all those which have followed it, that these traits vanish as soon as the children become absorbed in a piece of work that attracts them. The so-called bad qualities, together with the good and the superior, *all vanish* and there remains only one kind of child. He has none of those qualities.

This means that the world has not yet been able to evaluate the good and the bad traits in child character, nor those which superseded them. What we have always thought turns out to have been wrong. I am reminded of a mystical saying: "There is no Truth but in Thee, O Lord: everything else is illusion." The children in our schools have proved to us that their real wish is to be always at work—a thing never before suspected, just as no one had ever before noticed the child's power of choosing his work spontaneously. Following an inner guide, the children busied themselves with something (different for each) which gave them serenity and joy.

Then another thing happened never before seen in a group of children. It was the arrival of "discipline," which sprang up spontaneously. This, more than anything else, struck the public imagination. Discipline in freedom seemed to solve a problem which had hitherto seemed insoluble. The answer lay in obtaining discipline by giving freedom. These children, who sought their work in freedom, each absorbed in a different kind of task, yet all belonging to the same group, gave an impression of perfect discipline. During the last forty years this has been verified in the most widely different parts of the world, and it shows that when children are placed in surroundings which permit them to evolve an orderly activity they come to have this new aspect. In other words, they evolve a psychological type common to the whole of mankind. This had been invisible before, because hidden by characteristics not proper to the child.

This change, which creates almost a uniformity of type, does not occur gradually, but appears all of a sudden. In any given child, it follows invariably upon a spell of deep concentration on some activity. This does not mean the directress has to urge a lazy child to do something. It is enough for her just to put him in touch with the various means for purposive action that are awaiting his use in the environment prepared for him. No sooner has he found his work than his defects disappear. It does not help to reason with the children. Something within them seems to break out and fasten itself to the external activity. This attracts the child's energy which thus becomes held in a constant piece of work actively repeated.

The human being is a united whole, but this unity has to be built up and formed by active experiences in the real world, to which it is led by the laws of nature.

The embryonic development of each of its parts, which is at first carried on separately from birth till three, must in the end become integrated, when it will be so organized that all of these parts act together in the service of the individual. This is what is happening during the next period, from 3 to 6, when the hand is at work and the mind is guiding it.

If outer conditions prevent this integration from occurring, then the same energies go on urging each of the partial formations to continue their activities apart from the others. This results in unequal development, divorced from its proper ends.

The hand moves aimlessly; the mind wanders about far from reality; language takes pleasure in itself; the body moves clumsily. And these separate energies, finding nothing to satisfy them, give rise to numberless combinations of defective and deviated growth, which become sources of conflict and despair.

Such deviations cannot be attributed to the personality itself. They come from a failure to organize the personality.

They are ephemeral characteristics, yet they are not correctible, because they can only be corrected when all the powers are functioning as one to serve the ends of the whole individual.

But when the attractions of the new environment exert their spell, offering motives for constructive activity, then all these energies combine and the deviations can be dispersed. A unique type of child appears, a "new child"; but really it is the child's true "personality" allowed to construct itself normally.

In the drawing we see on the right hand side the different characteristics of children, as we used to know them. These are shown by a number of lines radiating outward fan-wise. The halfway line, wide and perpendicular, symbolizes concentration on something specific; it is the line of normality. Once the children begin to concentrate, all the lines to the right of this mid-line disappear, and there remains only one type which has the characteristics shown by the lines on the left. The loss of all these superficial defects is not brought about by an adult, but by the child himself, who passes into the central line with his whole personality, and this means that his normality has been attained.

We find this phenomenon repeated unfailingly in all our schools, with children belonging to different social classes, races and civilizations.[1]

It is the most important single result of our whole work.

The transition from one state to the other always follows a piece of work done by the hands with real things, work accompanied by mental concentration.

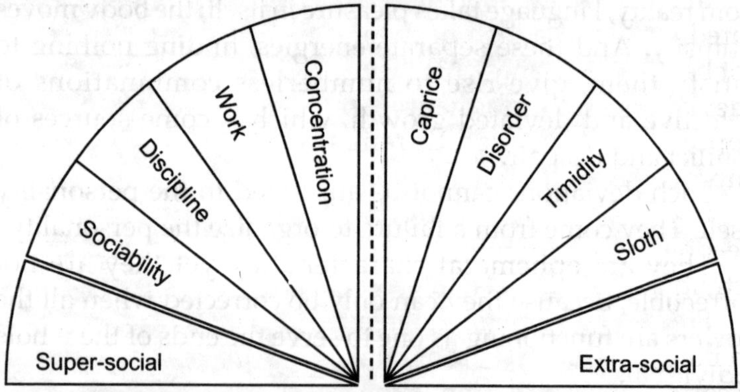

Fig. 10. *Normal and deviated character traits in children.*

This psychological event, which brings to mind the cure of adults by psychoanalysis, we have called by the technical term, "normalization."

Today, after so many years, and so vast an experience, the truth of it is established. In the *Child Guidance Clinics*, which are being so widely founded for the treatment of "difficult children," what is done is just this, to offer the child an environment rich in motives for activity, in which he can choose what he will take and use. In this choice he is free from any teacher's control, or indeed from adult control in general.

"Play therapy," too, leaves the child free to choose between many toys and imitative games—a more varied selection than the home can usually offer.

It is found that this, combined with interpretations by the psychiatrist (leading to advice which improves the child's treatment at home), can bring about improvements in the child's character, though this is also attributable to social life with other children.

But the scope of these institutions is far too limited. They are just places for "cure," like nursing homes for the sick. What is still needed is a general understanding that if work and freedom can cure defects of growth, it means that work and freedom are normally needed for the child's development.

In fact, it often happens that when children, after being cured or improved, go back to live in conditions that have not been altered, and which were the original causes of their "deviations, from normality," they lack the power, or the opportunities, needed to remain normalized, and their improvement is purely temporary.

In some countries efforts have been made to apply freedom and activity in the schools also; but freedom and activity have then been interpreted much too loosely.

Freedom is understood in a very elementary fashion, as an immediate release from oppressive bonds; as a cessation of corrections and of submission to authority. This conception is plainly negative, that is to say, it means only the elimination of coercion. From this comes, often enough, a very simple "reaction": a disorderly pouring out of impulses no longer controlled because they were previously controlled by the adult's will. "To let the child do as he likes," when he has not yet developed any powers of control, is to betray the idea, of freedom.

The result is children who are disorderly because order had been arbitrarily, imposed upon them, children lazy because previously forced to work, children disobedient because their obedience had been enforced.

Real freedom, instead, is a consequence of development; it is the development of latent guides, aided by education. Development is active. It is the construction of the personality, reached by effort and one's own experiences; it is the long road which every child must travel to attain maturity.

Anyone can dominate and repress the weak and subdued; but no one can cause another to develop. Development cannot be taught.

If freedom is understood as letting the children do as they like, using or more likely misusing the things available, it is clear that only their "deviations" are free to develop; their abnormalities will increase.

Normalization comes about through "concentration" on a piece of work. For this we must provide "motives for activity" so well adapted to the child's interests that they provoke his deep attention. Their success in this is dependent on the use of the objects for the purposes they are designed to serve, a thing which is also conducive to the child's "mental order." If they are used with care and precision, this leads the child to the "coordination of his movements."

Mental order and the coordination of movement guided by scientific standards are what prepare for concentration, and this, once it has occurred, "frees the actions of the child," and leads him to the cure of his defects. We say "concentration," and not just "occupation," because if the children go indifferently from one thing to another, even if they use them all properly, this is not enough to remove their defects.

The essential thing is for the task to arouse such an interest that it engages the child's whole personality.

In our schools, this "moment of healing" is not the point of arrival, as it is in the clinics for difficult children, but it is the point of departure, after which "freedom of action" consolidates and develops the personality.

Only "normalized" children, aided by their environment, show in their subsequent development those wonderful powers that we describe: spontaneous discipline, continuous and happy work, social sentiments of help and sympathy for others.

Activity freely chosen becomes their regular way of living. The healing of their disorders is the doorway to this new kind of life.

Its principal feature never changes. It is "application to work." An interesting piece of work, freely chosen, which has the virtue of inducing concentration rather than fatigue, adds to the child's energies and mental capacities, and leads him to self-mastery.

Now, to help such development, it is not enough to provide objects chosen at random, but we have to organize a world of "progressive interest." The result is an educational technique based on the psychology of infantile development.

In our schools, not only is character strengthened but the children's intellectual life becomes insatiable in its search for knowledge.

One is tempted to say that the children are performing spiritual exercises, having found the path of self-perfectionment and of ascent to the inner heights of the soul.

Their work, in its development, reminds one of principles to be found in the Indian book of wisdom, the *Gita*.

"It is important to give the right work. The mind needs to work continuously. Spiritual development is to keep it always busy in healthy occupations. The devil enters the idle mind. The indolent man cannot be spiritual."

Our concept also agrees with the words of Gibran, "Work is love made visible."[2]

REFERENCES

1. See *The Secret of Childhood*.
2. See Kahlil Gibran: *The Prophet* (Heinemann, London, and Knopf, New York, 1948, p. 33)

20

Character Building is the Child's Own Achievement

As explained in the preceding chapter children construct their own characters, building up in themselves the qualities we admire. These do not spring from our example of admonishments, but they result solely from a long and slow sequence of activities carried out by the child himself between the ages of three and six.

At this time no one can "teach" the qualities of which character is composed. The only thing we can do is to put education on a scientific footing, so that children can work effectively without being disturbed or impeded.

Only later on is it possible to tackle the child's mind in a direct way, by means of reasoning and exhortation. Not till six can we become missionaries of morality because it is between six and twelve that conscience begins to function and the child is able to visualize the problems of good and evil. Still more can be done between twelve and eighteen, when the boy begins to have ideals (patriotic, social, religious, and the like). Then we can act as missionaries towards him, as we can to adults. The pity of it is that after six, children can no longer develop character and its qualities spontaneously. Thenceforward the missionaries, who are also imperfect, find themselves faced by considerable difficulties. They are working on the smoke, not on the fire.

Teachers of youth often complain that, although they can teach the subjects of science, literature, and so on, the pupils before them are unable to learn, and this not for lack of intelligence, but for lack of character. Without character there is no "drive." Only those who—despite early tantrums and wrong treatment—have succeeded in keeping some, or all, of the basic gifts of character, have any personality left. Too often the majority have none.

To tell these to concentrate is now useless, for this is just the power they cannot exert. How can we expect them to do their work carefully and patiently, if care and patience are among their missing gifts? It is like saying,

"Walk nicely!" to a person without legs. *Qualities like this can only be given by practice, never by commands.*

So what is to be done? Society usually replies,

"Be patient with young people: we can only influence them by our own good will and example." And one hopes, with time and patience, to achieve something. But nothing, in fact, is achieved. We get older as the time passes, but nothing comes out of it. Time and patience can effect nothing by themselves. We have to profit by the chance offered in the creative period.

Another thing becomes clear if we consider mankind as a whole. Adults, like children, seem to differ from one another *mainly in their defects,* but hidden in their hearts there is something deep, common to all. All have a tendency, however vague and unconscious, to raise themselves up; they aspire to something spiritual. And this tendency, however slight be its action on the defects of character, exerts sooner or later a pressure towards improvement. Both the individual and society have this in common: a continuous tendency to progress. Whether on the outer or inner plane, there is a tiny light in the unconscious of mankind, which guides it toward better things. In other words, man's behaviour is not invariable, like that of the animals, but it can progress, and it is natural for man to feel this urge to go forward.

In the drawing is a central circle, the centre of perfection.

Around this is an area which represents the stronger and more balanced type of human being, those approximating to the ideal, or "normal" type. The space surrounding this indicates the great mass of people who—in varying degrees—have not attained normality. On the periphery, we see a circle of smaller area which represents the class of people who are outside normality—the very few extrasocial, or antisocial folk (the extra social are insane, and the antisocial delinquent). Lunatics and criminals have not been able to adapt themselves to social life. All the rest have made the adaptation, more or less. Problems of education, therefore, concern those who have been able up to a point to remain within the compass of adaptation.

This adaptation to the world about one occurs in the first six years. Here, then, are to be found the origins of character. What a tremendous problem this is of becoming adapted! The inner circle beyond the core includes those fairly near to perfection. They are the strongest, either because they were possessed of more vital energy, or because they were luckier in their environmental conditions; while those of the next circle had less energy or had encountered greater obstacles. In social life, the first named are held to be persons of strongest character, while the others are regarded as weaker. The first feel in themselves a natural attraction to the centre, toward perfection; the second tend to slip toward the outer ring, the anti and extrasocial. These are always feeling tempted and, unless they make constant efforts, feel they will become inferior. Therefore they need moral support to protect them from temptation. It is not an attraction toward pleasure, for no one can enjoy the idea of becoming criminal or insane. But it is an almost irresistible force, like the pull of gravity which demands a constant struggle and defence. The effort to resist evil is regarded as virtuous because it does in fact prevent us from falling into the moral abyss. These sufferers impose rules upon themselves to save them from falling. They attach themselves to someone better than themselves. They pray Omnipotence to help them in temptation. More and more they clothe themselves in virtue, but it is a difficult life. Penance is not a joy. It is an effort like that of a mountaineer clinging to some projecting rock to keep his balance. Youth feels this terror of the void, and the educator tries to help by persuasion and example. He offers himself as a model, though not seldom feeling the same impulse and the same terror. How often he says, "I must set a good example or what will become of my pupils?" and this burden weighs on his shoulders. Both pupils and teachers belong to the category of the virtuous (third circle). And this, today, is the atmosphere in which we train character and teach morals, and, because no other is known, it has become accepted. It follows that the great majority of people live always within these limits, and humanity in general regards it as natural to be on the defensive.

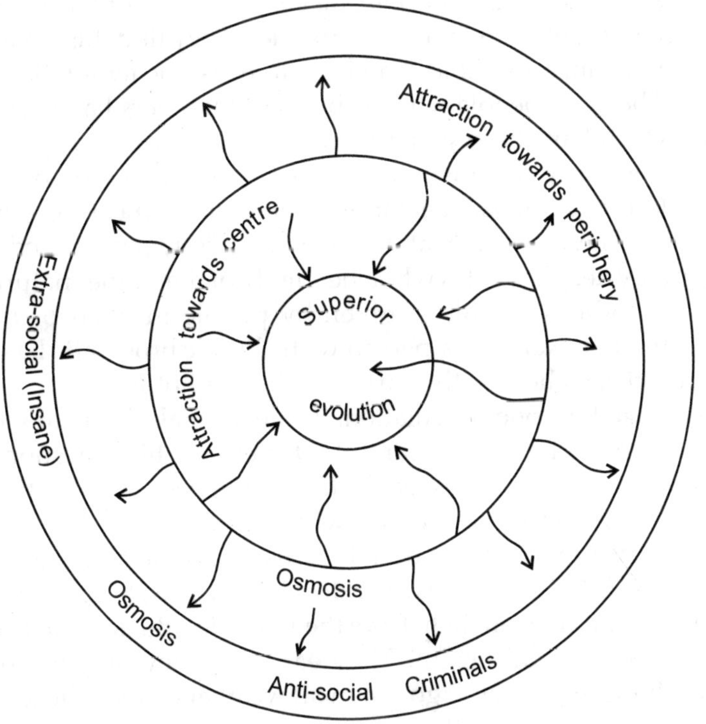

Fig. 11. *Circles of attraction for superior and inferior social types.*

In the inner circle are the stronger types attracted by perfection. Here, there is no force of gravity, but a *true* wish to become better. Often there is aspiration without the prospect of absolute perfection, but in any case these people are drawn towards perfection, naturally and without effort. It is not the fear of imprisonment that stops them from stealing; they do not win a desperate battle over a longing to possess the property of others; nor are they tempted to acts of violence from which they refrain by a pretence of virtue. They simply do not want other people's things, and violence repels them. Perfection attracts them because it is in their nature. Their search for it is not sacrificial, but is pursued as if it satisfied their deepest longings.

We have a difference not unlike that between vegetarians and non-vegetarians. Many eaters of meat abstain from it on certain days of the week. During Lent they fast for forty days, or go without meat and other luxuries. They find this a really long penance and hold it a virtue to resist the temptation.

These are people who keep rules that others have made, or which have been given them by their spiritual directors. But the inner circle would not contain these: it would be a circle for celestials, vegetarians, men whom meat does not tempt. These avoid meat. For them no missionary is needed, for they keep the rules wholeheartedly of their inner natures.

Another example is given by people in good or bad health. For example, a person with chronic bronchitis has to protect his chest with warm wool, take hot baths, and be massaged for poor circulation. While normal in appearance, he needs to be always careful. Or perhaps his digestion is bad, and to keep on his feet he has to eat special food at fixed hours. These people keep up with the others, but only with great care and with the dread of hospital or death always in their hearts. They live in their doctors' pockets, keep a nurse, or demand constant help from their families. But look at those who enjoy good health. They eat what they like without troubling about rules, go out in all weathers, break the ice to have a swim. The others, meanwhile, stay indoors hardly daring to put their noses out. In the third circle of the weak, spiritual mentors are needed on every hand. They act as brakes against the dangers of sliding into the abyss of temptation and degeneracy. But those in the inner circle have no need of such help, not in the same degree. Joys are open to them that the others cannot dream of.

Let us think, now, about this central circle, the circle of perfection. We must try to put character on a basis of facts. What is perfection? Is it the possession of all the virtues, carried to the highest level, and if so to reach what? Here again, we must try to be clear. By character we mean the behaviour of men driven (though often unconsciously) to make progress. This is the general tendency. Humanity and society have to progress in evolution. There is naturally an attraction toward God. But here let us consider a purely human centre of perfection, the progress of mankind. Someone makes a discovery and society progresses along that line. The same thing happens in the spiritual field, a person reaches a high level and gives society a push forwards. Everything we know, spiritually speaking, and all that we see, speaking physically, has been the work of some person. If we consider what is known of geography and history, we see this constant progress, because in every age some man has added a point to the circle of perfection which fascinated him and drove him to action. This was a man in the third circle who, being sure of himself, did not have to waste his energies in wrestling with temptation. Those same energies could then engage in what might have seemed impossible to persons always in strife against their own miserable selves. Admiral Byrd undertook the humiliating task of collecting money in order to explore the South Pole. Then he exposed himself to all the torments of a polar expedition. But all he felt was the attraction of doing something never before done, and so he planted his banner among the others in the zone of perfection.

In conclusion, we may say that humanity, from the point of view of character, is too rich in people of the third circle type. Too many need crutches to hold them up, and if the world keeps on with education as it is, the level of mankind will sink ever lower.

Suppose a missionary were to come from the third circle, and preach to children in the second. He might say, "Avoid meat. It can be the occasion of sin." The children would reply, "That is all right. We don't like meat." Or he might turn to some others and say: "You will catch cold in those clothes. Wear something warmer." To which the answer would be: "The cold doesn't harm us. We are quite warm enough." It is plain that teachers from the third circle tend to lower the children's level, instead of bringing them nearer to the centre of perfection.

If we examine the programmes of work recommended for use in schools, we see at once their poverty and dullness. The education of today is humiliating. It produces an inferiority complex and artificially lowers the powers of man. Its very organization sets a limit to knowledge well below the natural level. It supplies men with crutches when they could run on swift feet. It is an education based on man's lower powers, not on his higher ones. And it is man's own fault if the majority of human beings are inferior, for the formation of their characters during the constructive period has been prevented. We have to make an effort to recapture the true human level, letting our children use their creative powers. And then, it may well be, the second circle, which is not that of perfection, but tends towards it; which is not on the defensive, but seeks to conquer; will invade the whole of the third circle. If in man's whole life there is only one time for mental construction, and if at that time, it cannot occur, or occurs badly owing to faulty conditions, then it is not surprising that the human masses are underdeveloped. But if character were allowed its natural way of formation, and if we gave not moral dissertations but the chance to act constructively, then the world would need a very different kind of education.

Away would go artificial restrictions and great things to

be done would meet men's gaze. One can read the whole of history and the whole of philosophy, and still remain incapable. But let the *means* that inspire great efforts be given, and the results will be very different. But for this we must use things to which the human being responds. The qualities to be encouraged are those formed in the creative period, and if at that time they have no chance to establish themselves, they will not appear later. Neither sermons nor good examples will be able to revive them.

This is the difference between the old and the new education. We want to help the auto construction of man at the right time, so that mankind can go forward to something great. Society has built up walls, barriers. These the new education must cast down, revealing the free horizon. The new education is a revolution, but without violence. It is *the* non-violent revolution. After that, if it triumphs, violent revolution will have become forever impossible.

21

Children's Possessiveness and its Transformations

Having made a general survey of the facts that have come to light in the course of our experiments, let us now study them one at a time and give our interpretations of them. Both the ages of the children, and the deep interests they show, have given us much noteworthy material; the more so as their actions have so much in common with the highest characteristics of mankind.

In all these phenomena one can see a process of construction going on. It is not unlike the work of caterpillars when they reach a certain stage in their development. Instead of crawling about in the foliage, as they did till then, they stop at a joint between two stems and begin a mysterious activity which is peculiar to them. After a bit, one may see a tiny cloud of very fine and diaphanous threads. It is the beginning of the cocoon. So in the case of children, the first thing that strikes us is a phenomenon of concentration on some one thing. In a little girl of three and a half, who attended our first school, the intensity of this was amazing. With many interesting things on all sides, she could not be distracted from her work. Such a depth of concentration is seldom seen except among adults and then only in exceptional personalities. It is usually taken as a sign of genius. Naturally, in a child so young, it could not be of the same calibre, but finding it always present in different children, we had to accept it as something fundamental. Just as in using a compass, the fixing of the point is what enables us to draw the circle, so in the child's formation the fixing of his attention is basic to all that comes afterwards. No one says it must always fixate in the same way, or on the same things, but unless it does fixate formation cannot begin. Without concentration it is the objects about him which possess the child. He feels the call of each, and goes from one to another. But once his attention has been focused, he becomes his own master and can exert control over his world.

All of us know that in the grown-up world, a man who keeps changing his profession will never be fit for a responsible post. But a man whose aim is clearly defined, and who knows how to organize his work, will surely succeed. We give so much importance to this that we are never tired of telling even university students how pleased we should be to see them concentrating. But how little difference it makes! Good advice by itself is never enough. And if this be true for grown-ups, how can any teacher expect to induce concentration in a child of three and a half? One thing certain is that no child concentrates just by making an effort of will.

So the concentration shown by our little ones brings to light something new in child psychology. It shows how nature proceeds to bring about the formation of character. Her method is to give the child special interests, interests of exceptional intensity for doing that special creative work necessary for each part of his developing personality.

After concentration will come perseverance. This is another trait of character which now has its turn to unfold. I have, in fact, already spoken of the way in which children repeat exercises which, because they have no external purpose, must clearly have an internal purpose. This repetition, which begins after the first concentration, produces a kind of consolidation. It marks the beginning of yet another stage in human character formation. Here, also, the will which acts is not the child's will; it is nature's will. By its means, she builds the power which enables people to carry out the projects they have undertaken. There is something else, in fact, which the child shows in conjunction with his repetition of the exercise. It is the ability to carry through what he has begun. The children in our schools choose their work freely, and show this power unmistakably. They practise it daily for years. If, in the grown up world, we find ourselves in the company of people who never know what they want, we say they have no will-power. But of those who know what they want, and see clearly what line to take, we say they are strong willed and capable.

Children decide on their actions under the prompting of natural laws. Adults do it by taking thought. If the child is to exercise this power, it is clearly necessary that he be not directed by someone telling him what to do at every moment of his life. Inner forces affect his choice, and if someone usurps the function of this guide, the child is prevented from developing either his will or his concentration. So if we want him to acquire these traits, the first thing we must do is to make him independent of the adult. Besides this, the child's own strongest instinct is to free himself from adult control and this is very logical as we can see by the purposes it serves. But the child does not act from logic, he acts by nature. It is nature which marks out the path he must follow. See what a strange parallel exists between man's development and the lives of the animals, for these also have a path laid down for them, and they follow it by freeing themselves from dependence on the adults of their kind. There are natural laws which guide growth and formation, and the individual *must* follow these laws if he is to build up his character, his inner self.

One may await the formation of each separate part of man's mental side, and observation will always confirm that what happens is not caused only by education, but it comes out of the great and complex processes that guide the universe itself. It is nature's will, not our doing. It is a part of creation, not of education. This is well shown by another remarkable change that accompanies those we have seen. Children who have been prevented from developing fully often show character traits that disappear when they become normalized through work.

A very common one is possessiveness. In the normalized child, his freedom to take an interest in all kinds of things, leads to his focusing his attention not on the things themselves, but on the knowledge he derives from them. Hence his longing to possess undergoes a transformation. How strange it is to see a child who has been longing ardently to possess something, lose it or break it, as soon as it is his. It seems as if the hunger to possess is accompanied by a passion to destroy, yet this can easily be understood if we remember that no object is ever of perpetual interest. It only attracts for a moment and is then put aside. Take, for example, a watch. This is made to tell us the time and that is its real value. But a little child, who does not even know what time means, cannot grasp this; and so, when he happens to get hold of a watch, he nearly always breaks it. An older child, knowing what the watch is for, may become absorbed in seeing how it is made. He opens it carefully to look at the wheels and levers which interlock to make it go. But this means he is no longer interested in the watch. His interest now is in the working of its complex mechanism; he wants not the object but the understanding of the object.

Here, then, is a secondary type of possessiveness: the interest in knowing how things work. We can see it in many forms. Children who pick flowers just because they want them soon throw them aside or pull them to pieces. Here, the mania for possession does go side by side with the mania for destruction. But if the child knows the parts of a flower, the kind of leaf it has, or the branching pattern of its stem, then it will not occur to him to pick it or to damage it. He will want to study it. His interest has become intellectual and his possessiveness takes the form of knowledge. In the same way, he might kill a butterfly to possess it, but if he takes an interest in the lives of the insects and in the part they play in nature, his interest will still be focused on the butterfly but with the idea of watching it, not of capturing it or killing it. This intellectual possessiveness shows itself when the child is so strongly attracted by his environment that we may almost say he is "in love" with it. This love for his environment makes the child treat it with great care and handle everything in it with the utmost delicacy.

If the passion to possess is dictated by an intellectual interest, we may say it has been raised to a higher level and this will lead the child on towards knowledge. Instead of possessiveness there is, in this higher interest, an aspiration to know, love and serve. In the same way is curiosity sublimated in scientific research. Curiosity is an impulse to investigate. Once the child has felt the fascination of *one* object, he will become zealous in the conservation of *all* objects. It was the changes wrought in children in our first school that showed us how they pass from possessiveness to a sense of love and care for the things we had entrusted to them. The exercise books in which they wrote never had a creased page, an ink blot or an erasure. They were neat, tidy and often decorated.

When we think of man in all the greatness that history and evolution reveal, we see that this aspiration toward the best is part of his nature. In every way he tries to understand life, so as to protect and improve it, and he ends by helping living things by his intelligent insight. Does not the farmer spend all his time in looking after plants and animals, and the scientist in managing his microscopes and lenses? Humanity begins by seizing and destroying, and ends by loving and serving by means of his intelligence. The children who tore up the plants in the garden now watch their growth, count their leaves and measure their height. They no longer speak of *my* plant, but *of the* plant. This sublimation, and this love, are due to a new consciousness born in their minds. We can never cure destructiveness by preaching. If the child wants things for himself or in order that others may not have them, and we try to correct him by giving him a sermon or by appealing to his better feelings, he may stop for a few minutes but will soon begin again. Only work and concentration, bringing knowledge and love, can induce a transformation which discloses the spiritual man previously lying hidden.

To know, to love and to serve is the trinomial of all religions, but the child is the true maker of our spirituality. He teaches us the plan of nature for giving form to our conduct and character, a plan fully traced out in all its details of age and work, with its need for freedom and intense activity in accordance with the laws of life. What matters is not physics, or botany, or works of the hand, but the will, and the components of the human spirit which construct themselves by work. The child is the spiritual builder of mankind, and obstacles to his free development are the stones in the wall by which the soul of man has become imprisoned.

22

Social Development

The first essential for the child's development is concentration. It lays the whole basis for his character and social behaviour. He must find out how to concentrate, and for this he needs things to concentrate upon. This shows the importance of his surroundings, for no one acting on the child from outside can cause him to concentrate. Only he can organize his psychic life. None of us can do it for him. Indeed, it is just here that the importance of our schools really lies. They are places in which the child can find the kind of work that permits him to do this.

Any enclosed space, of course, favours concentration. All the world over, when people wish to concentrate, they seek out a place set aside for it. What do we do in shrine or temple? These create an atmosphere favourable to concentration. They are forcing houses for character formation. Children are seldom admitted to the ordinary schools before they are five and then the most formative period is over. But our schools offer the tinies a sheltering refuge in which the first elements of character can take shape, each of which has its own importance.

When I first pointed out the great value of an environment specially adapted in this way to the needs of little children, this idea aroused great interest in architects, artists, and psychologists, some of whom collaborated with me to settle the ideal size and height of the rooms, and the decorations desirable in a school where concentration was to be favoured. Such a building was more than protective and might almost be called "psychological." Yet its value did not depend entirely on dimensions and colouring—which are not enough in themselves—but it depended on the things provided for the children's use, for the child needs tangible things on which to focus his attention. Yet these things, in their turn, were not decided upon arbitrarily, but only as a result of prolonged experimentation with children themselves.

We started by equipping the child's environment with a little of everything, and left the children to choose those things they preferred. Seeing that they only took certain things and that the others remain unused, we eliminated the latter. All the things now used in our schools are not just the result of elimination in a few local trials but in trials made in schools all over the world. So we may truly say that these things have been chosen by the children. We found there were objects liked by *all* children, and these we regard as essential. There were others that they seldom used, contrary to the beliefs of most adults, and this also happened in all countries. Wherever our normalized children were allowed to choose freely, we always obtained the same results, and I used to think of those insects which only, and always, got to the particular flowers that are suited to them. It was very clear that the children needed these things. A child chooses what helps him to construct himself. At first we had many toys, but the children always ignored them. There were also many devices for displaying colours, but they chose one type only, the flat silk-wound spools that we now use everywhere. In every country this was confirmed. Even as to shape and intensity of the coloured area, we let the children's preferences guide us. This close determination of all the objects provided, has its reflection also in the social life of the class. For if there are too many things, or more than one complete set for a group of thirty or forty children, this causes confusion. So we have few things, even if there are many children.

There is only one specimen of each object, and if a piece

is in use when another child wants it, the latter—if he is normalized—will wait for it to be released. Important social qualities derive from this. The child comes to see that he must respect the work of others, not because someone has said he must, but because this is a reality that he meets in his daily experience. There is only one between many children, so there is nothing for it but to wait. And since this happens every hour of the day for years, the idea of respecting others, and of waiting one's turn, becomes an habitual part of life which always grows more mature.

Out of this comes a change, an adaptation, which is nothing if not the birth of social life itself. Society does not rest on personal wishes, but on a combination of activities which have to be harmonized. From their experiences another virtue develops in the children: the virtue of patience, which is a kind of denial of impulses by means of inhibition. So the character traits that we call virtues spring up spontaneously. We cannot teach this kind of morality to children of three, but experience can, and because in other conditions normalization is prevented—so that people the world over see children fighting for what they want—the fact that our children waited struck them as all the more impressive. I was often asked, "But how do you make these tinies behave so well? How do you teach them such discipline?" It was not I. It was the environment we had prepared so carefully and the freedom they found in it. Under these conditions, qualities formerly unknown in children of three to six were able to show themselves.

When adults interfere in this first stage of preparation for social life, they nearly always make mistakes. When children are "walking on the line" one of them may go in the opposite direction to all the others, and collision seems inevitable. One's impulse is to seize the child and turn him around. But he looks out very well for himself, and solves the difficulty—not always in the same fashion, but always satisfactorily. Such problems abound at every step, and it gives the children great pleasure to face them. They feel irritated if we intervene, and find a way if left to themselves. This is all social experience, and it provides constant practice in dealing suitably with situations that no teacher would be able to invent. The teacher, instead, usually intervenes, but her solution differs from that of the children and this disturbs the harmony of the group. Apart from exceptional cases, we ought to leave such problems to the children. We can then study their behaviour objectively, and of this very little is known. It is through these daily experiences that a social order comes into being.

Teachers who use direct methods cannot understand how social behaviour is fostered in a Montessori school. They think it offers scholastic material but not social material. They say, "If the child does everything on his own, what becomes of social life?" But what is social life if not the solving of social problems, behaving properly and pursuing aims acceptable to all? To them, social life consists in sitting side by side and hearing someone else talk: but that is just the opposite.

The only social life that children get in the ordinary schools is during playtime or on excursions. Ours live always in an active community.

When the classes are fairly big, differences of character show themselves more clearly, and wider experience can be gained. With small classes this is less easy. The higher levels of perfection all come through social life.

What is the constitution of this society of children? It has come together by chance, but not a casual chance. The children who find themselves in this circumscribed world are of mixed ages (between three and six). This does not usually happen in schools unless the older ones are mentally retarded. Grouping is commonly based on age, and only in a few schools does one find our "vertical classification."

When some of our own teachers wanted to apply the principle of one age for one class, it was the children themselves who showed what great difficulties sprang from this. It is just the same at home. A mother with six children finds them easy to manage. But when there are twins, or if other children are brought in of the same age, things become harder, since it is very tiring to cope with children who are all wanting the same thing at the same time. The mother with six children of different ages is far better off than the mother with one. "Only children" are always difficult, not so much because of spoiling, as because they suffer more from lack of company. Parents often have more trouble with the first born than they do with later children. They put this down to their own inexperience, but actually it is because the later children have companionship.

The charm of social life is in the number of different types that one meets. Nothing is duller than a Home for the Aged. To segregate by age is one of the cruellest and most inhuman things one can do, and this is equally true for children. It breaks the bonds of social life, deprives it of nourishment. In most schools the sexes are first of all separated, then the ages each, more or less, in a different room. This is a fundamental mistake, which breeds a host of evils. It is an artificial isolation and impedes the development of the social sense. In our schools the sexes are usually mixed, but putting boys and girls together is not really very important. They can quite well go to different schools. What matters is to mix the ages. Our schools show that children of different ages help one another. The younger ones see what the older ones are doing and ask for explanations. These are readily given, and the instruction is really valuable, for the mind of a five-year-old is so much nearer than ours to the mind of a child of three, that the little one learns easily what we should find it hard to impart. There is a communication and a harmony between the two that one seldom finds between the adult and the small child.

There are many things which no teacher can convey to a child of three, but a child of five can do it with the utmost ease. There is between them a natural mental "osmosis." Again, a child of three will take an interest in what a five-year-old is doing, since it is not far removed from his own powers. All the older ones become heroes and teachers, and the tinies are their admirers. These look to the former for inspiration, then go on with their work. In the other kind of school, where children in the same class are all of the same age, the more intelligent could easily teach the others, but this is hardly ever allowed. The only thing they may do is to answer the teacher's questions when the less intelligent cannot. The result is that their cleverness often provokes envy. Envy is unknown to little children. They are not abashed by an older child knowing more than they do, for they sense that when they are bigger their turn will come. There is love and admiration on both sides; a true brotherhood. In the old type of school, the only way to raise the level of the class was by emulation, but this too often aroused the depressing and antisocial feelings of envy, hatred and humiliation. The brighter children became conceited and dominated the others, whereas in our schools the five-year-old feels himself a protector of the younger one. It is hard to believe how deep this atmosphere of protection and admiration becomes in practice. The class gets to be a group cemented by affection. Finally, the children come to know one another's characters and to have a reciprocal feeling for each other's worth. The only thing they used to say in schools of the old kind was, "So and so has won the first prize," or "That boy has scored zero." True fellow feeling does not develop in such a fashion. Yet this is the age in which social or antisocial qualities are going to be evolved according to the nature of the child's surroundings. This is their point of origin.

People sometimes fear that if a child of five gives lessons, this will hold him back in his own progress. But, in the first place; he does not teach all the time and his freedom is respected. Secondly, teaching helps him to understand what he knows even better than before. He has to analyse and rearrange his little store of knowledge before he can pass it on. So his sacrifice does not go unrewarded.

The classroom for those of three to six is not even rigidly separated from that of the children from seven to nine. Thus, children of six can get ideas from the class above. Our dividing walls are only waist-high partitions, and there is always easy access from one classroom to the next. Children are free to pass to and fro between classrooms. If a child of three goes into the room for sevens, eights and nines, he does not stay there long because he soon sees that it contains nothing useful to him. There are demarcations but no separations, and all the groups can intercommunicate.

Each has its appointed place but is not isolated: one can always go for an intellectual walk! A child of three may see another of nine using beads to perform the arithmetical operation of extracting a square root. He may ask him what he is doing. If the answer makes him no wiser, he will return to his own room, where there are things of greater interest. But a child of six may comprehend a little of what the nine year old is doing, and may stay to watch, learning something from it. Freedom like this enables the observer to note the limits of understanding at each age. In fact, this was how we came to realize that children of eight or nine could understand the square root operations, which they saw being done by children of twelve to fourteen. In the same way, it was brought to our notice that children of eight can be interested in algebra. The child's progress does not depend only on his age, but also on being free to look about him.

Our schools are alive. To understand what the older ones are doing fills the little ones with enthusiasm. The older ones are happy to be able to teach what they know. There are no inferiority complexes, but everyone achieves a healthy normality through the mutual exchange of spiritual energy.

All this, and more, serves to show that the events which seemed at first so astonishing in our schools are really due only to the working of natural laws.

Studying the behaviour of these children and their mutual relationships in an atmosphere of freedom, the true secrets of society come to be revealed. These are facts so delicate and refined that a spiritual microscope is needed to discern them, but their interest is immense, for they show us the true nature of man. Therefore, we look on these schools of ours as laboratories of psychological research, though we mean by this, not research as commonly understood, but that these are places especially suited for child observation. Here are some other noteworthy facts.

Children, as we have said, solve their own problems, but we have not yet explained how. If we watch them without interfering, we see something apparently very strange. This is that they do not help one another as we do. If a child is carrying something heavy, none of the others run to his aid. They respect one another's efforts, and give help only when it is necessary. This is very illuminating, because it means they respect intuitively the essential need of childhood which is not to be helped unnecessarily. One day it happened that a little one had spread out all the wooden geometric figures with their cards on the floor.[1] Suddenly a band heading a procession was heard passing in the street right under the schoolroom window. All the children ran to look except this one, because he would never have dreamed of leaving so much work lying about loose. It must all be put back in its right place, and no one seemed inclined to lend him a hand. But his eyes filled with tears, as he would dearly have loved to see the procession. The others noticed this and many turned back to help him. Adults are lacking in this fine power of discrimination by which an emergency can be recognized. More often than not they give unnecessary help. How often will a gentleman, in the name of good manners, move the chair forward as a lady is seating herself at table, although the lady can quite well do it for herself; or he offers her an arm when going downstairs, though she is far from needing any support. But, in cases of real want, everything changes. No one comes running when there is dire need of help; but when there is no need, everyone helps! So here is a field in which children have nothing to learn from grown ups. I believe the child has an unconscious memory of his own early wish (and deeply felt need) to make the maximum effort, and that is why he does not help others when his help would be an obstacle.

Another interesting point in children's conduct concerns their treatment of those who disturb the class. Let us suppose, for example, that a child recently admitted to school and not yet acclimatized, is restless, troublesome and a nuisance to everyone. The teacher, in the ordinary way, says, "That won't do; it isn't at all nice," or perhaps, "You are a very naughty little boy!"

But his companions react quite differently. One of them may approach the newcomer and say, "It is true you are very naughty, but don't worry about it. We were just as bad when we came!"

He has felt pity for him, regarded his ill behaviour as a misfortune, tried to comfort him and perhaps to bring out in him all the good of which he was capable.

How the world would change if wickedness always awakened pity, and if we made an effort to confront the criminal with the same sympathy, as we do the sick! Besides, wrongdoing is often pathological and may be due to bad home conditions, to a misfortune at birth, or some other kind of mishap, and it ought to excite compassion and the wish to help. This alone would raise the very substance of our society.

With our children, if there is a mishap, like the breaking of a vase, the child who has dropped it is often desperate. He takes no pleasure in breaking things and feels ashamed of himself for not being able to carry it safely.

The grown-up's instinctive reaction is to shout:

"Now you've broken it. How often have I told you never to touch those things?" Or, at least, the grown-up will tell him to pick up the pieces, thinking this will impress him the more.

But what do our children do? They all run to help, saying with an encouraging tone in their little voices, "Never mind, we shall soon find another vase," and, while some collect the pieces, others wipe up the spilled water. They have an instinct to help the weak, encouraging and comforting them, and this is really an instinct for social progress. Indeed, the greatest step forward in human evolution was made when society began to help the weak and the poor, instead of oppressing and despising them.

The whole science of medicine has grown up from this principle and thence comes the wish not only to help those who awaken pity, but mankind itself. It is not a mistake to encourage the weak and inferior, but a contribution to general social progress. The children show that they possess these sentiments as soon as they have become normalized, and they show them not only for one another, but also for animals.

The usual belief is that respect for animal life has to be taught, because we think of children as being naturally cruel or insensitive. But this is untrue. Normalized children feel protective toward animals. In the school at Laren[2] we had a goat which I used to feed daily, and I held the food up high so that to reach it the goat had to balance on its hind legs. I found it interesting to see the animal adopt this posture, and it too gave the impression of being entertained by it. But one day, a very small child came and put his hands under the animal's belly to help keep it up. The anxious look in his face showed clearly that he was afraid the effort to stand on two legs would be too much for it. Beyond question this showed a most kindly and spontaneous thought.

Something else very uncommon can be seen in our schools: it is admiration for the best. Not only are these children free from envy, but anything well done arouses their enthusiastic praise. This happened in the now famous "explosion" into writing. The first word to be written by one of them, brought a great outburst of joy and laughter. Everyone looked admiringly at "the writer," and thus they felt moved to follow his example. "I can do it, too!" they cried. The achievement of one started off the whole group. It was the same with the letters of the alphabet, so much so that once, the whole class formed a procession holding up the cards bearing the sandpaper letters like banners. So great was their joy, and so loud their cheering, that people on the floor below (the school was on the roof) came running to see what was going on. The teacher had to explain: "They are so delighted at learning their letters."

There is among children an evident sense of community. This rests on the noblest feelings and creates unity in the group. These examples are enough to teach us that under conditions in which the emotional life reaches a high level and the children's personalities are normalized, a kind of attraction makes itself felt. Just as the older ones are drawn to the younger, and vice versa, so are the normalized drawn to the newcomers, and these to those already acclimatized.

REFERENCES

1. About 100 pieces all told.
2. Laren in Holland. Here Dr. Montessori was conducting a psychopedagogical research centre and experimental school, when war broke out in 1939.

23

Cohesion in the Social Unit

A society like this seems to be more united by the *absorbent mind* than it does by the conscious mind. The manner of its construction is observable and may be compared to the work of the cells in the growth of an organism. It seems clear that a society goes through an embryonic phase which we can follow among little children in the course of their development. It is interesting to see how, little by little, these become aware of forming a community which behaves as such. They come to feel part of a group to which their activity contributes. And not only do they begin to take an interest in this, but they work on it profoundly, as one may say in their hearts. Once they have reached this level, the children no longer act thoughtlessly, but put the group first and try to succeed for its benefit.

The first step towards a social consciousness recalls the "spirit of the family or the tribe," for in primitive societies, as is well known, the individual loves, defends and values his own group, as the end aim of his existence. The first signs of this phenomenon amazed us, because they occurred quite independently of us, or of any influence that we could have exerted. They appeared all of a sudden just like any other proof that development is going on, as when a child cuts his teeth at the age prescribed by nature. This unity born among the children, which is produced by a spontaneous need, directed by an unconscious power, and vitalized by a social spirit, is a phenomenon needing a name, and I call it *"cohesion in the social unit."*

The idea was forced upon us by the children's spontaneous actions, which left us speechless with astonishment. To give an example, it so happened that the Argentinian ambassador, hearing it said that in our schools children of four and five worked entirely on their own, read and wrote spontaneously, and had an excellent discipline not imposed by authority, found himself unable to believe this. So he thought he would pay a surprise visit. Unfortunately, it happened to be a holiday, so he found the school shut. This was a school called "The Children's House" in a block of working men's flats where the children lived with their parents. Just by chance, one of the children was in the courtyard and heard the ambassador's expression of annoyance. Guessing he was a visitor, the child said, "Don't worry about the school being shut. The caretaker has the key and we are all here." The door was soon opened and all the children went in and began to work. Here, then, was an example of action for the group. Each did his part without hope of reward. They cooperated for the honour of their community. Only on the day following did the teacher hear what had happened.

This sense of solidarity, not instilled by any instruction, completely extraneous to any form of emulation, competition or personal advantage, was a gift of nature. Yet it was a point to which those children had reached by their own efforts. As Coghill says, "Nature herself determines the child's early conduct, but this can only evolve by contact with the world about him."[1] It seems clear enough that nature lays down a plan for the construction both of personality and of social life, but this plan becomes realized only through the children's activity when they are placed in circumstances favourable to its fulfilment. In doing this, they reveal to us the phases through which social life must pass in the course of its natural unfolding. This corporate life, which rules and unites a social group, corresponds closely to what the

American educator, Washburne, has called "social integration." He holds that this is the key to social reform, and that it should be made the basis of all education. Social integration has occurred when the individual identifies himself with the group to which he belongs. When this has happened, the individual thinks more about the success of his group than of his own personal success.

To illustrate his thesis, Washburne instances the Oxford and Cambridge boat race. "Every man rows his hardest for the boat, knowing full well that this will bring him no personal glory nor special reward. If this became the rule in every social undertaking, from those which embrace the whole country down to the smallest industrial concern, and if all were moved by the wish to bring honour to his group rather than to himself, then the whole human family would be reborn. This integration of the individual with his group must be cultivated in the schools, because it is just this that we lack, and the failure and ruin of our civilization is due to this lack."[2]

An example may be given of a human society not lacking in this integration. It is the society of little children who are guided by the magical powers of nature. We must value it and treasure it, because neither character nor the social sentiment can be given by teachers. They are products of life.

But we must not confuse this natural social solidarity with the organization of adult society which governs man's destinies. It is simply the last phase of children's unfolding, the almost divine and mysterious creation of a social embryo.

Soon after six years of age, when the child starts another phase of development (marking the change from a society in embryo to a society just born), another form of existence sets in spontaneously in which the group is organized entirely on the conscious plane. Children then want to know the customs and laws which men have adopted to guide their conduct: they seek to have someone in control who will govern the community. Obedience to the head and to the laws acts obviously like a kind of connective tissue in this society. We know that this obedience has been prepared in the preceding embryonic stage.

The British psychologist McDougall has described this kind of society which our little ones have already begun to establish by the time they are six or seven years old. They subordinate themselves to children older than themselves as if they were driven by an instinct which he calls the gregarious instinct.[3] Abandoned and forgotten children often organize themselves into groups and gangs in rebellion against authority and adult-made regulations. These natural needs, which almost always result in rebellious attitudes, have been sublimated in the Boy Scout movement which answers to a real requirement of social development, inherent in the nature of young boys and adolescents.

But McDougall's "gregarious instinct" is not the same as the force of cohesion which lies at the root of an infantile society. All the later social forms that evolve in children right up to the level of adult society are organized consciously, and need rules given by a man or even by a chief, who makes himself respected.

Life in association is a natural fact and belongs, as such, to human nature. It grows like an organism and shows a succession of different characteristics in the course of its unfolding. An illuminating comparison may be made with the Indian village industry of hand woven cloth practised by the villagers in their homes.

To start at the beginning, let us first consider the white tuft or "flock" which the cotton plant produces around its seed. In social life, we must first consider the baby and the kind of home life into which he has been born. The first thing to be done with cotton is to purify it after picking, to free it from the black seeds attached to the flock, and this also is the first work to be done by children in Gandhi's rural schools. This corresponds to our work when we gather the children from their various homes and correct their defects, helping them to concentrate and to become normalized individuals.

Now let us turn to the spinning. This, in our analogy,

corresponds to the formation of the personality which is brought about by work and living in a group. This is the basis of everything. If the thread has been well spun and is strong, the cloth made from it will also be strong. The quality of the material we weave depends on the quality of the yarn. This, clearly, is the first thing to be sure of, for a tissue made of weak threads is worthless.

Then comes the moment when the threads are placed on the frame, stretched parallel without touching and held by little hooks along the sides. These form the warp for a piece of cloth, but they are not yet the cloth. Yet without the warp the cloth could not be woven. If the threads break, or get out of place, not being made fast in the same direction, the shuttle cannot pass between them. This warp corresponds to social cohesion. Preparation for human society is based on the activities of children who act, urged on by the needs of their nature, in a limited world corresponding to the frame. They end by becoming associated, all with the same end in view.

Now begins the real weaving when the shuttle passes between the threads and joins them, fixing them solidly together by means of the weft. This stage corresponds to the organized society of man which is ruled by laws and controlled by a government which all obey. When we have a real piece of stuff it remains intact after removal from the frame. It has an independent existence and can be used. One can make it in unlimited quantities. Men do not form a society just by having individual aims and undertaking each his own work, as the children do in our schools. The final form of human society is based on organization.

Yet the two things interpenetrate. Society does not depend entirely on organization, but also on cohesion, and of these two the second is basic and serves as foundation for the first. Good laws and a good government cannot hold the mass of men together and make them act in harmony, unless the individuals themselves are orientated towards something that gives them solidarity and makes them into a group. The masses, in their turn, are more or less strong and active according to the level of development, and of inner stability, of the personalities composing them.

The Greeks based their social order on the formation of personality. Alexander the Great, at one time their ruler, conquered the whole of Persia with only a few men. The Moslem world also presents a formidable unity, not so much because of its laws and rulership as on account of a common ideal. A mass pilgrimage to Mecca is made periodically. Strangers to one another, these pilgrims serve no private or ambitious ends. No one drives them, or commands them; yet in the fulfilment of their view, their capacity for sacrifice is immense. These pilgrimages are an example of cohesion.

The Middle Ages of European history saw something that in our own days, lacerated by war, all our leaders try in vain to reach: real union of the European nations. How was it done? The secret of this triumph lay in the religious faith which had captured all the people who lived in the various empires and European kingdoms, uniting them by its tremendous force of cohesion. Those days really saw all kings and emperors (each of whom governed in his own fashion) subject to Christianity, and dependent on its strength.

But cohesion alone is not enough to set up a society which can play a practical part in the world, evoking therein a civilized life of work and thought. An example in our own day, is that of the Jews who have been united by the force of cohesion for thousands of years, but only now are becoming a nation. They are like the warp from which a people has yet to be woven. Recent history has presented us with still another example. Mussolini and Hitler were the first to grasp that rulers, who wish to make sure of a new social order surviving, must train people to it from infancy. They drilled children and youths for years, imposing on them from outside an ideal to unite them. Whatever one may think of its morality, this was a logical and scientific procedure. These heads of the state felt the need to have a "cohesive society" as a basis on which to build, and they prepared its roots accordingly.

But the cohesive social order is a natural fact and must build itself spontaneously under the creative stimuli of nature. No one can replace God, and anyone who tries to do so becomes a devil, just as when the overbearing adult oppresses the creative energies of the infantile personality. Even the force of cohesion among adults is something that needs to be directed by an attachment to ideals; that is to say, to something higher than a mere organizing mechanism. There ought to be two societies interwoven with one another. One, so to speak, should have its roots in the unconscious creative zone of the mind, the other should come from the world of conscious activity. In other words, one begins in infancy, and the other is superimposed upon this by the hands of the adult, for (as we saw at the beginning of this book) it is the absorbent mind of the child which takes in the characteristics of the race. The child's characteristics, during his life as "the spiritual embryo," are not discoveries of the intellect, nor made by human work, but are mental qualities that we find in the cohesive part of society. The child collects and incarnates them, and by this means constructs his own personality. So he becomes a man with a particular language, a particular religion, and a particular set of social customs. Whatever is stable and fundamental ("basic," to use the modern term) in a social order which is constantly being revolutionized, is the cohesive part. When we let the infant develop, and see him construct from the invisible roots of creation that which is to become the grown man, then we can learn the secrets on which depend our individual and social strength.

Instead—and we have only to look about us to see it—men judge and act and regulate their lives only on the organizational and conscious part of society. They want to strengthen and ensure the organization as if they alone were its creators. They think not at all of the indispensable basis of the organization, but worry about its human control; and their highest aspiration is to find a leader.

How many place their hopes in a new Messiah, a genius

who will have the strength to take over and to organize? A proposal was made after the First World War to found a training centre for leaders, because it appeared that none of the existing leaders had the necessary qualities, or could dominate events. Efforts were actually made to discover superior persons by means of "mental tests," young men who had shown the right dispositions in their school days, and to steer such persons toward positions of authority. But who could instruct them if there was no one suited to the task?

It is not leaders who are lacking, or at least the question is not limited to this. The problem is infinitely more vast. It is the masses themselves who are totally unprepared for social life in our civilization. Hence the problem is to educate the masses, to reconstruct the character of individuals, to garner the treasures hidden within each one of them and to develop its value. No single head of the state can do this, however great his genius. Out of multitudes of the underdeveloped no one can ever solve this problem.

This is the most urgent and troublesome question of our time: the great mass of folk are inferior to what they should be. We have already seen the diagram of the two attractive forces one which draws to the centre and the other to the periphery (see Fig. 11). The great task of education must be to secure and to preserve a normality which, of its own nature, gravitates towards the centre of perfection. Today, instead, all we do is to prepare artificially men who are abnormal and weak, predisposed to mental illness, constantly needing care not to slip outward to the periphery where, once fallen, they become social outcasts. What is happening today is truly a crime of treason to mankind, and its repercussions on everyone could destroy us. The great mass of illiterates, which covers half the earth, does not really weigh upon society. What weighs upon it is the fact that, without knowing it, we are ignoring the creation of man, and trampling on the treasures which God himself has placed in every child. Yet here lies the source of those moral and intellectual values which could bring the whole world on to a higher plane. We cry out in the face of death, and long to save mankind from destruction, but it is not safety from death, but our own individual elevation, and our destiny itself as men that we ought to have in mind. Not the fear of death, but the knowledge of our lost paradise should be our tribulation.

The greatest danger lies in our ignorance. We know how to find pearls in the shells of oysters, gold in the mountains and coal in the bowels of the earth, but we are unaware of the spiritual germs, the creative nebulae that the child hides in himself when he enters our world to renew mankind.

If the spontaneous forms of organization we have just described could be admitted to the ordinary schools, this would work wonders. Instead, teachers do not believe that children are active learners. They drive and encourage or give punishments and rewards to stimulate work. They use competition to arouse effort. One may say that all are forced into a hunt for evil for the sake of combating it, and a typical attitude of the adult is to be always looking for vice in order to suppress it. But the correction of errors is often humiliating and discouraging and, since education rests on this basis, there follows a lowering in the general quality of social life. In the schools of today no one may copy another's work, and to help someone else is regarded as a crime. To accept help is as guilty as to give it, so the union we spoke of fails to be formed. Normal standards are debased by a rule arbitrarily imposed. At every turn one hears: "Don't play about," "Don't make a noise," "Don't help others with their work," "Don't speak unless you are spoken to." Always the injunction is negative.

What can be done in such a situation? Even if the teacher does try to elevate her class, she never does it as the children would. At the best she says, "Don't be jealous if someone does better than you do," "Don't retaliate if someone hurts you." Still we have nothing but negations. The general idea is that everyone is crooked and we must straighten them as much as possible. But often the children do things that the educator would never dream of as being possible. They admire those who do better than they do. This is more than just not being envious. Certain spiritual attainments cannot be awakened if they do not already exist; but if they exist, and are instinctive (as truly they are), it is even more important to encourage and cultivate them. The same may be said about not retaliating. The child often makes friends with his enemy, but no one can oblige him to do so. One can feel love and sympathy even for the wrongdoer, but no one can impose this sympathy on another. One may like to help a more stupid companion, but not to be forced into it. These natural sentiments ought, as I have said, to be encouraged. But too often they are made sterile, and all the work of the schools evolves at this low level, that is to say, in the third zone (see Fig. 11), wherein people feel drawn towards the periphery of the anti-social and the outcast. First, the teacher thinks that the child is incapable and must be taught. Then she thinks it is good to keep on saying, "Don't do this, don't do that," in other words "Do not slide towards the periphery." But normalized children show the strongest attraction towards good. They do not find it necessary to "avoid evil."

Another negative action is the interruption of work, at fixed times in the daily programme. They say to the child, "Don't apply yourself for too long at any one thing. It may tire you." Yet he shows an evident need to put out his best efforts. The schools we have today cannot help the creative instincts of the children, who feel in themselves a true delight in activity, a real joy in hard work, in finding the beauty of work, in comforting the unhappy, and helping the weak.

I would like to compare the relation between ordinary schools and normalized schools to that between the Old and the New Testament. In the Ten Commandments of the Old Testament, "Thou shalt not kill," "Thou shalt not steal," and the others, we have the negations of a law that men needed only because they were still dark and confused in their minds. But in the New Testament, Christ—like the children—gives positive commandments, such as "Love your enemies," while, to those who felt superior to others because they keep the law and wished to be admired for this, He said "I came to bring sinners to repentance."

Yet to teach men these precepts is not enough. It is useless to say, "Love your enemies," if all we do is to say it in church and not in battle, where the contrary is happening. When we say, "Thou shalt not kill," we focus all attention on the evil thing from which we wish to defend ourselves, as if goodness were impracticable. To love one's enemies seems impossible, so much so that it remains on the whole a vain ideal.

And why? Because the root of goodness does not exist in the soul of man. Perhaps it was there once, but now it is dead and buried. If rivalry, emulation and ambition have been encouraged throughout the whole period of education, how can we hope that people who have grown in that atmosphere will become good at the age of twenty, or thirty, simply because someone preaches goodness? I say it is impossible because no preparation has been made for the life of the spirit.

Not sermons but creative instincts are important, because they are realities. Children act in accordance with their natures, and not because of the teacher's exhortations. Goodness must come out of reciprocal helpfulness, from the unity derived from spiritual cohesion. This society created by cohesion, which children have revealed to us, is at the root of all social organizations. For this reason I maintain that we adults cannot teach children from three to six years of age. We can but observe them with intelligence and follow their development, at every hour of every day, in their endless exercises. What nature has given them develops with work. Nature offers an interior guidance, but to develop anything in any field, continuous effort and experience are required. Without the possibility of this no amount of preaching will avail. Growth comes from activity, not from intellectual understanding. Education, therefore, of little ones is important, especially from three to six years of age, because this is the embryonic period for the formation of character and of society (just as the period from birth to three is that for forming the mind, and the prenatal period that for forming the body). What the child achieves between three and six does not depend on doctrine but on a divine directive which guides his spirit to construction. These are the germinal origins of human behaviour and they can only be evolved in the right surroundings of freedom and order.

REFERENCES

1. G.E. Coghill, *Anatomy and the Problem of Behaviour*, Cambridge University Press, 1929.
2. Carleton Washburne, *The Living Philosophy of Education*, John Day Company, New York.
3. See William McDougall, *An Introduction to Social Psychology*, Methuen, London, 1948. Revised edition.

24

Mistakes and Their Correction

The children in our schools are free, but that does not mean there is no organization. Organization, in fact, is necessary, and if the children are to be free to *work*, it must be even more thorough than in the ordinary schools. The child gains experience in our environment and so perfects himself, but special things for him to do are indispensable. Once concentration has begun, he may maintain it in occupations of many kinds, and the more active he is the less active will be the teacher; in fact, she may end by standing almost completely aside.

As we have already indicated, children following this path become fused into a social group, so much more perfect than our own that one feels they should always be left free from adult interference. Their life together is a vital phenomenon as delicate as the life of the embryo, and we must see it is not spoiled. Once we have created an environment in which all the objects are attuned to children's developmental needs, we have done all that is needed to produce this phenomenon.

In this new world a precise relationship exists between the teacher and the children. The teacher's task will be described in another chapter, but there is one thing she must never do and that is, to interfere by praising a child's work, or punishing him if it is wrong, or even by correcting his mistakes. This may sound absurd and many people find it a stumbling block.

"How," they say, "can you get the child on if you never correct his mistakes?"

Most teachers think it is their main business to be always criticizing, and they do this just as much in the field of learning as they do in moral matters. The child's training has, they think, to be guided by two reins: prizes and punishments.

But if a child has to be rewarded or punished, it means he lacks the capacity to guide himself; so this has to be supplied by the teacher. But supposing he sets himself to work; then the addition of prizes and punishments is superfluous; they only offend the freedom of his spirit. Hence, in schools like ours which are dedicated to the defence of spontaneity and which aim at setting the children free, prizes and punishments obviously have no place. Moreover, the child who freely finds his work shows that to him they are completely unimportant.

Prizes we might have abolished without serious protest. After all, this is economical; it affects few children, and then only once a year. But punishments! That is another story. These are given every day. What is meant by correcting exercise books? It means marking them from 0 to 10. How can a zero correct anyone's defects? Then the teachers says, "You keep on making the same mistake. You don't listen to what I say. You will never pass your examinations like that!"

All the crosses made by the teacher on the child's written work, all her scoldings, only have a lowering effect on his energies and interests. To tell a child he is naughty or stupid just humiliates him; it offends and insults, but does not improve him. For if a child is to stop making mistakes, he must become more skilful, and how can he do this if, being already below standard, he is also discouraged? In olden times teachers used to fasten asses' ears to stupid children, and smacked their fingers for writing badly. But even if they had wasted all the paper in the world to make donkeys' ears, and if they had reduced the tiny fingers to pulp, this would not have brought any fresh powers into being. Only exercise and experience can correct a disability, and it takes long practice to acquire the various kinds of skill that are needed. The undisciplined child enters into discipline by working in the company of others; not by being told that he is naughty. If you tell a pupil that he lacks the ability to do something, he might as well rejoin, "Then why talk about it? I can see that for myself."

This is not a correction. It is a statement of fact. Improvement and rectification can only come about when the child practices voluntarily for a long time.

True, it may happen that the child makes a mistake without knowing it; but also the teacher can err unconsciously. Unfortunately, teachers usually have the idea that they must never make a mistake themselves, for fear of setting a bad example. Hence, if the teacher does make a slip, she will certainly not admit it to the child. Her dignity rests on being always right. The teacher has to be infallible. However, this is not entirely the fault of teachers. The whole school system is to blame, resting as it does on a false foundation.

Supposing we study the phenomenon of error in itself; it becomes apparent that everyone makes mistakes. This is one of life's realities, and to admit it is already to have taken a great step forward. If we are to tread the narrow path of truth and keep our hold upon reality, we have to agree that all of us can err; otherwise we should all be perfect. So it is well to cultivate a friendly feeling towards error, to treat it as a companion inseparable from our lives, as something having a purpose, which it truly has.

Many errors correct themselves as we go through life. The tiny child starts toddling uncertainly on his feet, wobbles and falls but ends by walking easily. He corrects his errors by growth and experience. We deceive ourselves if we imagine we are always following life's highway towards perfection. The truth is that we make mistake after mistake, and do not correct ourselves. We fail to realize our faults; we live in a state of illusion shut off from reality. The teacher who sets out with the idea that she is perfect, and never notices her own mistakes, is not a good teacher. Whichever way we look, a certain "Mr. Error" is always to be seen! If we seek perfection, we must pay attention to our own defects, for it is only by correcting these that we can improve ourselves. We have to face them in the full light of day and realize their existence as something unavoidable throughout life.

Even in the exact sciences (mathematics, physics, chemistry, etc.), errors play an important part, because they have to be taken into account. The coming of positive science made it necessary to study the error scientifically. Science is only considered to be immune from error because it makes use of exact measurement to evaluate error. When measurements are made, there are two things that matter, one is to obtain a precise figure, the other is to know the extent to which it may be wrong. Whatever science has to say is stated as an approximation, never as an absolute, and this is allowed for in the conclusions drawn. For example, an antibiotic injection is found to be successful in 95 per cent of cases. But it is important to know there is this 5 per cent element of uncertainty. Even a linear measurement is cited as correct only to a certain fraction of a unit. No figure is ever given, or accepted, without an indication of its probable error and it is the calculation of this that makes it valuable. Probable errors are as important as the data themselves, which are not taken seriously without them. If the evaluation of error is so important in the exact sciences, it is even more so in our work. For mistakes, to us, have a particular importance, and to correct or eliminate them, we have first of all to know them.

So we come to a scientific principle which is also a path to perfection. We call it "the control of error." Whatever is done in school, by teachers, children, or others, there are bound to be mistakes. So we need this rule as a part of school life: namely, that what matters is not so much correction in itself as that each individual should become aware of his own errors. Each should have a means of checking, so that he can tell if he is right or not. I need to know whether I am doing well or badly, and if—at first—treated my own mistakes as unimportant, I have now become interested in them.

Children in schools of the usual kind often have no idea that they are making mistakes. They make them unconsciously and with complete indifference, because it is not their business to correct them but the teacher's! How far this is from our own idea of freedom!

But, unless I can correct myself, I shall have to seek the help of someone else, who may not know any better than I do. How much better it is if I can recognize my own mistakes, and then correct them! If anything is likely to make the character indecisive, it is the inability to control matters without having to seek advice. This begets a discouraging sense of inferiority and a lack of confidence in one's self.

What we know as a "control of error" is any kind of indicator which tells us whether we are going toward our goal, or away from it. Supposing I want to visit a certain town, but do not know the way. This happens often enough in daily life. For safety I consult a map, and also I find signposts *en route*. Seeing one which says, "Ahmedabad—two miles," I feel reassured. But if, all of a sudden, I see one saying, "Bombay—fifty miles," then I know I am wrong. The map and signposts are a help, without which I should have had to ask the way and would have received—as likely as not—contradictory answers. Reliable guidance, and the possibility of checking as we go, are the indispensable conditions for getting anywhere.

So, what science and practical life both need must surely be accepted from the start as necessary in education. This is the possibility of "recognizing one's own mistakes." We must provide this *as well* as instruction and materials on which to work. The power to make progress comes in large measure from having freedom and an assured path along which to go; but to this must also be added some way of knowing if, and when, we have left the path. If this principle be realized, both in school and in daily life, then it does not matter whether teachers and mothers are perfect or not. Errors made by adults have a certain interest, and children sympathize with them, but in a wholly detached way. It becomes for them one of the natural aspects of life, and the fact that we can all make mistakes stirs a deep feeling of affection in their hearts; it is one more reason for the union between mother and child. Mistakes bring us closer and make us better friends. Fraternity is born more easily on the road of error than on that of perfection. A "perfect person" is unable to change. If two "perfect people" are put together they invariably quarrel, because neither can comprehend the other nor tolerate any differences.

It will be remembered that one of the first exercises done by our children is that with a set of cylinders of equal height but varying diameter, which fit into corresponding sockets in a block of wood. The first thing is to realize that all are different; the second is to hold them by the knob at the top of each, using the thumb and first two fingers. The child begins fitting them one at a time into their sockets, but finds when he comes to the end that he has made a mistake. One cylinder is left which is too large for the only remaining hole, while some of the others fit too loosely. The child looks again and studies them all more closely. He is now faced by a problem. There is that cylinder left over, which shows that he has made a mistake. Well, it is just this that adds interest to the game and makes him repeat it time after time. So this piece of apparatus meets two requirements: (1) that of improving the child's perceptions, and (2) that of providing him with a control of error.

Our apparatus is always designed to have this property of offering visible and tangible checks. A little one of two may start using it, and quickly gets the idea of correcting his own mistakes. This sets his feet upon the path to perfection.

By daily practice he becomes sure of himself. But this does not mean he is perfect already, only that he acquires a sense of his abilities, and this bestirs in him the desire to try.

The child might say, "I am not perfect, I am not omnipotent, but this much I can do and I know it. I also know that I can make mistakes and correct myself, thus finding my way."

So here we have prudence, certitude and experience; a sure *viaticum* for the journey through life. To give this sense of security is not so simple as one might think; nor is it easy to set children upon a pathway toward perfection. To tell a person he is clever or clumsy, bright, stupid, good or bad, is a form of betrayal. The child must see for himself what he can do, and it is important to give him not only the means of education but also to supply him with indicators which tell him his mistakes.

Let us watch a somewhat older child who has been educated in this way. He works out sums in arithmetic, but is always shown how to check the answer, and this he forms a habit of doing. The checking often attracts him even more than the sum! The same thing happens in reading. In one exercise the child puts cards with names on them against corresponding objects. As a check, there is a card kept apart on which the same objects are pictured with their names written beneath them. The child's greatest pleasure is to use this to see if he has made any mistakes.

If in the daily routine of school we always arrange for errors to become perceptible, this is to place us on a path to perfection. The child's interest in doing better, and his own constant checking and testing, are so important to him that his progress is assured. His very nature tends towards exactitude and the ways of obtaining it appeal to him. A little girl in one of our schools saw a "reading command" worded like this: "Go outside, close the door, and come back." She studied it intently and then moved to obey, but she stopped in mid-career and went to the teacher. "How do I come back if I have shut the door?"

"You are quite right," said the teacher. "It was my mistake," and she rewrote the sentence.

"Yes," the child said with a smile, "now I can do it."

From all this awareness of mistakes, there springs up a kind of brotherhood. Errors divide men, but their correction is a means of union. It becomes a matter of general interest to correct errors wherever they may be found. The error itself becomes interesting. It becomes a link, and is certainly a bond of fellowship between human beings. It helps especially to bring harmony between children and adults. To detect some small error in a grown-up person does not produce lack of respect in the child or loss of dignity in the grownup. The error becomes impersonal and is then amenable to control.

In this way, small things lead to great.

25

The Three Levels of Obedience

Discussions on character training usually turn upon the questions of will and obedience. These, in the minds of most people, are opposed ideas, since education is so largely directed towards the suppression or bending of the child's will, and the substitution for it of the teacher's will, which demands from the child unquestioning obedience.

Let me try to clarify these ideas, basing my views not on opinions, but on observed facts. But first it must be noted what a great confusion there is in this field of thought. As we saw in Chapter 8, there are theories which suggest that man's will proceeds from a great universal power (*horme*), and that this universal force is not physical, but is the force of life itself in the process of evolution. It drives every form of life irresistibly towards evolution, and from it come the impulses to action. But evolution does not occur by luck, or by chance, but is governed by fixed laws, and if man's life is an expression of that force, his behaviour must be moulded by it.

In the little child's life, as soon as he makes an action deliberately, of his own accord, this force has begun to enter into his consciousness. What we call his will has begun to develop, and this process continues henceforward, but only as a result of experience. Hence, we are beginning to think of the will not as something inborn, but as something which has to be developed and, because it is a part of nature, this development can only occur in obedience to natural laws.

Further confusion springs from the belief that children's natural actions are bound to be disorderly and even violent. Usually this belief is based on the fact that people seeing a child act in a disorderly way, always assume that these actions proceed from his will. But this is far from the truth. Such actions have no place in the universal *horme*. Suppose, in adult behaviour, we took a man's convulsions for his voluntary acts, or supposed that all the things he did in a fury were rational. This would be silly. In fact, our habitual use of the word "will" implies that there is an end, or goal, in view, and that there are difficulties to be overcome. If, instead, we found that our voluntary actions almost always consisted in disorderly movements, then we too should feel the need of dominating the will, or of "breaking" it, as people used to say, and, having found this to be necessary, the logical result would be to substitute our will for the child's and oblige him to obey us.

But the real facts of the situation are that the will does not lead to disorder and violence. These are signs of emotional disturbance and suffering. Under proper conditions, the will is a force which impels activities beneficial to life. Nature imposes on the child the task of growing up, and his will leads him to make progress and to develop his powers.

A will in agreement with what the individual is doing finds the path open for its conscious development: Our children choose their work spontaneously, and by repeating the work they have chosen, they develop an awareness of their actions. That which at first was but a vital impulse (*horme*) has become a deliberate act. The little child's first movements were instinctive. Now, he acts consciously and voluntarily, and with this comes an awakening of his spirit.

The child himself feels the difference, and one of them has expressed it in a fashion which will always be one of our most treasured memories. A lady of high rank once paid the school a visit and, being old-fashioned in her views, she said to a little boy, "So this is the school where you do as you like?"

"No, ma'am," said the child. "It is not that we do as we like, but we like what we do." The child had grasped the subtle difference between doing a thing because it gives one pleasure, and enjoying a piece of work that one has decided to do.

One thing ought to be very clear. Conscious will is a power which develops with use and activity. We must aim at cultivating the will, not at breaking it. The will can be broken in a moment. Its development is a slow process that evolves through a continuous activity in relationship with the environment. It is so much easier to destroy. The devastation of a building, by bombardment or earthquake, can be wrought in a few seconds. But how hard it was to construct. For this was needed a knowledge of the laws of equilibrium, of the strength of materials, and even of the rules of art, to make it please the eye.

If all this be required to set up a lifeless structure, how much more is needed to construct the human spirit? But this is a building which constructs itself in secrecy. So its builder can be neither the mother nor the teacher. Nor are they even the architects. All they can do is to help the work of creation which is going on in their presence. To help: this must be their task and their aim. Yet they still have the power to break the will and can destroy it by tyranny. Many prejudices converge on this point making the issue obscure. It is worthwhile to clear it up.

The commonest prejudice in ordinary education is that everything can be accomplished by talking (by appealing, that is, to the child's ear), or by holding one's self up as a model to be imitated (a kind of appeal to the eye), while the truth is that the personality can only develop by making use of its own powers. The child is usually considered as a receptive being instead of as an active being, and this happens in every department of his life. Even imagination is so treated; fairy tales and stories of enchanted princesses are told with a view to encouraging the child's imagination. But when he listens to these and other kinds of stories, he is only receiving impressions. He is not developing his own powers to imagine constructively. That creative imagination which has so high a place among man's mental powers, is not at work in him. This error, when applied to the will, is even more serious, for the ordinary school not only denies the child every opportunity for using his will, but it directly obstructs and inhibits its expression. Every protest on the child's part is treated as rebellion, and one may truly say that the educator does everything possible to destroy the child's will.

Meanwhile, the principle of educating by example causes the teacher—apart from her storytelling—to offer herself as the model to be copied, so that imagination and will both remain idle, and the children are reduced to watching what the teacher does and listening to her words.

We must free ourselves finally from these prejudices and have the courage to face reality.

In old time education, the master reasoned in a way that might seem fairly logical. He said, "To educate, I must be good and perfect. I know what should or should not be done, so if the children imitate me, and obey me, all will be well." Obedience was the fundamental secret of everything. I forget which of the famous educators it was who enunciated this maxim: All the virtues of childhood can be summed up in a single virtue, obedience.

This made the lot of the teacher an easy and even a proud one. He was able to argue: "This person before me is empty and distorted. I will straighten him and change him into one like myself." And in this way he attributed to himself those powers of which we read in the Bible, when it says: "God made man in his own image."

Naturally, the adult does not realize that he is putting himself in God's place, and he forgets still more those other Biblical words which tell us how it was that the devil became the devil, that is to say, because in his pride he wanted to take God's place.

Within the child is the work of a creator much more exalted than the teacher, the mother or the father, yet in spite of this he is at their mercy. Teachers, at one time; used the cane to enforce their orders, and not long ago, in a highly civilized country, the teachers collectively made a public protest in these terms: "If you want us to give up the cane, then we must stop trying to teach." Even in the Bible, among the proverbs of Solomon, we find that famous text saying that parents do wrong who spare the rod, since this condemns their child to hell! Discipline is made to rest on threats and fear, so we end by concluding that the disobedient child is wicked and the obedient one good.

If, in this present age of freedom and of democratic theories, we reflect on this attitude, we are bound to perceive that the kind of education still in vogue condemns the teacher to be a dictator. Except, of course, that dictators (being of necessity far more intelligent than teachers) are wont to combine with their orders some little originality and a modicum of imagination, while teachers of the older school hold firmly to irrational rules and have little to guide them but illusion and prejudice. Between the tyranny of dictators and the tyranny of teachers there is a real difference, for while the first may use harsh means constructively, the same means in the hands of a second can only be destructive.

The basic error is to suppose that a person's will must necessarily be broken before it can obey, meaning before it can accept and follow another person's directions. Were this reasoning to be applied to intellectual education, we should have to destroy a person's mind before we could give him any knowledge.

But when people have fully developed their own powers of volition and then freely chosen to follow another person's orders, we have something very different. This kind of obedience is a form of homage, a recognition of superiority, and the teacher who receives it from her children may well feel complimented.

Will and obedience then go hand in hand, inasmuch as the will is a prior foundation in the order of development, and obedience is a later stage resting on this foundation. The word "obedience" now has a higher meaning than the one usually given to it. It may well imply a sublimation of the individual's own will.

It is easy, in fact, to identify obedience as a natural phenomenon of human life; it is a normal human characteristic. In our children we may watch its development as a kind of unfolding. It shows itself spontaneously and unexpectedly at the end of a long process of maturation.

Indeed, if the human soul did not possess this quality, if men had never acquired, by some form of evolutionary process, this capacity for obedience, social life would be impossible. The most casual glance at what is happening in the world is enough to show us how obedient people are. This kind of obedience is the real reason why vast masses of human beings can be hurled so easily to destruction. It is an uncontrolled form of obedience, an obedience which brings whole nations to ruin. There is no lack of obedience in our world: quite the contrary! Obedience, as a natural aspect of the soul's development, is plain enough. What, unhappily, is absent is the control of obedience.

What we have been able to observe in children under conditions of life designed to help them in their natural development, has shown us very clearly the growth of obedience as one of the most striking features of the human character. Our observations throw much light on this subject.

Obedience is seen as something which develops in the child in much the same way as other aspects of his character. At first it is dictated purely by the *hormic* impulse, then it rises to the level of consciousness, and thereafter it goes on developing, stage by stage, till it comes under the control of the conscious will.

Let us try to depict what obedience really means to a person. At bottom, that is what it has always meant: teachers and parents tell the children what to do, and the children respond by carrying out their orders.

But if we study the natural unfolding of this obedience, we find that it occurs in three stages, or levels. At the first level, the child obeys sometimes, but not always, and this may strike one as capricious, but it has to be subjected to a deeper analysis.

Obedience does not depend solely on what we are accustomed to call "good will." On the contrary, the child's actions in the first period of his life are controlled by *horme* alone. This is manifest to all, and it is a level lasting till the end of the first year. Between the first and the sixth year, this aspect becomes less marked, as the child unfolds his consciousness and acquires self-control. During this period, the child's obedience is closely connected with the stages of ability that he happens to have reached: To carry out an order, one must already possess some degree of maturity and a measure of the special skill that it may need. So obedience, at that time, has to be judged in relation to the powers that exist. It would be absurd to order a person to walk on his nose, because that is physiologically impossible; but it is equally absurd to demand of an illiterate that he write a letter. Hence we first have to know whether the child's obedience is practically possible at the level of development he has reached.

Before the child is three he cannot obey unless the order he receives corresponds with one of his vital urges. This is because he has not yet formed himself. He is still busy in the unconscious building up of the mechanisms needed by his own personality, and he has not yet reached the stage when these are so firmly founded that they can serve his wishes and be directed by him consciously. To exercise mastery over them is to have reached a new level of development. In fact, the ordinary behaviour of grown-ups living with children shows an implicit acceptance of the fact that obedience from a child of two is not to be expected.

By instinct and logic (or perhaps through the mutual sharing of life with children for thousands of years) the adult knows that all one can do at this age is to forbid, more or less violently, those actions that the child continues to do notwithstanding.

Yet obedience is not always negative. It consists, above all, in acting in accordance with the will of someone else. While the life of a slightly older child is no longer in the primitive preparatory phase of the child from 0 to 3 (conducted, as we have seen, in the sanctuary of his inner life) nevertheless, in this later period, we still meet with similar stages. Even after three, the little child must have developed certain qualities before he is able to obey. He cannot, all of a sudden, act in conformity with another person's will, nor can he grasp, from one day to the next, the reason for doing what we require of him. Certain kinds of progress come from interior formations which have several phases to pass through. While these formations are going on, the child may sometimes succeed in performing an action on request, but this means he is using an interior acquisition which has only just been formed, and it is only when the acquisition is firmly established that his will can always make use of it.

Something like this happens when the child is first urging himself to acquire the elements of movement. When he is about one year old, he ventures to take the first footsteps, but he often falls and for a short while he does not repeat the experiment. But when the walking mechanism is secure, he can use it at any moment.

Here, then, is another point of the first importance. The child's obedience in this stage is dependent, above all, on the development of his powers. He may succeed in obeying an order once, but he cannot do it next time. This is often thought to be due to malice, and the teacher's insistence or scolding may easily impede the development that was going on. A point of much interest, connected with this, may be found in the life of Pestalozzi, the famous Swiss educator, whose work still exerts a profound influence on schools the world over. Pestalozzi was the first to introduce a fatherly note into the treatment of school children. He invariably sympathized with their difficulties and was most ready to condone or forgive. But there was one thing excluded from pardon, and that was caprice: he could not tolerate the child who obeyed one minute and not the next. If the child had once done what was asked, it meant he could do it if he wished, and Pestalozzi accepted no excuses for failure to do it again. This was the one occasion on which his kindness failed him. If even Pestalozzi felt like this, how often must other teachers be making the same mistake?

There is nothing more harmful than discouragement just when new formations are being made. If the child is not yet master of his actions, if he cannot obey even his own will, so much the less can he obey the will of someone else. That is why he may succeed in obeying sometimes, but not always. Nor is it only in infancy that this may happen. How often a beginner in music plays a piece beautifully the first time, but if asked to repeat it the next day he fails miserably. It is not that the will is absent, but that the skill and sureness of the accomplished artist have not yet been formed.

So, what we call the first level of obedience is that in which the child can obey, but not always. It is a period in which obedience and disobedience seem to be combined!

The second level is when the child can always obey, or rather, when there are no longer any obstacles deriving from his lack of control. His powers are now consolidated and can be directed not only by his own will, but by the will of another: This is a great step forward in the path of obedience. It is like being able to translate from this language to that. The child can absorb another person's wishes and express them in his own behaviour. And this is the highest form of obedience to which present day education ever aspires. The ordinary teacher asks only that she be obeyed.

But the child, when allowed to develop in accordance with the laws of his nature, goes much further than this: further than we should ever have expected.

He goes on to the *third level of obedience.*

This does not stop at the point where he just makes use of a newly acquired ability, but his obedience is turned towards a personality whose superiority he feels. It is as if the child had become aware that the teacher could do things beyond his own powers, and had said to himself, "Here is someone so far above me that she can exert an influence on my mind and make me as clever as she is. She acts inside me!" To feel like this seems to fill the child with joy. That one can take direction from this superior life is a sudden discovery that brings with it a new kind of enthusiasm, and the child becomes anxious and impatient to obey. A wonderful, yet natural phenomenon; is there anything we can compare it with? On another plane it resembles, perhaps, the instinct of the dog who loves his master, and gives effect to his will by obedience. He gazes intently at the ball his master shows him, and when this is thrown to a distance, runs for it and brings it back triumphantly. Then he waits for the next order. He longs to be given orders, and runs joyfully to obey them, wagging his tail. The child's third level of obedience is not unlike this. Certain it is that he obeys with astonishing readiness, and seems anxious to do so.

Some interesting proofs have been provided by a directress of ten years' experience. She had a class which she conducted extremely well, but often she could not restrain herself from giving suggestions. One day she said, "Put everything away before you go home tonight." The children did not wait for her to finish the sentence, but directly they heard her say, "Put everything away," they started to do it with great care and speed. Then, with surprise, they heard the words, "when you go home tonight." Their obedience had become so prompt that the teacher had to be very careful how she expressed herself. In fact, she ought on this occasion to have said, "Before you go home tonight, put everything away."

Things like this kept happening, she said, every time she expressed herself without enough thought. The promptitude of the children's response gave her a feeling of responsibility. And this was a strange new experience, for one usually thinks it natural for the person in charge to give what orders they like. Instead, she felt her position of authority to be quite a burden. So readily did the children make "the silence" that it was enough for her to write "Silence" on the blackboard, and before she had finished the letter, S, everyone had become still.

My own experience (and it was this that led me to introduce the "Silence Game") was another proof, but this time obedience took on a collective aspect. A marvellous and quite unexpected unity grew up by which a whole group of children almost identified itself with me.[1]

Perfect silence can only be obtained if all those present are willing. A single person can break it. Success therefore depends on conscious and united action. From this comes a sense of social solidarity.

The game of silence offers us a means of testing the children's will power. We found that this grew as the game was repeated and the periods of silence became longer. Then we added a kind of "call" in which the child's name was barely murmured, and each child, on hearing his name, had to come up quietly, while the others stayed motionless as before. Those called moved very slowly in their efforts to make no noise, so one can imagine how long the last child had to keep still, while awaiting his turn! It was incredible what will power these children developed. The exercise called for an inhibition of impulse as well as for the control of movement. Much of this method rests on that. There is, on the one hand, freedom to choose and to be diligent, and on the other hand there is inhibition. Children under these conditions can use their will power, both for the purposes of action and of restraint from action. They ended by forming a group that was truly admirable. We saw obedience appear among them, because all the elements for it had been prepared.

The power to obey is the last phase in the development of the will, which in its turn has made obedience possible. Among our children the level reached is so high that the teacher is obeyed immediately, whatever her request may be. She feels she must be cautious not to exploit for her own ends so selfless a dedication. And she comes to realize what kind of qualities a person in charge should have. A good manager does not have to be assertive in manner, but he must have a deep sense of responsibility.

REFERENCE

1. See *The Discovery of the Child*.

26

Discipline and the Teacher

The inexperienced teacher, filled with enthusiasm and faith in this inner discipline which she expects to appear in our little community, finds herself faced by no light problems.

She understands and believes that the children must be free to choose their own occupations just as they must never be interrupted in their spontaneous activities. No work may be imposed—no threats, no rewards, no punishments. The teacher must be quiet and passive, waiting patiently and almost withdrawing herself from the scene, so as to efface her own personality and thus allow plently of room for the child's spirit to expand. She has put out a great deal of the apparatus, almost all of it, but this instead of diminishing the disorder increases it alarmingly.

Are the principles she has learned mistaken? No. Between her theories and the results to which they lead, something is missing. It is the teacher's practical experience. At this point the inexpert beginner needs help and advice. It is not unlike that which happens to the young physician, or to anyone who has mastered certain ideas and principles, and who then finds himself alone with the living facts which seem to him a good deal more mysterious than the unknown quantities in a mathematical equation!

Let us always remember that inner discipline is something to come, and not something already present. Our task is to show the way to discipline. Discipline is born when the child concentrates his attention on some object that attracts him and which provides him not only with a useful exercise but with a control of error. Thanks to these exercises, a wonderful integration takes place in the infant soul, as a result of which the child becomes calm, radiantly happy, busy, forgetful of himself and, in consequence, indifferent to prizes or material rewards. These little conquerors of themselves and of the world about them are real supermen, who show us the divine worth of man's soul. The teacher's happy task is to show them the path to perfection, furnishing the means and removing the obstacles, beginning with those which she herself is likely to present (for the teacher can be the greatest obstacle of all). If discipline had already arrived our work would hardly be needed; the child's instinct would be a safe enough guide enabling him to deal with every difficulty.

But the child of three, when he first comes to school, is a fighter on the verge of being vanquished; he has already adopted a defensive attitude which masks his deeper nature. The higher energies which could guide him to a disciplined peace and a divine wisdom, are asleep. All that remains active is a superficial personality which exhausts itself in clumsy movements, vague ideas, and the effort to resist or avoid adult constraint.

But wisdom and discipline are waiting to be awakened in the child. Oppresion has worked against him, but he is not yet completely defeated or so fixed in his deviations that our efforts will be vain. The school must give the child's spirit space and opportunity for expansion. At the same time, the teacher must remember that his habitual reactions of defence, and in general the lowered characteristics which his nature has acquired, are obstacles to the unfolding of his spiritual life and from these the child will have to free himself.

This is the starting point of education. If the teacher cannot recognize the difference between pure impulse, and the spontaneous energies which spring to life in a tranquillized spirit, then her action will bear no fruit. The true foundation of the teacher's efficiency consists in being able to distinguish between two kinds of activities, each of which has the appearance of spontaneity, because the child in both acts of his own free will, but which are in fact directly opposed. Only when the teacher has learned to discriminate can she become an observer and a guide. The necessary preparation is not different from that of the doctor, who must learn above all how to distinguish the physiologically normal state from the pathological, or diseased, one. If he cannot separate health from sickness, if all he can do is to know the living from the dead, he will never come to recognize the still finer distinctions between different pathological states, and so he will remain unable to diagnose illness correctly. This power to know good from bad is the light which disperses the shadows hiding the path to that discipline which leads to perfection. Is it possible to specify the symptoms or syndromes, with sufficient clarity and precision to permit even a theoretical description of the stages through which the infant soul has to pass in its ascent towards discipline? Yes, it is possible, and some landmarks can be set up as guides to the teacher.

Let us consider the child of three or four, who has not yet been touched by any of the factors which can act upon him to produce inner discipline. Simple description enables one to recognize three types and their characteristics:

1. Disorder of the voluntary movements. This does not refer to the intentions behind the movements, but to the movements themselves, which show a fundamental disharmony or lack of coordination. This symptom, which means far more to the specialist in nervous disorders than it does to a philosopher, is of the greatest importance. When a patient is seriously ill (for example, in the first stages of a creeping paralysis) the physician will note the most trifling defects of voluntary movement, knowing that these are fundamental. On them he will base his diagnosis far more than on mental aberrations or disorderly behaviour, which are also among the symptoms of this disease. The child who is clumsy in his movements will show other traits, such as

ill-mannered behaviour, jerky actions, wriggling movements and shouting, but these have less diagnostic value. An education which brings about a delicate coordination of the earliest movements will of itself diminish disorder in voluntary movement. Rather than try to correct the thousand and one visible signs of a deviation from normal development, the teacher needs only to offer, in an interesting form, means for the intelligent development of more harmonious movements.

2. Another feature that always accompanies the disorder of which we have spoken, is the child's difficulty, or inability, to concentrate his attention on real objects. His mind prefers to wander in the realm of fantasy. While playing games with stones or dried leaves, he talks as if he were preparing delicious banquets on immense tables, and his imagination will probably take the most extravagant forms when he grows up. The more the mind is divorced from its normal function the more exhausted it becomes, and useless as a servant of the spirit; which needs to have as its goal the development of the inner life. Unfortunately, many people think that these fanciful activities which disorganize the personality are those which develop the spiritual life. They maintain that fantasy is creative in itself; on the contrary, it is nothing by itself, or just shadows, pebbles and dried leaves.

The spiritual life is really built upon the fundamental basis of a unified personality, well attuned to the outer world. The wandering mind that breaks away from reality, breaks away also—it must be said—from healthy normality. In the world of fantasy, wherein it thrives, there is no control of error, nothing to coordinate thought. Attention to real things, with all the future applications that derive from this, becomes impossible. This life of the imagination—falsely so-called—is an atrophy of organs on the functioning of which the spiritual life depends. The teacher who tries to focus the child's attention on something real—but making reality accessible and attractive—who succeeds, let us say, in interesting him in the laying of a real table, and the serving of real food, speaks with the voice of a trumpet to the vague mind, wandering far from the pathway of its own good. And the coordination of perfected movements, together with the recapture of an attention which has escaped from reality, is all that is needed to effect a cure.

We are not called upon to correct one by one all the signs of a fundamental deviation; as soon as the ability of fixing the mind on real things is acquired, the mind will return to its state of health, and begin again to function normally.

3. The third phenomenon, which is closely allied to the other two, is the tendency to imitate, which becomes ever readier and more rapid. It is a sign of deep seated weakness, a magnification of those characteristics which would be normal in children of two. (The imitativeness of much younger children is quite different, and has been dealt with already.)[1] This tendency is the sign of a will which has not prepared its instruments, has found no proper course, but merely follows in the wake of others. The child is not following the path to perfection, but is at the mercy of every wind, like a ship without a rudder. Anyone who watches a two-year-old, with the limited range of ideas suggested by imitation as his whole sum of knowledge, will recognize the degenerated form of mind of which I am speaking. It is a form connected with disorder, with mental instability, and it tends to lower the child, like going downstairs.

A child has only to do something wrong or noisy; for example, throw himself on the floor, laughing and shouting, and many, or perhaps all the children will follow his example, or do something worse. The foolish act is multiplied in the group, and may even extend outside the classroom. This kind of "gregarious instinct" produces a collective disorder which is the opposite of social life, for that is founded on work and the orderly behaviour of individuals. In a crowd, the spirit of imitation spreads and enhances individual defects; it is the point of least resistance, where degeneration originates.

The further this kind of degeneration goes, the harder it becomes for the children to obey a person calling them to better things. But set them once upon the right track, and an end soon comes to the manifold consequences of the single source of this disorder.

When called on to direct a class of such children, the teacher may find herself in an agonizing situation if she is armed with no other weapon than the basic idea of offering the children the means of development and of letting them express themselves freely. The little hell that has begun to break loose in these children will drag to itself everything within reach, and the teacher, if she remains passive, will be overwhelmed by confusion and an almost unbelievable noise. On finding herself in such a situation—whether it be due to inexperience, or to overrigid (or oversimple) principles and ideas—the teacher must remember the powers which lie dormant in these divinely pure and generous little souls. She must help these tiny beings, who are scampering downhill towards a precipice, to turn about and climb again. She must call to them, wake them up, by her voice and thought. A vigorous and firm call is the only true act of kindness toward these little minds. Do not fear to destroy evil; it is only good that we must fear to destroy. Just as we must call a child's name before he can answer, so we must call the soul vigorously if we wish to awaken it. The teacher must remove her apparatus from the school and take away the principles from what she has learned; then she must face this question of the call, practically and alone. Only her intelligence can solve the problem, which will be different in every case. The teacher knows the fundamental symptoms and the certain remedies; she knows the theory of the treatment. All the rest depends on her. The good doctor, like the good teacher, is a person. Neither of them are machines, merely prescribing drugs, or applying pedagogical methods. The details must be left to the judgement of the teacher, who is also just starting on a new path. It is for her to judge whether it is better for her to raise her voice amid the general hubbub, or to whisper to a few children, so that the others become curious to hear, and peace is restored again. A chord played loudly on the piano may end the discord like a whiplash.

A teacher of experience never has grave disorder in her class because, before she draws aside to leave the children free, she watches and directs them for some time, preparing them in a negative sense, that is to say, by eliminating their uncontrolled movements. To this end there is a series of preparatory exercises which the teacher should bear in mind, and those children whose minds are wandering from reality will come to feel what a powerful help the teacher can give them. Calm, firm and patient, her voice reaches their hearts in praise or exhortation. Some exercises are particularly useful, such as the one to put all the chairs and tables in their proper places without making any noise; to make a row of chairs and sit on them; to run from end to end of the room on tiptoe. If a teacher is really sure of herself this alone will be enough, before she can say, "Now, children, let us all keep quite still," and a calm will be born as if by magic. The simplest exercises of practical life will lead the little wandering spirits back to the solid earth of real work, and this reclaims them. Little by little the teacher will offer the apparatus, though she will never place it freely at their disposal till they understand its use.

Now we see the class calm. The children come into contact with reality; their occupations have a definite aim, such as to dust a table, remove a stain, go to the cupboard, take a piece of the apparatus, use it properly, and so on.

It is clear that the capacity for free choice is strengthened by exercise. Usually the teacher is satisfied, but it seems to her that the apparatus established by the Montessori method is insufficient and she feels the necessity of adding more. In a week a child has used and re-used all the material. Many of the schools get no further than this.

One, and only one, factor betrays the insecurity of this apparent order, and threatens the collapse of the whole: it is that the children keep going from one thing to another. They do each thing once; then they go and fetch something else.

There is an endless stream going to and from the cupboard. Not one of these children, in the world into which he has descended, has yet found an interest strong enough to awaken the divine and powerful nature that is his. His personality is not being exercised, he is not developing, is not growing stronger. In these fugitive contacts, the outer world cannot exercise on him that influence which brings harmony to the spirit. The child is like a bee flying from flower to flower, without finding one on which to stop, from which it can take the nectar and be satisfied. He will not be able to work till he feels the awakening within him of that tremendous instinctive activity which is destined to construct his character and his mind.

The teacher, when this unstable situation has been reached, feels her work to be difficult; what is more she keeps running from child to child, thus spreading the contagion of her own anxiety and wearisome lack of calm. Many of the children, who are tired and bored, play with the material as soon as her back is turned, and use it in the most stupid ways. While the teacher is busy with one child, the others misbehave. The moral and intellectual progress so loyally awaited, does not occur.

The appearance of discipline which may be obtained is actually very fragile, and the teacher, who is constantly warding off a disorder which she feels to be "in the air," is kept in a state of tension. The great majority of teachers, in the absence of sufficient training and experience, end by thinking that the "new child," so eagerly expected and of whom so much has been said, is nothing but a myth or an ideal. They may also conclude that a class held together by such an effort of nervous energy, is both tiring for the teacher and not profitable for the children.

It is necessary for the teacher to be able to understand the children's condition. These little spirits are in a transitory phase. The real door to progress is not yet open to them. They are knocking and waiting outside. In fact, there is little progress of any kind to be seen. The situation is nearer to chaos than discipline. The work of children like this is bound to be imperfect. Their elementary coordinated movements lack strength and grace, while their actions are capricious. In comparison with the first stage, when they were out of touch with reality, they have made hardly any progress. It is like the state of convalescence after an illness. We have here a crucial moment in development and the teacher must carry out two different functions: she must supervise the children and also give them individual lessons. This means she must present the material regularly, showing its exact use. General surveillance and individual teaching, given with precision, are two ways in which the teacher can help the child's development. In this period she must take care never to turn her back on the class while she is dealing with a single child. Her presence must be felt by all these spirits, wandering and in search of life. These lessons, exact and fascinating, given in an intimate way to each child separately, are the teacher's offering to the depths of the child's soul. Then, one day, one of these tiny spirits will awaken, the inner "self' of some child will go out to an object which it will temporarily possess, his attention will focus on the repetition of an exercise the doing of which brings increased skill, and the child's radiant and contented manner will show that his spirit has been reborn.

Free choice is one of the highest of all the mental processes. Only the child deeply aware of his need for practice and for the development of his spiritual life, can really be said to choose freely. It is not possible to speak of free choice when all kinds of external stimuli attract a child at the same time and, having no will power, he responds to every call, passing restlessly from one thing to another. This is one of the most important distinctions that the teacher must be able to make. The child who cannot yet obey an interior guide is not that free being who sets out to follow the long and narrow path towards perfection. He is still a slave to superficial sensations which leave him at the mercy of his environment. His spirit bounces back and forth like a ball. Manhood is born within him when his soul becomes aware of itself, when he sets himself a task, finds his way and chooses.

This simple but sublime phenomenon is to be seen in all created beings. Every living creature possesses the power to choose, in a complex and many-sided environment, that thing, and only that, which is conducive to its life.

The roots of every plant seek out, from among the many substances which the soil contains, only those which they need. The choice of the insect is not indeterminate but it fastens on the particular flower made to receive its visits. In man the same marvellous discernment is apparent but in his case it is no longer instinctive but has to be acquired. Yet children, especially in their first years, have an intimate sensitiveness as a spiritual necessity. A misdirected or repressive education can cause this to disappear and to be replaced by a sort of slavery of the outer senses to every object in the neighbourhood. We ourselves have lost this deep and vital sensitiveness, and in the presence of children in whom we see it reviving, we feel as if we were watching a mystery being unfolded. It shows itself in the delicate act of free choice, which a teacher untrained in observation can trample on before she even discerns it, much as an elephant tramples the budding flower about to blossom in its path.

The child whose attention has once been held by a chosen object, while he concentrates his whole self on the repetition of the exercise, is a delivered soul in the sense of the spiritual safety of which we speak. From this moment there is no need to worry about him except to prepare an environment which satisfies his needs, and to remove obstacles which may bar his way to perfection.

Before such attention and concentration have been attained, the teacher must learn to control herself so that the child's spirit shall be free to expand and show its powers; the essence of her duty is not to interrupt the child in his efforts. This is a moment in which the delicacy of the teacher's moral sensitiveness, acquired during her training, comes into play. She must learn that it is not easy to help, nor even, perhaps, to stand still and watch. Even when helping and serving the children, she must not cease to observe them, because the birth of concentration in a child is as delicate a phenomenon as the bursting of a bud into bloom. But she will not be watching with the aim of making her presence felt, or of helping the weaker ones by her own strength. She observes in order to recognize the child who has attained the power to concentrate and to admire the glorious rebirth of his spirit.

The child who concentrates is immensely happy; he ignores his neighbours or the visitors circulating about him. For the time being his spirit is like that of a hermit in the desert: a new consciousness has been born in him, that of his own individuality. When he comes out of his concentration, he seems to perceive the world anew as a boundless field for fresh discoveries. He also becomes aware of his classmates in whom he takes an affectionate interest. Love awakens in him for people and for things. He becomes friendly to everyone, ready to admire all that is beautiful. The spiritual process is plain: he detaches himself from the world in order to attain the power to unite himself with it. To admire the vastness of a panorama, do we not leave the town? Seen from an aeroplane, the earth is better disclosed to our eyes. So it is with the human spirit. To exist and mix with our fellow men we must sometimes retire into solitude and acquire strength, only then do we look with love on the creatures who are our fellows. The saint in solitude prepares himself to view with wisdom and justice those social necessities which remain unknown to the masses of men. It is the preparation made in the desert that prepares the great mission of love and peace.

The child adopts with simplicity an attitude of deep seclusion, and there forms in him also a strong and calm character radiating love to those about him. From this attitude is born the sacrifice of self, regular work obedience, and, together with these, the joy of life gushing out clear as a spring from its rocky bed, a joy and a help for all those who dwell near by.

The result of concentration is an awakening of the social sense, and the teacher must be ready to follow this. She will be a person to whom the hearts of these children will turn directly they are awakened. They will "discover" her, just as they now notice the blue sky and the hardly perceptible scent of flowers hidden in the grass.

The demands of these children, rich in their enthusiasms and explosive in their amazing rush forward, may overwhelm an unpractised teacher. As in the first stage, when she must not waste time on the many confused actions of the children but focus entirely on the indications they give of fundamental requirements, so now she must not be overcome by the innumerable signs they show of this moral wealth and beauty. She must always aim at something simple and central, something which behaves like the hinge of a door. Naturally, this is hidden, for it functions independently and without relation to the decorations of the door which it controls.

The teacher's mission always has for its aim something constant and exact. She begins by feeling unnecessary, for the children's progress is disproportionate to the part she has played, or to what she has done. She sees the children becoming ever more independent in choosing their work and in the richness of their powers of expression. Sometimes their progress seems miraculous. She feels worthy only to serve, in the humble sense of preparing the environment and keeping out of sight. She bears in mind the words of John the Baptist after the Messiah had been revealed to him: "He must grow while I diminish."

This, however, is the moment in which the child has the greatest need of her authority. When a child has accomplished something using his own intelligence and activity (for example he has just done a drawing, written a word, or done any other small piece of work), he runs to the teacher and asks her to say if it is all right. The child does not want to be told what to do or how to do it—he defends himself from such help. Choice and execution are the prerogatives and conquests of a liberated soul. But after he has done the work, he wants his teacher's approval.

The same instinct that makes children defend their

spiritual privacy—the obedience they give to the mysterious guiding voice that each seems to hear within himself—this same instinct leads them to submit their work to an external authority, so as to be sure they are following the right path. It makes us think of the first tottering steps of the baby, when he still needs to see an adult's outstretched arms waiting to catch him, although he may already have within him the power to begin walking and of learning to do it perfectly. The teacher must then respond with a word of approval, encouraging him with a smile, like that of a mother to her baby. For perfection and confidence must develop in the child from inner sources with which the teacher has nothing to do.

The child, in fact, once he feels sure of himself, will no longer seek the approval of authority after every step. He will go on piling up finished work of which the others know nothing, obeying merely the need to produce and perfect the fruits of his industry. What interests him is finishing his work, not to have it admired, nor to treasure it up as his own property. The noble instinct that drives him on is far removed from pride or avarice. Many visitors to our schools will remember how the teachers showed them the children's best work without pointing out who had done it. This apparent neglect comes from the knowledge that the children do not care. In any other kind of school a teacher would feel guilty if, when showing a child's lovely piece of work, she was not careful to introduce the doer. Should she forget to do so, she would hear a plaintive, "I did that!"

In one of our schools, the child who has done the admired piece of work is probably busy in a far corner on some new effort, and is only wanting to be left in peace. This is the period in which discipline becomes established: a form of active peace, of obedience and love, when work is perfected and multiplied, just as when the flowers in spring get their colours and prepare a distant harvest of sweet and nourishing fruit.

REFERENCE

1. See Chapter 15.

27

The Teacher's Preparation

The first step an intending Montessori teacher must take is to prepare herself. For one thing, she must keep her imagination alive; for while, in the traditional schools, the teacher sees the immediate behaviour of her pupils, knowing that she must look after them and what she has to teach, the Montessori teacher is constantly looking for a child who is not yet there. This is the main point of difference. The teacher, when she begins work in our schools, must have a kind of faith that *the child will reveal himself* through work. She must free herself from all preconceived ideas concerning the levels at which the children may be. The many different types of children (meaning they are more or less deviated) must not worry her. In her imagination she sees that single normalized type, which lives in a world of the spirit. The teacher must believe that this child before her will show his true nature when he finds a piece of work that attracts him. So what must she look out for? That one child or another will begin to concentrate. To this she must devote her energies, and her activities will change from stage to stage, as in a spiritual ascent. What she does will usually have three aspects.

First Stage. The teacher becomes the keeper and custodian of the environment. She attends to this instead of being distracted by the children's restlessness. From this will come healing, and the attraction that captures and polarizes the child's will. In our countries, where each wife has her own home, the wife tries to make the home as attractive as possible for herself and her husband. Instead of giving her whole attention to him, she gives much also to the house, so as to make surroundings in which a normal and constructive life can flourish. She tries to make the home a place of comfort and peace, with full and varied interests. The essential charm of a house is its cleanliness and order, with everything in its place, dusted, bright and cheerful. She makes this her first consideration. The teacher in the school must not do otherwise. All the apparatus is to be kept meticulously in order, beautiful and shining, in perfect condition. Nothing may be missing, so that to the child it always seems new, complete and ready for use. This means that the teacher also must be attractive, pleasing in appearance, tidy and clean, calm and dignified. These are ideals that each can realize in her own way, but let us always remember, when we present ourselves before children, that they are *"of the company of the elect."* The teacher's appearance is the first step to gaining the child's confidence and respect. The teacher should study her own movements, to make them as gentle and graceful as possible. The child of this age idealizes his mother. We may not know what kind of woman she is, but we often hear a child say, when he sees a pretty woman, "How lovely she is —just like my mummy!" Quite possibly the mother is not at all beautiful, but she is so to the child, and everyone he admires is, to him, as beautiful as she. So, care for one's own person must form part of the environment in which the child lives; the teacher herself is the most vital part of his world.

The teacher's first duty is therefore to watch over the environment, and this takes precedence over all the rest. Its influence is indirect, but unless it be well done there will be no effective and permanent results of any kind, physical, intellectual or spiritual.

Second Stage. Having considered the environment, we must ask how the teacher shall behave toward the children. What can we do with these disorderly little people, with these confused and uncertain little minds that we hope to attract and cause to fasten upon work? Sometimes I use a word easily misunderstood: the teacher must be seductive, she must entice the children. Were the environment to be neglected, the furniture dusty, the apparatus broken and out of place, and if—above all—the teacher herself were slovenly, ill-mannered and harsh to the children, then the basic essentials would be lacking for the goal at which she aims. The teacher, in this first period, before concentration has shown itself, must be like the flame which heartens all by its warmth, enlivens and invites. There is no need to fear that she will interrupt some important psychic process, since these have not yet begun. Before concentration occurs, the directress may do more or less what she thinks best; she can interfere with the children's activities as much as she deems necessary.

I once read of a saint who tried to gather together some children whom he had found abandoned in the streets of a city in which the people's conduct was far from refined. What did he do? He tried to amuse them. This is what the teacher must do at this juncture. She can tell stories, have some games and singing, use nursery rhymes and poetry. The teacher who has a gift for charming the children can have them do various exercises, which, even if they have no great value educationally, are useful in calming them. Everyone knows that a lively teacher attracts more than a dull one, and we can all be lively if we try. Anyone, for example, can say cheerfully, "Let's move all the furniture today!" and work with the children, encouraging and praising them all in a bright and pleasing manner. Or she may say, "What about this brass water jug? It needs polishing." Or, again, "Let's go in the garden and pick some flowers." Every action of the teacher's can become a call and an invitation to the children.

This is the second phase of the teacher's work. If at this stage there is some child who persistently annoys the others, the most practical thing to do is to interrupt him. It is true that we have said, and repeated often enough, that when a child is absorbed in his work, one must refrain from interfering, so as not to interrupt his cycle of activity or prevent its free expansion; nevertheless, the right technique, now, is just the opposite; it is to break the flow of disturbing activity. The interruption may take the form of any kind of exclamation, or in showing a special and affectionate interest in the troublesome child. These distracting demonstrations of affection, which grow more numerous with the disturbing activities of the child, act on him like a series of electric shocks and they have their effect in time. Often a question will serve, such as, "How are you, Johnny? Come with me, I have something for you to do." Probably, he won't want to be shown, and the teacher will say, "All right, it doesn't matter. Let's go into the garden," and either she will go with him or send her assistant. In this way, he and his naughtiness will pass directly into the hands of the assistant, and the other children will cease to be disturbed by him.

Third Stage. Finally, the time comes in which the children begin to take an interest in something: usually, in the exercises of practical life, for experience shows that it is useless and harmful to give the children sensorial and cultural apparatus before they are ready to benefit from it.

Before introducing this kind of material, one must wait till, the children have acquired the power to concentrate on something, and usually, as I say, this occurs with the exercises of practical life. When the child begins to show interest in one of these, the teacher must *not interrupt,* because this interest corresponds with natural laws and opens up a whole cycle of new activities. But the first step is so fragile, so delicate, that a touch can make it vanish again, like a soap bubble, and with it goes all the beauty of that moment.

The teacher, now, must be most careful. Not to interfere means not to interfere in *any way*. This is the moment at which the teacher most often goes wrong. The child, who up to that moment has been very difficult, finally concentrates on a piece of work. If, as she passes, the teacher merely says, "Good," it is enough to make the trouble break out all over again. Quite likely, it will be two weeks before the child takes an interest in anything else. If another child is finding it hard to do something, and the teacher goes to help him, he may leave it to her instead. The child's interest is not only focused on the operation itself, but more often it is based on his wish *to overcome the difficulty*. "If the teacher wants to overcome it instead of me, let her. I am no longer interested." That is his attitude. If the child is trying to lift something very heavy and the teacher tries to help him, it often happens that he leaves the object in her hands and runs away. Praise, help, or even a look, may be enough to interrupt him, or destroy the activity. It seems a strange thing to say, but this can happen even if the child merely becomes aware of being watched. After all, we too sometimes feel unable to go on working if someone comes to see what we are doing. The great principle which brings success to the teacher is this: *as soon as concentration has begun, act as if the child does not exist*. Naturally, one can see what he is doing with a quick glance, but without his being aware of it. After this, the child who is no longer a prey to the boredom which made him go from one thing to another without ever fastening upon any, starts choosing his work purposefully, and this may produce problems in a class where many want the same thing at the same time. But even to solve these problems, one should not interfere unless asked; the children will solve them by themselves. The duty of the teacher is only to present new things when she knows that a child has exhausted all the possibilities of those he was using before.

The teacher's skill in not interfering comes with practice, like everything else, but it never comes very easily. It means rising to spiritual heights. True spirituality realizes that even to help can be a source of pride.

The real help that the teacher can give does not lie in obeying a sentimental impulse, but it comes from subjecting one's love to discipline, using it with discernment, because the doer of a kindness reaps greater happiness than the receiver. True kindness serves the needy without disclosing itself or, when it is discovered, it poses not as a help, but as something natural and spontaneous.

Although the relationship between child and teacher is in the spiritual field, the teacher can find a very good model for her behaviour in the way a good valet looks after his master. He keeps his master's dressing table tidy, puts the brushes in place, but he does not tell his master when to use the brushes; he serves his meals, but does not oblige his master to eat; having served everything nicely, without a word, he discreetly disappears. So we must behave when the child's spirit is being forged. The master whom the teacher serves is the child's spirit; when it shows its needs she must hasten to respond to them. The valet never disturbs his master when alone, but if the latter calls, he hurries to find out what is wanted, and replies, "Yes, Sir." If he finds that admiration is expected, he expresses it, and may even say, "How lovely!" of something he does not find beautiful at all. In the same way, if a child does a piece of work with great concentration, we must keep out of the way, but if he shows a wish for our approval, we should give it generously.

In the psychological realm of relationship between teacher and child, the teacher's part and its techniques are analogous to those of the valet; they are to serve, and to serve well: to serve the spirit. This is something new, especially in the educational field. It is not a question of washing the child when he is dirty, of mending or cleaning his clothes. We do not serve the child's body, because we know that if he is to develop he must do these things for himself. The basis of our teaching is that he should *not* be served in this sense. The child has to acquire physical independence by being self-sufficient; he must become of independent will by using in freedom his own power of choice; he must become capable of independent thought by working alone without interruption. The child's development follows a path of successive stages of independence, and our knowledge of this must guide us in our behaviour towards him. We have to help the child to act, will and think for himself. This is the art of serving the spirit, an art which can be practised to perfection only when working among children.

If the teacher meets the needs of the group of children entrusted to her, she will see the qualities of social life burst surprisingly into flower, and will have the joy of watching these manifestations of the childish soul. It is a great privilege to be able to see them. It is the privilege of the traveller when he reaches an oasis and hears the water surging from the sandy breast of the desert which had seemed so arid, fiery and hopeless; for the higher qualities of the human soul are usually hidden in the deviated child, and when they appear, the teacher by whom they had been foreseen welcomes them with the joy of a faith rewarded. And in these qualities of the child, she sees man as he ought to be: the worker who never tires, because what drives him on is a perennial enthusiasm. She sees one who seeks out the greatest efforts because his constant aspiration is to make himself superior to difficulties; he is a person who really tries to help the weak, because in his heart there is the true charity which knows what is meant by respect for others, and that respect for a person's spiritual efforts is the water that nourishes the roots of his soul. In the possession of these characteristics, she will recognize the true child, who is father of the true man.

But this will only happen little by little. At first the teacher will say, "I have seen the child as he ought to be, and found him better than I could ever have supposed." This is what it means to understand infancy. It is not enough to know that this child is called John, that his father is a carpenter; the teacher must know and experience in her daily life the secret of childhood. Through this she arrives not only at a deeper knowledge, but at a new kind of love which does not become attached to the individual person, but to that which lies in the hidden darkness of this secret. When the children show her their real natures, she understands, perhaps for the first time, what love really is. And this revelation transforms her also. It is a thing that touches the heart, and little by little it changes people. Once these facts have been seen, one cannot cease from writing and talking about them. The names of the children may become forgotten, but nothing can cancel the impression their spirits have made and the love they were able to awaken.

There are two levels of love. Often, when we speak of our love for children, we refer to the care we take of them, the caresses and affection we shower on those we know and who arouse our tender feelings, and if a spiritual relationship binds us to them, we show it by teaching them their prayers.

But I am speaking of something different. It is a level of love which is no longer personal or material. To serve the children is to feel one is serving the spirit of man, a spirit which has to free itself. The difference of level has truly been set not by the teacher but by the child. It is the teacher who feels she has been lifted to a height she never knew before. The child has made her grow till she is brought within his sphere.

Before this, she used to feel that her task was a noble one, but she was glad when the holidays came and hoped, like all human beings who work for others, that her working hours would be reduced and her salary raised. Her satisfactions were, perhaps, to exert authority and to have the feeling of being an ideal to which the children looked up and tried to emulate. It would make her happy to become a headmistress, or even an inspectress. But to go from this level to the higher one is to understand that true happiness does not lie in these things. One who has drunk at the fountain of spiritual happiness says good-bye of his own accord to the satisfactions that come from a higher professional status, and this is shown by the many heads of schools and inspectors who have abandoned their careers to dedicate themselves to small children, and to become what others call contemptuously "infant teachers."

I know two doctors of medicine in Paris who left their profession to devote themselves entirely to our work and to enter into the reality of these phenomena. They felt they had gone from a low level to a higher one.

What is the greatest sign of success for a teacher thus transformed? It is to be able to say, "The children are now working as if I did not exist."

Before the transformation, her feelings were just the contrary; she thought it was she who had taught the children, she who had raised them from a low level to a higher one. But now, with the manifestations before her of the child's spirit, the greatest value she can ascribe to her own contribution is expressed in the words: "I have helped this life to fulfil the tasks set for it by creation."

This is truly satisfying. The teacher of children up to six years of age knows that she has helped mankind in an essential part of its formation. She may know nothing of the children's circumstances, except what they have told her freely in conversation; possibly she takes no interest in their future: whether they will go on to secondary schools and the university, or end their studies sooner; but she is happy in the knowledge that in this formative period they were able to do what they had to do. She will be able to say: "I have served the spirits of those children, and they have fulfilled their development, and I kept them company in their experiences." The teacher; quite apart from the authority to whom she is responsible, feels the value of her work, and of what she has accomplished, in the form of a satisfied spiritual life, which is "life everlasting" and a prayer in itself from each morning to the next. This is hard to understand for one who has not adopted this life. Many think it is due to a virtue of self-sacrifice and say, "How humble these teachers are, not to be interested even in their own authority over the children," and many say: "How can your method succeed if you ask your teachers to renounce all their most natural and spontaneous desires?" But what no one understands is that not sacrifice, but satisfaction, is in question; not renunciation, but a new life in which the values are different, where real life values, hitherto unknown, have come to exist.

Moreover, all the principles are different; justice for example. In schools and in society, and in democratic countries, justice often means only that there is a single law for all; for the rich and powerful and for those dying of hunger. Justice is generally thought of in connection with lawsuits, with prisons and sentences. Courts of law are called Palaces of Justice, and to say, "I am an honest citizen," implies that one has nothing to do with legal administration (police or law courts). Even in the school, the teacher has to be careful about caressing a child, otherwise he might have to caress them all: he must be just. This is a kind of justice that puts everyone on the lowest level; as if, in a spiritual sense, we were to behead the tallest in order to have them all of the same height.

On this higher educational level justice is something truly spiritual; it tries to ensure that every child shall make the best of himself. Justice, here, is to give every human being the help he needs to bring about his fullest spiritual stature, and service of the spirit at every age means helping those energies that are at work to bring this about. This, perhaps, will be the basis on which society will be organized in the future. Nothing of these spiritual treasures should be lost. In comparison with these, economic treasures have no value. Whether I be rich or poor does not mater: if I can attain to the full measure of my powers, the economic problem solves itself. When mankind as a whole can fully perfect its spirit, it will become more productive, and the economic aspect of life will cease to preponderate. Men do not produce with their feet and their bodies, but with their spirit and intelligence, and when these shall have reached the level of development which is proper to them, then all our "insoluble problems" will have become solved.

Children unaided can construct an orderly society. For us adults, prisons, police, soldiers and guns are necessary. Children solve their problems peacefully; they have shown us that freedom and discipline are two faces of the same medal, because scientific freedom leads to discipline. Coins usually have two faces, one being more beautiful, finely chiselled, bearing a head or allegorical figure, while the other is less ornate, with nothing but a number or some writing. The plain side can be compared to freedom, and the finely chiselled side to discipline. This is so true that when her class becomes undisciplined, the teacher sees in the disorder merely an indication of some error that *she* has made; she seeks this out and corrects it. The teacher of the traditional school would feel this to be humiliating; but it is not humiliating, it is a part of the technique of the new education. In serving the child, one serves life; in helping nature one rises to the next stage, that of super-nature, for to go upward is a law of life. And it is the children who have made this beautiful staircase that mounts ever higher. The law of nature is order, and when order comes of itself, we know that we have re-entered the order of the universe. It is clear that nature includes among the missions she has entrusted to the child, the mission of arousing us adults to reach a higher level. The children take us to a higher plane of the spirit and material problems are thereby solved. Permit me to repeat, as a form of farewell, words which have helped us to keep in mind all the things of which I have been speaking. It is not a prayer, but rather a reminder, and for our teachers, an invocation, a kind of syllabus, our only syllabus:

> "HELP US, O GOD, TO ENTER INTO THE SECRET OF CHILDHOOD, SO THAT WE MAY KNOW, LOVE AND SERVE THE CHILD IN ACCORDANCE WITH THE LAWS OF THY JUSTICE AND FOLLOWING THY HOLY WILL."

28

Love and its Source—The Child

On our social occasions we always have a typically Montessorian gathering. Often the students bring relatives or friends, so that one may see babes in arms, infants, boys, girls, young men and women, grown-ups, professional and non-professional people, those of highest education and the reverse, all mingled together, and none of us feels it the least bit necessary to regulate or direct these groups. This heterogeneity gives our meetings a different appearance from those typical of other fields of study. The students who attend our courses of training must have reached a certain educational standard and this is the only condition: among them may be matriculates and professors, lawyers, doctors, and those who could be their clients or patients. In Europe we used to have students from all parts of the world, and in America one of them was an anarchist. But in spite of all this mixing, there was never any friction. What made that possible? It came about because we were drawn together by a common ideal. In Belgium—such a small country that it could easily be placed in a tiny corner of India—there are two languages, Flemish and French. The population is also divided politically, and this division is complicated by the differences between Catholics and Socialists and other political groups. It is rare in the ordinary way for people so divided (each tied by loyalty to his own group) to meet together in a single conclave. Yet it never failed to happen in our courses. So strange did this seem that even the newspapers remarked on it.

"For years", they said, "we have striven to have meetings attended by all the parties, and here it is happening by itself."

Such is the child's power. Whatever be our political or religious affiliations, we are all near to the child and we all love him. It is from this love that comes the child's power for unity. Adults have strong, and often fierce, convictions which separate them into groups, and when they fall to discussing these they easily come to blows. But there is one point—the child—on which all have the same feelings. Few people realize how great is the child's importance owing to this.

Let us try to comprehend the nature of love. Let us think of what the prophets and the poets have said about it, for it is these who have given the best expression to the great energy that bears this name. What is lovelier and more ennobling than these songs of the great emotion from which all life springs? Do they not stir the hearts even of the most barbarous and violent of men? Even those who carry death and destruction to whole populations, feel themselves moved by the beauty of these words. This is a sign that, despite the nature of their acts, these men have retained that energy within them and that, when it is awakened, a vibration from that energy reaches their hearts. Were it otherwise, the beauty of these expressions would be lost on them; they would think them vain and senseless. If they feel this beauty, it is because, however little love seems to be at work in their lives, they are under its influence and thirst for it unconsciously.

If we want to produce harmony in the world, it is clear that we ought to think more about this. We should study its implications. The child is the only point on which there converges from everyone a feeling of gentleness and love. People's souls soften and sweeten when one speaks of children; the whole of mankind shares in the deep emotions which they awaken. The child is a well-spring of love. Whenever we touch the child, we touch love. It is a difficult love to define; we all feel it, but no one can describe its roots or evaluate the immense consequences which flow from it, or gather up its potency for union between men. Despite our differences of race, or religion, and of social position, we have felt during our discussions of the child a fraternal union growing up between us. This has conquered our shyness and dispelled those defences which are always ready to spring up between man and man, and between groups of men in the daily affairs of life.

In the vicinity of children mistrust melts away; we become sweet and kindly, because, when we are gathered about them, we feel warmed by that flame of life which is there, where life originates. In adults there is an impulse for defence which coexists with the impulse of love. Of these two, the fundamental one is love, the other being superimposed upon it. Love, like that which we feel for the child, must exist potentially between man and man, because human unity does exist and there is no unity without love.

How strange it is to observe that in times like ours, when war has achieved a destructiveness without parallel, and has stretched out to embrace the farthest corners of the earth, when one would have supposed that to speak of love would be the sheerest irony, people still talk about it as obstinately as ever. Future plans for unity are made, which means not only that love exists, but that its power is fundamental. And today—when it would seem that everything were saying to man, "Enough of this dream called love: let us face reality, which is, as we see, nothing but destruction; or is it perhaps untrue that towns, forests, women and children have all perished?" We continue to speak of reconstruction and love. Love is spoken of by the Church and by her enemies; the radio, the press, passers by, educated and ignorant, rich and poor, the followers of every creed and theology; all, all of them talk about love.

If this be so (and no greater proof could there be that the force of love exists), why should we not make a study of this tremendous phenomenon? Why should it only be discussed when hatred is working its havoc? Why should it not always be a subject for study and analysis, so that its power can become beneficent? And why not ask ourselves how it comes about that no one has ever thought of studying this primordial energy, and of combining it with the other forces that we know? Man has devoted so much intelligence to the study of other natural facts; he has sifted and dissected them, and made innumerable discoveries concerning them. Why not spend a little of this vigour in the study of a force that might unite mankind? Every contribution able to bring out the latent power of love, and to throw light upon love itself, should be welcomed with avidity and considered of paramount importance. I have already said that prophets and poets speak often of love as it if were an ideal; but it is not just an ideal, it is, has always been, and will ever be, a reality.

And we must come to learn that if we feel the reality of this love, it is not because we were taught it in school.

Even if we had been made to learn by heart the sayings of poets and prophets their words are not very many, and we should have forgotten them by now in the stresses and turmoil of life. If people are calling vehemently for love, it is not because they have heard it spoken of, or read about it. Love and the hope of it, are not things one can learn; they are a part of life's heritage. It is life that really speaks, not just the poets and the prophets.

Love may be considered, in fact, from another aspect than that of religion and poetry can be considered from the point of view of life itself. Then we see it not only as something imagined or desired, but as the reality of an eternal energy that nothing can destroy.

I would like to say a word about this reality, and also about the sayings of the poets and the prophets. This force that we call love is the greatest energy of the universe. But I am using an inadequate expression, for it is more than an energy: it is creation itself. I should put it better if I were to say: "God is love."

I should like to be able to quote from all 'the poets, the prophets and the saints, but they are not all known to me, nor could I do so in their various tongues. But perhaps I may quote one that I do know, and who, in speaking of love, expresses himself so strongly that today, after two thousand years, his words still echo emphatically in Christian hearts.

"If I speak with the tongues of men and of angels, and have not Charity, I am become as sounding brass or a tinkling cymbal. And if I should have prophecy, and should know all mysteries, and all knowledge, and if I should have all faith, so that I could remove mountains, and have not Charity, I am nothing. And if I should distribute all my goods to feed the poor, and if I should deliver my body to be burned, and have not Charity, it profiteth me nothing." (Paul to the Corinthians, 1. XIII.).

Any one of us might be forgiven for saying to the apostle, "You feel this so deeply that you must certainly know what love is. It must be something very wonderful. Will you not explain it to us?" Because, when we try to describe this loftiest of sentiments, we find it not so easy. We can indeed find the words of St. Paul mirrored in our existing civilization, for can we not move mountains and work even greater miracles? Can we not speak in a whisper and be heard at the ends of the earth? Yet all this is nothing without love. We have set up huge organizations to feed and clothe the poor, but unless there is a heart at work in them, they are like the beating of a drum, which is heard only because it is empty. So what is the nature of this love? St. Paul, whose word, quoted above, describe its grandeur, goes on, but without providing any philosophical theory. He says:—

"Charity is slow to anger, is kind: charity envieth not, dealeth not perversely: is not puffed up. Is not ambitious, seeketh not its own, provoketh not opposition, plans no evil. Rejoiceth not in injustice, but delighteth in the truth; beareth all things, believeth all things, hopeth all things, endureth all things."

It is a long list of facts, a description of mental pictures, but all these pictures remind one strangely of the qualities of childhood. They seem to be describing the *Absorbent Mind* of the child! This mind, which receives all, does not judge, does not refuse, does not react. It absorbs everything and incarnates it in the coming man. The child performs this work of incarnation to achieve equality with other men and to adapt himself to live with them. The child endures all things. He enters into the world, and whatever the conditions into which he is born, he forms and adapts himself to live there, and the adult he is to become will be happy under those conditions. If he happens to see the light in a torrid zone, he will so construct himself that he will not be able to live and be happy in any other climate. Whether it be the desert which receives him, or plains bordering on the sea, or mountain slopes or the frozen fields of the arctic, he enjoys them all, and only where he was born and bred does he feel at his best.

The Absorbent Mind welcomes everything, puts its hope in everything, accepts poverty equally with wealth, adopts any religion and the prejudices and habits of its countrymen, incarnating all in itself.

This is the child!

And if it were otherwise, the human race would not achieve stability in any of the different quarters of the earth; nor could it progress continuously in civilization if it always had to be starting fresh.

The Absorbent Mind forms the basis of the society created by man, and we see it in the guise of the gentle and tiny child who solves by the virtue of his love the mysterious difficulties of human destiny.

If we study the child better than we have done hitherto, we discover love in all its aspects. Love has not been analysed by the poets and by the prophets, but it is analysed by the realities which every child discloses in himself.

If we think of St. Paul's description, and then look at the child, we are obliged to say, "In him is to be found all that has been said. Here is personified the treasure which includes every kind of charity."

Primarily, therefore, this treasure is to be found not only in those few who express it in poetry and religion, but it is present in every human individual. It is a miracle offered to all; everywhere we find the personification of this great force. Man makes a desert of discord and strife, and God continues to send this rejuvenating rain. So can we understand easily how everything man creates, even when called progressive, leads to nothing without love. But this love, which is the gift of every tiny child who is brought into our midst—if this were realized in its potentialities, or if the fullness of its values were developed, our achievements, already so vast, would become immeasurable. Grown-ups and children must join their forces. In order to become great, the grown-up must become humble and learn from the child. Strange, is it not, that among all the wonders man has worked, and the discoveries he has made, there is only one field to which he has paid no attention; it is that of the miracle that God has worked from the first: the miracle of children.

But love is much more than we have said so far. In man's mind it has been exalted by fantasy, but in us it is no other than one aspect of a very complex universal force, which—denoted by the words "attraction" and "affinity"— rules the world, keeps the stars in their courses, causes the conjunction of atoms to form new substances, holds things down on the earth's surface. It is the force which regulates and orders the organic and the inorganic, and which becomes incorporated into the essence of everything and of all things, like a guide to salvation and to the endlessness of evolution. It is generally unconscious, but in life it sometimes assumes consciousness, and, when felt in man's heart, he calls it "love."

All animals have periodically the instinct of reproduction, which is a form of love. This form of love is a command of nature, because without it there would be no perpetuation of life. So, a small modicum of this universal energy is lent to the living forms for a moment, so that the species shall not die out.

They feel it for a moment and then it disappears from their consciousness. This shows how economical and measured is nature in her bestowal of love: how precious, therefore, must this energy be which she grants in such small doses, as if commanded to do so. When the young ones come into the world, the gift of love is renewed to the parents; a special love which leads them to feed their offspring, keep them warm, and to defend them to the point of death. The mother's fondness for her young keeps her constantly near them, day and night. This is the form of love which insures the survival, safety and well-being of the little ones. This special aspect of the energy has a limited task: "The species must be cared for and defended, and you are to dedicate yourself to this, until the youngsters no longer need help." And, lo! no sooner are the young grown up than this love vanishes, from one moment to the next! Those who seemed, till then, to be united by an unbreakable bond of affection, separate. If they meet again, they behave as if they had never known one another, and if the youngster dares to take a mouthful of food from the mother, who used to deny him nothing, she attacks him fiercely.

What can this mean? It means that the little ray of energy passing through the clouds of consciousness which is lent to everyone, is withdrawn again the moment its purpose has been accomplished.

In man, it is not so. Love does not disappear when the children are grown up, and not only that but it extends beyond the confines of the family. Have not we ourselves found it ready to appear and to unite us, directly an ideal touched our hearts?

Love is permanent in mankind, and its consequences are felt outside the individual's life. For, what is the social organization which goes on extending till the whole of humanity is embraced by it, if not the consequence of a love which others have felt in the centuries of the past?

If nature bestows this energy for exact purposes, if she measures it out so accurately to other forms of life, the generosity she shows to man cannot be purposeless.

If in all its aspects this energy leads to salvation, it is inevitable that when ignored it should lead to destruction.

The value of this portion of energy which we have been given is immeasurably beyond all those material conquests of civilisation to which man is so attached. These are only temporary expressions of the same energy and, after a little while, when new conquests have superseded them, they will disappear; but the energy itself will go on to develop its own ends of creation, of protection and salvation, even after no trace of man is left in the universe.

Love is conceded to man as a gift directed to a certain purpose, and for a special reason, and in this it resembles everything lent to living beings by the cosmic consciousness. It must be treasured, developed and enlarged to the fullest possible extent. Man, alone among living creatures, can sublimate this force which he has received and can develop it more and more. To treasure it is his duty. It holds the universe together because it is a real force, and not just an idea.

By its means man, also, will be able to hold together all that he creates with his hands and with his intelligence. Without it, all he creates will turn (as so often it has) to the bringing of disorder and destruction. Without it, with the growth of his own powers, nothing of his can last, all will collapse.

Now we can understand the words of the Saint, that all is nothing unless there be love. Love is more than the electricity which lightens our darkness, more than the etheric waves that transmit our voices across space, more than any of the energies that man has discovered and learned to use. Of all things love is the most potent. All that men can do with their discoveries depends on the conscience of him who uses them. But this energy of love is given us so that each shall have it in himself. Although the amount given to man is limited and diffused, it is the greatest of all the forces at his disposal. That part of it which we possess consciously is renewed every time a baby is born and, even if circumstances at a later stage cause it to become dormant, we still feel for it a fervent desire. Therefore, we must study it and use it, more than any of the other forces that surround us, because it is not lent to the environment, as these are, but is lent to us. The study of love and its utilization will lead us to the source from which it springs, The Child.

This is the path that man must follow in his anguish and his cares if, as his aspirations direct, he wishes to reach salvation and the union of mankind.

Index